ADDICTION
AND
COMPULSIVE
BEHAVIORS

Contributors

Fred S. Berlin, M.D., Ph.D.
Director, National Institute
  for the Study, Prevention
  and Treatment of Sexual Trauma
Baltimore, Maryland

Rev. David M. Carey, B.A., C.A.C.
Counselor and Presenter
  in Spirituality in Recovery
Fr. Martin's Ashley
Havre de Grace, Maryland

Patrick J. Carnes, Ph.D., C.A.S.
Clinical Director
  of Sexual Disorder Services
The Meadows
Wickenburg, Arizona

Rev. Romanus Cessario, O.P., S.T.D.
Professor of Systematic Theology
St. John's Seminary
Brighton, Massachusetts

Anna Rose Childress, Ph.D.
Researcher
Treatment Research Center
School of Medicine
University of Pennsylvania
Philadelphia, Pennsylvania

Archbishop Paul Josef Cordes, S.T.D.
President
Pontifical Council *Cor Unum*
Vatican City State

Rev. Wojciech Giertych, O.P., M.A., S.T.D.
Assistant of the Master
  of the Dominican Order
  for Central and Eastern Europe
Rome, Italy

Scott E. Lukas, Ph.D.
Director, Behavioral
  Psychopharmacology Research
  Laboratory
McLean Hospital
Belmont, Massachusetts

Michael M. Miller, M.D., F.A.S.A.M.
Director, Meriter Behavioral Services
Meriter Hospital
Madison, Wisconsin

Robert M. Morse, M.D.
Consultant in Psychiatry
Mayo Clinic
Rochester, Minnesota

Patricia L. Owen, Ph.D.
Vice President
Research & Development
Hazelden Foundation
Center City, Minnesota

Sally L. Satel, M.D.
Lecturer in Psychiatry
School of Medicine
Yale University
New Haven, Connecticut

Charles W. Socarides, M.D., F.A.C.PSA.
Clinical Professor of Psychiatry, Emeritus
Albert Einstein College of Medicine
New York, New York

Alfonso Cardinal López Trujillo
President
Pontifical Council for the Family
Vatican City State

Rachel A. Volberg, Ph.D.
President
Gemini Research, Ltd.
Northhampton, Massachusetts

ADDICTION
AND
COMPULSIVE
BEHAVIORS

Seventeenth
Workshop for Bishops

Edward J. Furton, M.A., PH.D.
Editor

Veronica McLoud Dort, M.A., M.T.S.
Assistant Editor

Nihil Obstat: Rev. James A. O'Donohoe, J.C.D.

Imprimatur: Bernard Cardinal Law

November 21, 2000

The Nihil Obstat and Imprimatur are a declaration that a book or pamphlet is considered to be free from doctrinal or moral error.
It is not implied that those who granted the Nihil Obstat and Imprimatur agree with the contents, opinions, or statements expressed therein.

Cover Design
Thomas Gannoe

Cover Art
Courtesy: National Gallery of Art
"The Return of the Prodigal Son"
1667–1670
(oil on canvas)
Bartolomé Esteban Murillo

© 2000 The National Catholic Bioethics Center
Boston, Massachusetts

Special thanks to Amanda Parish

Library of Congress Cataloging-in-Publication Data

Workshop for Bishops of the United States and Canada (17th : 1999 : Dallas, Tex.)
    Addiction and compulsive behaviors : proceedings of the Seventeenth Workshop for Bishops / Edward J. Furton, editor; Veronica McLoud Dort, assistant editor.
    P. cm.
    Includes bibliographical references.
    ISBN 0-935372-43-1
    1. Compulsive behavior--Religious aspects--Catholic Church--Congresses. 2. Substance abuse--Religious aspects--Catholic Church--Congresses. 3. Compulsive behavior--Congresses. 4. Substance abuse--Congresses. I. Furton, Edward James. II. Dort, Veronica McLoud. III. Title.

BX1795.C68 W67 2000
261.8'322--dc21

00-048711

Contents

Clinical Approaches

Theological Perspectives

Scientific Analysis

To My Brother Bishops
Taking Part in the Seventeenth Bishops' Workshop
Of the National Catholic Bioethics Center

With great joy, I greet you, the Bishops from Canada, Central America, Mexico, the Philippines, and the United States of America taking part in the Seventeenth Bishops' Workshop organized by the National Catholic Bioethics Center. An expression of the Church's gratitude is due to the organizers of this study session and to the Knights of Columbus whose generosity has made it possible.

This year, the theme of your reflections is "Addiction and Compulsive Behaviors." In your pastoral experience, you have frequently encountered men and women of all ages who have fallen victim to alcoholism, drug addiction, and various forms of compulsive behavior. I join you in praying for all who suffer from these disorders, for their families and friends, and for those engaged in helping them to overcome the causes of their difficulties. The Church encourages all who are burdened by the devastating effects of addiction and compulsive behavior to turn to Christ, the physician of soul and body, who can above all help them to overcome the sense of abandonment and the temptation to despair.

The Workshop will help you to increase your scientific knowledge of these disorders and to learn of the most recent developments in their treatment. I am confident that this study session, combined

1

with an appreciation of how Christian anthropology sheds light on the intimate relation of body and soul, will be of great assistance to you in developing pastoral initiatives to bring Christ's consolation to those in need. In helping them to recover their self-confidence and rediscover a sense of meaning and moral values, you will enable them to understand the slavery of addiction, to become aware of the possibility of overcoming dependence, and to commit themselves to a course of rehabilitation. Through faith in the God of life, they will come to see life in its deeper meaning, to grasp its utter gratuitousness, its beauty and its invitation to freedom and responsibility (cf. *Evangelium vitae*, 83).

I join you in praying that the liberating power of Christ may free all who are oppressed by drugs, alcohol, or forms of compulsive behavior, and I entrust them and those who assist them to the maternal protection of Mary, Comforter of the Afflicted. To all taking part in the Workshop I cordially impart my Apostolic Blessing as a pledge of unity, peace and love in the Lord Jesus Christ.

From the Vatican, January 18, 1999.

Joannes Paulus II
Pope John Paul II

Greetings from the Knights of Columbus
Dallas, Texas
February 1–5, 1999

In the name of our almost 1.6 million Brother Knights — plus our families— throughout the world, it is my privilege to greet all who are participating in this Seventeenth Dallas workshop.

It is a personal pleasure also to greet His Eminence Alfonso Cardinal López Trujillo, president of the Pontifical Council for the Family, of which my wife Ann and I are longtime members. I also greet His Excellency Archbishop Paul Josef Cordes, president of the Pontifical Council "Cor Unum," whose mission we have been able to assist.

Once again it is gratifying for the Order to be able to fund this important gathering, organized by the National Catholic Bioethics Center and its President, Dr. John Haas, to enable Your Excellencies to update your knowledge about one specific topic. The subject of these meetings has always had great relevance to the manner in which you fulfill your calling as shepherd and teacher within your Sees.

The subject this year: "Addiction and Compulsive Behaviors," is one that impinges upon all aspects of the human condition — fall-out, perhaps, from the original sin of Adam and Eve. The various forms of addiction and compulsion impact society, certainly. But they also impact the life and discipline of the Church insofar as they pertain to some of its priests and religious, to many of its families, indeed, to all the wounded members of the Mystical Body of Christ. As St. Paul said in Romans 7, quoted on the brochure developed for this meeting: "For I do not do the good I want, but the evil I do not want." St. Augustine also prayed: "Lord, give me chastity but not yet."

The addictions and compulsions to be discussed for you by experts in their fields include, among others, alcohol, drugs, gambling, and sexual behaviors. More importantly, there will also be discussions about the role played by the clinical, pastoral, and sacramental approaches in dealing with these conditions.

That is why it is important for you to be here; that is why it is important for the Knights of Columbus to make this workshop possible.

As you gather for the daily Liturgies, for the meetings and discussions, for the camaraderie that these days have been known to foster among Bishops from different lands, please know that our Knights stand in solidarity with Our Holy Father, with the Magisterium, and with each one of you. May you return to your Sees more empowered to understand and assist not only those who suffer from these disorders, but also those who are made to suffer by those who are so disordered.

I pray that this meeting be a source of grace and blessing to us all.

Virgil C. Dechant
Supreme Knight
Knights of Columbus

Clinical Approaches

Pastoral Care to the Suffering Alcoholic/Addict

Reverend David M. Carey, B.A., C.A.C.

I am honored to speak to you today as a person in recovery who happens to be a Roman Catholic priest. I choose to share some turning points in my personal spiritual journey in order to focus on the genuine pastoral approach afforded me through my church hierarchy and compassionate friends. Following this sharing, I will offer some suggestions encouraging the establishment of a *Pastoral Care Plan* (for lack of a better word) intended to be supportive of suffering alcoholics and addicts in their walk of recovery.

The Journey

I believe pastoral care is a shepherd's care; there is no other care. I received a shepherd's care; sadly, I know some who did not. The night before I left Sacred Heart Parish, Glyndon, Maryland, for treatment of alcoholism at Guest House, Lake Orion, Michigan, sixteen years ago, I received a phone call from Archbishop William D. Borders. "David, I want you to get well. Don't worry about anything. I am appointing an administrator in your absence; your pastorate will be here for you when you return." At the very moment I heard these words, I willed to get well! I suggest this is pastoral care; this is a shepherd's care, the care Jesus would offer. During my three-month stay at Guest House, I came to realize that not every priest's or brother's case was handled with the same shepherd's care I had experienced.

Alcoholic Anonymous has a beautiful and humble philosophy, which is the basis of its many success stories: "Remember how it was, remember what happened, and be grateful for how it is today." Remembering how it was before recovery? It was a nightmare. My drinking began immediately after ordination in 1962, in my first parish assignment. Over the course of twenty years of priestly ministry, I medicated life's hurts and celebrated life's joys with the sedation of alcohol. I progressed from social drinking, to problem drinking, to maintenance drinking on a daily basis while still managing my priestly duties to all appearances, for the most part.

"Alcohol is cunning, baffling and powerful," says the book of Alcoholics Anonymous. How true. I remember at one point being immobile, literally so stuck in the fear that people could see into my soul, that I could not offer Mass. I sought psychiatric help and received librium at one time, valium another. This medication simply compounded my addiction and quickened my dependency on drugs. Active addiction is a nightmare; I must never forget it.

As my alcoholism progressed through the years, drinking became the center of my existence and priesthood. How often I wished I was anything but a priest, who was expected to keep faith and smile each day. Sure, some people knew, my friends knew, and I knew, that I was a victim of alcoholism. How many times I set the alarm to 4 a.m. to take my valium, so I could offer the 8 a.m. Mass without shaking apart. How miraculous to hold the chalice and host today without the dreadful fear of shaking. In how many Masses my only prayer was "Please, Jesus, get me through this moment, and I'll never do this to myself again." By five o'clock that same day, I was eagerly awaiting the cocktail hour. And the whole frightful cycle began again. Still, in a secret part of my heart I wanted so desperately for someone to help stop the pain. Alcoholics and other addicts, you know, can't help themselves. Addiction robs us of the power to choose. Will power is no power at all. We need a power from the outside to intervene; otherwise talented and productive men die from benign neglect. For a Catholic priest, the power of authority lies in the bishop.

That day of confrontation arrived, December, 1981, and I was ready for it. Bishop Frank Murphy called me to his office and confronted me on my drinking. He asked me to see Father Joe Martin, a leading authority on alcoholism, I offered little resistance to Bishop Murphy. Even in my sickness, I sensed compassion in Bishop Murphy's eyes, as he strongly yet gently confronted a brother priest about his dysfunction. His pastoral approach was "tough love."

A religious sister on staff, my associate, a few selected parishioners had called Bishop Murphy expressing concern for me. That day I saw Bishop Murphy I cried openly, but with joy. What a release from years of secret oppression! "It's over, it's over," I cried to myself, "my bishop knows my problem and it's O.K. with me." The following day, I saw Fr. Joe Martin. It was the week after Christmas. Fr. Martin embraced me warmly and began by sharing his story. I listened and I identified. Someone knowledgeable about the subject of addiction is indispensable in the intervention process. "I know what you're going through, I've been there." There is no pastoral approach more intimate than that.

"David, you are a sick man and you deserve the best treatment there is," Fr. Martin said. "You must go to Guest House where I got sober," he continued. "Besides, Michigan is great this time of year!" It was December, and I smiled. Only Fr. Martin can jest about a life-or-death illness without offending. Again, I offered little resistance. I did feel, however, that I wasn't all that bad. After all, I was a pastor of a large parish, I was in good health and I was a good worker. To all appearances everything seemed fine to me. But, on the inside, I knew I was a sick man, spiritually and emotionally bankrupt, in need of healing.

Then came what I thought was the most difficult part of it all. "David, you must tell the people where you're going," Father Martin said. "And don't lie about it. Don't say you are going away to study alcoholism, you are it! You must get honest with yourself. Now is the time." I remember driving back to the rectory that day feeling a mixed blessing. I was glad it was over, but how will it all play itself out? How can I tell these people who have been so good to me for almost fifteen years that I was sick? As their pastor, I felt I was letting them down, and that they might even blame themselves for all those heated parish council meetings.

I followed Father Martin's direction and wrote up my "mixed blessing" report for publication in the following weekend bulletin. It included my Guest House address in Michigan. Much to my surprise, the experience of being honest with my parishioners was most therapeutic in my early recovery. I received many, many letters from parishioners, telling me how grateful they were that I was getting help and assuring me of their prayers that I would return to Sacred Heart. I knew then they had seen the sickness and pain I attempted to deny.

I arrived in Detroit January 13, 1982, with a fellow priest from Baltimore already in recovery, whom Bishop Murphy had arranged to accompany me. Once again, a pastoral approach deeply appreciated, not easily forgotten. Guest House personnel met us at the airport. As we arrived at the lovely snow-covered Scripps Estate in Lake Orion, I saw written over the doorway: "No one comes too early; no one comes too late." What a nice touch, I thought to myself, but how did they know? "I must be right on time," I remembered saying out loud. "Indeed you are," said Jo Holladay, my counselor for the next few months; my friend until she died a few years ago.

The advantage of in-patient treatment is removal from the stresses and obligation of the workplace to explore the reasons why one felt the need to self-medicate on drugs and alcohol. Through counseling, education, and prayer, I came to experience who I really was, how I actually felt, and how to relate to others without the protection of alcohol and mood-altering, mind-changing drugs. Despite all my education, I learned that I lacked some basic emotional skills in dealing with life on life's terms, and much more, after twenty years of an induced false identity.

9

My life at Guest House was the most transforming experience of my life. The census of Guest House fluctuated. For the next three months I lived with 25/30 men, priests and brothers from across the country. And it was the most healing community I had ever experienced. I almost regretted having to leave. But spring came, and I was ready to return home. It was Holy Week and I accepted an invitation to spend that Holy Week with a Sulpician priest friend who was directing a retreat with the Christian Brothers in Annandale, Maryland. What an Easter week that was. I felt the grace of Jesus' Resurrection flow through my veins for the first time in a very long time. I am most grateful to this day for having a second chance to be a priest again, to have been born again.

It was time to come home. I'll never forget my return to Sacred Heart parish that Easter week in 1982. The church was filled, and I spoke from the heart at all the Masses. It was a powerful experience. I was an answer to prayers of my parishioners. I was a miracle! The sick and broken priest they had witnessed a few months earlier returned, well into the recovery process. I remained in that parish five more years, and "cleaned up" the whole town! By this I mean people came out of the closet and admitted abusing children, spouses, money, food. This was the most fruitful time in my priestly ministry I can remember. People came to me because they saw in me a man who had problems, and who, with the grace of God, had been healed. I say healed, because I am not cured. I am not recovered; I am recovering. I can only say I will not drink today.

May I close by sharing some thoughts about Father Martin's Ashley founded in 1983 and built on the philosophy he had experienced at Austin Ripley's Guest House, begun in 1956. Alcoholism is a sickness of the soul, and we must offer the suffering alcoholic the best care, food, and accommodations. Slowly, the alcoholic (and other addicts) begins to see himself as a person of worth and value and begins to get well. I'm proud to be on the staff of Father Martin's Ashley and to work with Father Martin so closely. I'm proud also to serve as chaplain to the Baltimore Province of the School Sisters of Notre Dame. I have continued to participate in Guest House aftercare seminars held through the country whenever I can. Guest House opened its doors to women religious in 1994.

I am sober today through the grace of God, the fellowship of Alcoholics Anonymous, and the support of my pastoral church hierarchy. I truly believe the words of St. Paul "But for the grace of God, go I."

Professional Suggestions

While *alcoholism* is currently recognized by all health authorities as the third largest health problem in the United States today, outranked only by heart disease and cancer, there is also growing awareness that all too often, the sometimes subtle yet destructive nature of alcoholism and its sister, *drug addiction*, can be seen as the number one destroyer of family life in our country. This insight has become increasingly recognized by the Church, which has a long and fruitful ministry to families. In significant numbers, it has also been recognized in the Church itself. Alcoholism in a priest or religious is a pastoral problem in the priest himself and in those to whom he ministers.

The concept of alcoholism as a disease gives alcoholics the good news that they are sick rather than evil. May I venture to say alcoholism can be a particularly Catholic disease, given the high rate among people of Irish and Polish ethnicity. There is a solution pastorally sound, and profoundly Catholic—based on the psychology of conversion and the principles of spiritual growth. What is it? Confrontation, treatment, and Alcoholic Anonymous.

1. *Confrontation*: This is known as *intervention* by knowledgeable and caring persons around the alcoholic, who come together with a trained *interventionist* who will motivate the group, and show them how to present their accumulated data to the alcoholic in a compassionate way. In a diocesan or parish setting, this pastoral approach will include a member of the alcoholic's family, if possible; a bishop or his delegate; and a few concerned and compassionate friends. Their data would include written lists of explicit and specific incidences from these first hand observers, in order to legitimatize the severity of the confrontation. At least one practice session is suggested for simulating the forthcoming intervention.

The vow of obedience to one's superior is employed from the start: "We are asking you please, to listen to what we all believe is a serious matter affecting your present ministry." The *nature* of alcoholism (and chemical dependency) is such that these victims are incapable of recognizing the severity of their symptoms spontaneously; indeed, denial of the illness is a chief characteristic of the disease itself. To wait for its victims to "come to their senses" may be to watch them die. Instead, the first goal of the group is to help the victim of the illness identify their behavior as the primary problem. An example: "You were abrasive to the school principal at a Home School meeting on March 16, and again on April 23, 1998. In both instances alcohol was detected on your breath." Each person in turn might begin with the phrase, "Another reason I am concerned is that last week you ... " Remember the group has not gathered to debate the issue with the alcoholic, but to confront the problem and persuade the person into treatment.

The intervention is concluded by summarizing the concerns of the group, suggesting the options available, and the follow through which the group has agreed upon in advance. Immediate referral to inpatient treatment is the primary recommendation. The group must be prepared in advance to answer the usual excuses: "I cannot go to treatment now, my work load will not permit it." I can recall one priest telling me, "I can't go now, I have at least four funerals coming up." The primary purpose of the intervention is not to get a promise that the drinking will stop, but to get the victim into treatment immediately.

One value in using immediate family members as *intervenors* is that family members recognize and accept their own emotional involvement in the sickness, and gain awareness that they too need healing and care. Therefore, treatment models for family would include such programs as Alcoholics Anonymous, Adult Children of Alcoholics, Alateen, and Alanon.

2. *Treatment*: To be effective, the group itself must be familiar with various alternatives in the continuum of care. Today, awareness that alcoholism is a *primary* rather than a symptomatic condition, and, given specific treatment, is responsive to rehabilitation resulting in a high rate of recovery has gained acceptance from all health care professionals. This being true, alcoholism is one of the most treatable diseases of our day. Successful approaches have already been made in many industrial workplaces and in some dioceses across the country with positive results. Reaching a compromise with the alcoholic to go into outpatient treatment, or to attend a series of lectures is not enough. Active addiction is the problem; any complications that spring from the addiction must be explored with professional help only after the person is sober. This is the advantage of inpatient treatment.

Some of the better-known inpatient treatment facilities for men and women represented would include: Father Martin's Ashley, Havre de Grace, Maryland 21078, (1-800-799-4673); Guest House, Lake Orion, Michigan 48361, (1-800-626-6910); and Hazleden Foundation, Center City, Minnesota 55012, (1-800-328-9000).

3. *Alcoholics Anonymous*: Ongoing participation in AA's Twelve Step program for recovery is essential to the rediscovery of self. To quote Father Martin, "The Twelve Steps is the most powerful therapy known to humankind; the most effective therapy on earth." For the alcoholic to take on a life without alcohol, he must admit he is powerless over alcohol and that his life has become unmanageable because of it. The alcoholic must make this claim in his daily prayer. As Father Martin says, "Anyone can know how strong one is; it takes humility to know how weak one is." The life paradox here is that in acknowledging defeat by alcohol, the alcoholic gains victory over life!

To the millions of men and women who faithfully practice the Twelve Steps of AA and follow its principles in their daily affairs, there is a genuine, ongoing "spiritual awakening" changing their lives for the better. These have become God-centered, God-dependent, and God-blessed! When Bill Wilson and Dr. Bob Smith, cofounders of Alcoholics Anonymous, sat down to their first meeting, they were not theorizing about writing a manual of spirituality. They were baffled and beaten and desperately seeking a remedy for their disease. Still, what was born of their desperation may well go into history as the "greatest spiritual revolution of the twentieth century." Indeed, Alcoholics Anonymous is certainly recognized as America's most significant contribution to the history of spirituality.

In a keynote address to the National Association of Church Personnel Administrators, at their convocation in Forth Worth this past November, Father Thomas J. Reese, S.J., editor of *America Magazine*, cited "personnel" as the biggest problem facing Church leadership today. With the rise of alcoholism among the elderly and predominately aging clergy, the Church must remain open to recent findings from specialists in addictions in the public sector. In reading the mission statement of The National Catholic Bioethics Center, I was struck with its clear focus relating to Church ministry today: "Dedicated to promoting and safeguarding the dignity of the human person in the medical and life sciences." This ministry is directed not toward things, but toward persons.

May I suggest the establishment of a *Pastoral Care Plan on Alcoholism* as part of the overall health and well-being of a diocese? This *plan* would have a carefully stated and comprehensive policy with regard to the illness of addiction which can be applied unilaterally to all persons employed within a diocese. This includes bishops, priests, deacons, religious men and women, and all lay employees. This "commission" would engage knowledgeable, recovering clergy and lay people, who would provide current education on substance abuse, and the utilization of substance-abuse resources. Again, this would be considered pastoral care; this would be acknowledged as shepherd's care.

Once again, I thank you for this opportunity to share with you my most cherished gift of sobriety. In doing so, you have affirmed me as I continue to carry the message of life to others— through you. And God bless you in your ministry to the many still suffering alcoholic and drug addicts.

THE CLINICAL CARE OF ALCOHOL ADDICTS

PATRICIA L. OWEN, PH.D.

The goal of my presentation is to help you understand how alcoholics can enter into recovery through treatment, show you how the theory of change can be translated into effective treatment approaches, and give you appropriate expectations of treatment and outcomes.

In presenting this information to you today, I'll be asking—and answering— five questions:

First—if a person is obviously having serious trouble with alcohol, why doesn't he or she just stop drinking? Why is treatment needed at all?

Second—how *do* alcoholics change-and how long does it take?

Third—what are the critical components of treatment?

Fourth—what is the role of personal responsibility in recovery? Or—if it is a disease, can one hold an alcoholic responsible for not getting well?

Fifth—what is treatment success? Not drinking? Not drinking as much? Not drinking in a way that causes problems?

As I understand this conference is to be aimed at looking at the interplay between medicine and morality, I have intentionally framed my presentation to cover some of the moral questions involved in alcoholism treatment and recovery.

First—if a person is obviously having serious trouble with alcohol, why doesn't he or she just stop drinking?

Most alcoholics I've met are extremely intelligent people, with a great deal of willpower that has served them well in life. They've been able to make decisions and implement their decisions artfully ... as CEO's of major corporations, physicians, pilots, or professors. How is it, then, that these same people apparently can *not* make logical decisions about their use of alcohol?

(a) Denial is an inherent part of the disease of alcoholism. In fact, there is an inverse correlation between the severity of the disease, and the level of awareness a person has about it. This puzzled me when I first entered the field of addiction, twenty years ago. I did an assessment on a woman who was in a wheelchair because of her alcoholism; she had developed peripheral neuropathy and was no longer steady enough to walk. As I reviewed her chart, I thought certainly this person would now see the seriousness of her alcoholism, and be ready to address it. I was dumbfounded that, in fact, she not only denied problems with alcohol, she denied any use of alcohol at all—and convincingly. "How can I even get alcohol," she said, "when I have to be in a wheelchair?" If I didn't have another side of the story from her family and from her lab work, I would be hard pressed not to believe her. This was a very pleasant, reasonable woman.

How can it be that the more serious the alcoholism, the greater the denial? There are many reason. Alcohol is a socially acceptable chemical; people have negative stereotypes about alcoholics and therefore can't imagine being one; people have a lack of understanding of what alcoholism is, and therefore think, "whatever is going on with me, it's surely not alcoholism"; and finally, there's another, more profound reason: alcoholism is such an assault on a person's integrity—one's wholeness as a human being —that at some point the alcoholic cannot let the awareness of the devastation of disease into consciousness. Let me illustrate:

Before the development of alcoholism—and in "normal" people—we might view their sphere (*Figure 1*) of being as this: each small circle within the sphere represents an area of importance in life—relationships with family members, friends, God; interests such as music, sports, or other hobbies; doing well in a career; maintaining health; education and learning; all of these things. Maybe having a drink once in awhile is on the map, but small.

As alcoholism develops, this small circle becomes huge , displacing all the others into the very edge of existence. The first, and only, guiding force becomes obtaining and using alcohol. This is when a person risks a job in order to continue drinking, or would even leave a marriage or other important love relationship.

I believe a person cannot absorb this reality—and hence the denial—until they reach a point of readiness, and when they are in an emotionally and spiritually safe place to do so.

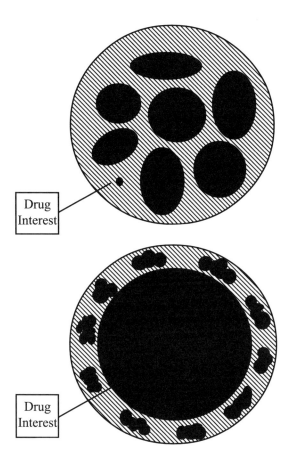

Drug Interest

Drug Interest

So one main reason that persons cannot just stop drinking if they have problems is denial—the absolute understanding of the need to quit is not yet in their awareness.

(b) But there's a second reason, and that also is in the nature of the disease of alcoholism. By definition, a person who is alcohol dependent, has crossed the thin line between choice and loss of control. By loss of control we mean that a person cannot reliably predict when drinking will stop, once it has begun. This is one of the distinctively characteristic features of alcoholism. A person who *can* reliably examine his or her use of alcohol and set limits on how much to drink and when, is most likely not an alcoholic. Research in recent years has helped us understand this from a biological point of view; for an alcoholic, after the brain has been "primed" by the initial intake of alcohol, the brain chemistry has changed, and the person needs more alcohol at that moment for the brain to function normally, or at least according to what has become "normal." Recovering alcoholics have understood this for decades; it's an old saying that for an alcoholic, "the person takes a drink, and then the drink takes a drink, and then the drink takes the person."

This, incidentally, is why controlled drinking works for alcohol abusers but not for alcoholics. If persons are simply abusing alcohol, they can learn to make better choices. If that line has been crossed, however, into alcoholism, the brain chemistry has irrevocably changed and choice is no longer possible.

Second — how do alcoholics change;
and how long does it take?

We tend to think of change as a moment in time when things become clear and new behaviors begin. For example, we might indicate a point (the person seeing the light) and say, "aha! This is where the change occurred!" But as a matter of fact, change is a process and not an event.

A team of researchers headed up by James Prochaska from University of Rhode Island have come up with an excellent model to explain how people change that I'd like to share with you, as it has a great deal of applicability to the treatment process. Here are the main components of the model:

Change Occurs in Stages

The first stage is called *Precontemplation*. This is the stage of denial that we just described: other people recognize that something is wrong, some-thing needs to change, but the person him or herself does not. I love the idea that this stage is not "before change." Even though a person may seem lost or unreachable, she or he is, in some way, on the path of change when they are in the Precontemplation phase.

The second stage is called the *Contemplation* phase. During this phase, the person recognizes that something is wrong, but is not sure what, or what to do about it. But there is growing awareness. At this point the person may be saying (at least to him or herself), "What would I be like if I didn't use alco-hol? Would other people like me more? Less? What would happen if I tried to change, and failed? Would I feel weak, guilty, coerced?"

The third stage is called the *Preparation* phase. At this point, alcoholic individuals are beginning to make visible moves toward action. They may start asking other people for advice or information. They might pick up a book or pamphlet, or read an article about getting help. They might try to limit their use by drinking later in the day, or only on certain days. They may even set a date for quitting drinking, or enter treatment, or go to an Alcoholics Anony-mous (AA) meeting.

The fourth stage of change is the one that people often think of as "real change" and it is called the *Action* phase. It is at this time that the person puts his or her heart into making changes, then making a personal commitment. We see behavior changes. A person in this stage seeks feedback and support, and small changes creates more change. It is the most stressful phase of change, because the person is taking risks with rejection and failure.

The fifth stage of change is the *Maintenance* phase. This is critical in alcoholism. In recovery, "change" is not something that just occurs once, in the past, but is ongoing. Specifically, for alcoholism, a person who has a sound plan for preventing or managing relapses has the best chance for successful maintenance. In maintaining change, the person engages in active behaviors that remind him or her of the commitment made and the need to continue. Sometimes these are "kindly daily disciplines" such as a daily meditation to maintain conscious contact with God, and a daily inventory; it includes continuing going to AA or other support groups; it might be using a key chain that has "easy does it" or another simple slogan on it. During the Maintenance phase, the person is able to demonstrate continued appropriate coping behaviors, and is becoming the kind of person he or she wishes to be.

The final stage of change is considered to be the *Termination* phase. Theoretically, this is when temptation to use is consistently at zero. However, because external or internal cues can unexpectedly trigger a thought or urge to use, most recovering alcoholics that I know consider it safest and wisest to stay in the Maintenance phase. For some problems, such as smoking, a person may be able to enter the Termination phase. For alcoholism, however, it is very realistic to expect to spend a lifetime in the Maintenance phase.

There are other important components of the model: Change is not linear, but most likely occurs in a spiral or repetitive fashion. Lessons learned are repeated, but at a higher or more complex level. Change is a process that often cannot be seen. For example, I sometimes hear people say something like, "that guy went through three treatments before he got sober; obviously those first two treatment programs weren't much good," or words to that effect. In fact, there might have been a tremendous amount of learning going on prior to the third treatment.

The Twelve Steps

Before we move on to specific treatments, I'd like to spend a few moments taking about the therapeutic principles of Alcoholics Anonymous, on which much treatment is based. Alcoholics Anonymous is essentially a program for change. Some excellent books have been written on the history of AA; briefly, it grew out of the Oxford Group movement in the United States and England in the earlier part of this century. The Oxford Group was comprised of people who came together to support each other in using the Bible and religion—specifically first-century Christianity—to find more meaning in their lives. AA itself began with a stockbroker and a physician—both alcoholics who had hit bottom.

As most of you know, AA has Twelve Steps. Essentially, here is what happens in these **Twelve Steps**:

1. Recognition and understanding of problem
2. Belief that God can help
3. Trust in God
4,5. Personal inventory and revealing to one other
6,7. Asking God for help
8,9. Amends, repairing personal relationships
10. Continued personal inventory and amends
11. Conscious contact with God
12. Carrying the message, and "practicing these principles in all our affairs"

There are three observations I'd like to make here:

First, the actual steps use the phrase, "Higher Power" or "God as we understand him." Often people in recovery from alcoholism, even those with strong religious backgrounds, need to reexamine, redefine, and reconnect with God in very basic, fundamental ways. Some people, through their disease, have decided that God has abandoned them, or punished them. Others have a quite narrow or limited relationship with God that may need to grow before they can progress in recovery. So the steps intentionally leave a lot of leeway for people in this regard, so as not to block people from even beginning.

Secondly, the Twelve Steps are, in themselves, a framework for change. One moves through the Steps as one is ready. The first time through the Steps, they may be guided, and the first three to five Steps may be complete during a treatment episode. The expectation is that people will return to these Steps— and all of the Steps—as needed. When a person repeats a Step, later in the recovery process, they usually do so with greater insight and awareness. For example, it's not surprising to hear someone who's relapsed say, "I forgot Step 1; somehow, I thought I could have just one drink on my vacation. I knew I couldn't drink at home. But somehow, I started thinking that one drink, a thousand miles away from home, couldn't hurt ... Now I understand that I am truly powerless over alcohol, no matter where I have the drink" This is a simple example; as years of recovery, and working the Steps continue, people can enter into profound levels of understanding about themselves—even beyond their alcohol use—through the Twelve Steps.

Third, entering into recovery through the Twelve Steps is not just "getting right with God." It is true that during the disease process, estrangement typically occurs. And, during recovery, a key component is the spiritual one, reconnecting with God. But it would be wrong to tell someone that they are alcoholic because they do not have a good relationship with God. AA is not a religion, but can lead people back to their religion in stronger ways.

Third—what are the critical components of treatment? How can I choose a treatment program, or tell if someone is getting good treatment?

Let me walk you through the important components of treatment in a sequential way. First, a person needs to be medically stabilized. This may include withdrawal medications. Some people think that the detoxification process for heroin or cocaine must be far more complex and dangerous than detoxification from alcohol. Actually, the opposite is true; we find that about 10–30% of the alcoholics who come to our facility need medications to safely withdraw them from alcohol. This earliest phase of treatment is focused on physical health issues; so many alcoholics have accompanying physical disorders, such as hypertension or recent trauma injuries. In fact, the severity of almost any physical disorder—diabetes, asthma, gastric disorders—is likely to be increased by the presence of alcoholism—and the symptoms may have been masked or treatment for them not sought or delayed.

The next phase of treatment is the assessment process. The best assessment for alcoholism is an interactive, iterative process where the alcoholic and the clinicians appear to reach the same conclusion at roughly the same point in time. If done well, the assessment process is a learning process for the alcoholic, increasing his or her motivation and readiness to change. If we do develop a biological litmus test for alcoholism, for example, like a pregnancy test, or a blood sugar test for diabetes, I am not certain that would effectively replace the necessity of the assessment process. What happens during the assessment process? The patient meets with each member of the multidisciplinary team individually—the nurse, the physician, the psychologist, perhaps the psychiatrist, the chemical dependency counselor, the chaplain, the fitness or wellness staff—and with each one tells part of his or her story. At the same time, he or she is reading, and filling out life questionnaires. At the end of this time—it may be three to seven days—the staff meets together and arrives at a diagnosis and initial individual treatment plan. The patient meets with his or her counselor, reviews the recommendations, and is ready to begin.

The individual treatment plan is the "meat" of the treatment process. A typical beginning for many patients for example, is to learn more about alcoholism as disease—and not as a moral failing—and to personalize the disease. This is when things start to make sense for the alcoholic; they can look back at incidents in their life and say, for example, "Gee, I see I switched jobs six times in the last ten years. I always thought it was because my employers didn't appreciate my talents or that I wasn't getting the right breaks. But seeing that now, in light of how my alcoholism was developing at the same time, maybe it was my alcoholism, and not just a string of bad luck." As they begin to understand the devastation that alcoholism has created in their life, they can begin to take some responsibility for it, and for the rest of their life.

A person's treatment plan is formalized, with goals and objectives. It includes a wide range of assignments: books and other readings, written assignments, holding or attending small groups, and practicing and demonstrating behavior changes. Some people with concomitant disorders such as depression, eating disorders, gambling, sexual compulsivity, post-traumatic stress syndrome, and other anxiety disorders will be given specific therapy for that. We used to think the wisest thing was to defer treatment for adjunct disorders until after treatment for the alcohol or drug problem. Now we typically treat it concurrently, as much as possible. If this doesn't happen, a person may be at a greater risk for relapse, triggered by the coexisting disorder.

A person continues to work on his or her assignments, until ready to make the transition to decreased services and support. Some may move on to a halfway house, where they continue to get daily services and support. Others may be ready to go home, if it is an environment conducive to recovery and a support network can be built.

Another way to look at treatment: It consists of three components; therapy, education, and fellowship.

1. Therapy includes individual counseling sessions and group counseling sessions, and it may include medication. Individual sessions are important for obtaining and reviewing the detailed assessment information, for discussion topics that may be too difficult or sensitive in a group setting, and for reviewing progress. Group sessions, contrary to many people's impressions, are not primarily for harsh confrontation or coercion. Instead, group sessions can be extremely helpful for what I would call vicarious learning. As one person is courageous enough to disclose some of the difficulties he or she is having with a problem, and receives some help, another person in the group can often identify with that person and apply much of the same information. Another advantage of group therapy is that people learn they are not alone in their difficulties. Third, they learn how to be comfortable participating in a group, which prepares them well for participation in Alcoholics Anonymous.

2. Education is a critical component of treatment: education about the disease, and about oneself. Education is typically provided through lectures and reading assignments; the latter is called "bibliotherapy." These forms of education—lectures and reading—provide the basis for "anonymous learning." That is, while listening to a lecture, or reading on a particular topic, a person does not have to disclose any personal information—and yet may find that the information is extremely relevant. This is particularly important in the treatment of alcoholism because of the high level of shame that is often present.

3. Fellowship: a critical component of the treatment process is introduction of the individual to a fellowship of other people where he or she can easily identify with others and be accepted. This is why some parts of treatment may seem to be informal or unstructured. In actuality, interaction with peers is intentionally built in during the treatment day. This interaction, being part of

a fellowship, provides alcoholics a mirror of themselves, an opportunity to try new ways of being, subtle lessons from recovering alcoholics just a bit further along, and helps fill the void that the absence of alcohol has left.

An important underpinning of treatment is the assumption of dignity and respect. An alcoholic may appear to be arrogant and self-centered by the time he or she enters treatment—but as a matter of fact, as we saw above, alcoholics are generally hanging on by their fingernails to some shred of belief that they are worth something. Unless that very belief is built upon—so they have the safety net, emotional and spiritual safety, they cannot go further. In one study, I asked alcoholics to name important turning points in their treatment process. One alcoholic simply said, "when I realized that people here would be so nice to a drunk like me."

Another important underlying aspect of treatment is that it must take the change process into consideration. That means (1) understanding that change does not occur quickly—in one or two sessions, or in three or five days; (2) that people will be at different stages in the change process, and therefore each approach will need to be individualized; and (3) that the process of change needs support and skilled management in all phases. Sometimes we will have a patient say, "I poured all my alcohol down the sink and have no more money anyway. So my problem's gone … I don't need any more treatment then, do I?" Or an insurance representative will say, "This person has not had any alcohol for five days, is stable, and not experiencing craving. Why is continued treatment needed?" These examples show how it is necessary to understand the change process; treatment, just as change, is a process rather than an event.

How then, can you tell that a person is "getting well"? There are some basic milestones, which are displayed on the accompanying slide *(Figure 3)*. As individuals make progress in the recovery process, they begin to accept and admit the fact that they have a problem with alcohol—specifically, a disease—and from that, move from denial and blame to personal responsibility and improved behavior changes. At the same time, craving and obsessive thoughts about drinking decrease, and a person makes a plan and a commitment to avoid people, places, and things that are most likely to trigger these thoughts and cravings.

Fourth—what is the role of personal responsibility in recovery? Or—if it is a disease, can one hold an alcoholic responsible for not getting well?

If one understands alcoholism as any other chronic disease, it's easier to understand and make sense of the implied paradox of this question. Let us use heart disease as an example. An individual may acquire heart disease almost purely as a result of genetics; another may acquire heart disease in large part through poor eating habits, lack of exercise, stressful reaction to life,

Figure 2

> ## Milestones of Recovery
> - Recognition of a problem
> - Understanding of disease (loss of control; not a matter of willpower; need for something greater)
> - Acceptance of others' input
> - Personal responsibility for recovery (as opposed to blame)
> - Demonstration of new behaviors & attitude
> - Daily pattern of living

and/or smoking. In any case, when the person arrives at the physician's office, the task at hand is to repair the damage as best as possible, teaching the patient how to live with his or her disease in a way that reduces or minimizes further episodes.

The same is true of alcoholism. Once a person has received a diagnosis of and treatment for alcoholism, the level of responsibility for it goes up. Not for having become an alcoholic, but for following clinical recommendations for the recovery process. We say to patients, "it's not your fault; but it is your problem." A person cannot be held responsible for becoming an alcoholic, but can—to varying degrees—for staying on the path of recovery. I hedge here because (1) denial and overuse of willpower is part of the disease process, and may deceive even a sincere recovering person: (2) if a person does have a relapse in the recovery process, his or her ability to choose and make responsible choices is, by very nature of the disease, going to be impaired: and (3) a person may have an underlying disorder—depression, anxiety, compulsive sexual behavior, gambling, eating disorder—that has gone undetected and may interfere with full recovery. It is fair to say that a person's responsibility for recovery increases proportionately and incrementally over time. I would expect someone with three years of sobriety to be able to accept far more responsibility for his or her recovery than someone with only three weeks.

Fifth—what is treatment success? Not drinking? Not drinking as much? Not having drinking problems?

The "gold standard" is continuous abstinence from alcohol and all other mood-altering drugs, beginning improved quality of life. These graphs (Figure 4) illustrate abstinence outcomes. The second graph is alcohol and other

Figure 3

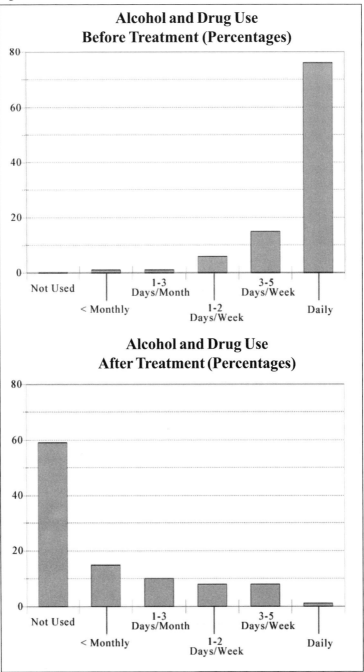

drug use for the year after treatment. As shown, in this group, 59% maintained complete abstinence; about 15% used less than monthly, and a descending proportion used more frequently. What is striking, of course, is the comparison before and after treatment. Behavior before treatment is indicated on the first graph. As you can see, during the year before treatment, most of the sample (76%) drank or used other drugs daily; after treatment, this figure fell to less than 5%. What we look for, though, to stress again, is total abstinence—and typically between 40–60% of patients will fall in this range with good treatment.

Not drinking is not enough. We know that it is possible for someone to quit drinking and to have a very unhappy life—and to make life difficult for those around him or her. Sometimes we see this with people who quit drinking purely by willpower or stubborn pride, but do not have a program for living such as AA to help them fill the void that alcohol has left and to learn how to continue to change.

After treatment we see improvements in the following areas:

Other Significant Areas of Improvement

- Relationships with Others
- Ability to Handle Problems
- Physical Health
- Employment Issues
- Legal Issues
- Overall Quality of Life

Typically over 70% report improvements in relationships with family, friends, and God. Most will report improved ability to handle problems and to deal with stress. We see significant decreases in health problems employment problems, and legal issues. These, as a matter of fact, in cost-benefit terms, generally produce significant savings to an employer, other payers, and to society in general.

Who does well? People who complete treatment and are actively involved in Alcoholics Anonymous do better, after treatment, than those who do not. The longer the person is actively involved in treatment or post-treatment support, the more likely is success in recovery. Probably the most critical time period is the six months after treatment; this is when a recovering person is most at risk for relapse, and is most likely to dive back into life as usual. It is extremely important that recovering persons face the fact that their lives will need to be rearranged to put recovery and recovery activities first.

A recovering alcoholic asked me a question. He asked, "Pat, as director of research at Hazelden, how do you measure 'success'?" I told him about our latest study, that we looked primarily at the percent of people who were able to maintain abstinence for the year after treatment. He then told me, "Well, I think you ought to know; I'm one of Hazelden's failures." I looked at him and laughed; he'd been sober for many years, had a great job and family. So I asked, "How can that be? What do you mean?" He explained that he had two relapses after treatment, before he got on track and solidly into sobriety.

He made a good point; the fact of the matter is that alcoholism is, by definition, relapsing—much like cancer or other chronic diseases. On the otherhand, we do expect total abstinence, in measuring success. But abstinence alone is not enough: successful recovery is a lifelong process of continued growth and change, which results in improved relationships with self, other, and God. We know that with treatment, this is possible.

References

Kurtz, E. *Not-God: A History of Alcoholics Anonymous*. Center City, MN: Hazelden Publishing.

Pittman, B. 1988. *AA: The Way It Began*. Seattle, WA: Glen Abbey Books.

Prochaska, J.O., C.C. DiClemente, and J.C Norcross. 1992. "In Search of How People Change: Applications to Addictive Behaviors." *American Psychologist*, 1102–1114.

THE CLINICAL CARE OF DRUG ADDICTS

ANNA ROSE CHILDRESS, PH.D.

Last night's dessert was terrific. There was a wonderful chocolate mousse cake—you may remember it, I know I do. And you may remember the smell of a chocolate mousse that you once encountered, the smell of mocha, a touch of coffee in the chocolate, maybe a kiss of Grand Marnier in the texture of the pudding. And although there was no whipped cream on top of this particular mousse, there really should have been, so you could remember what it feels like when the cream hits your throat and melts away.

I hope this is not too cruel. This does come after the break, and you did have a fair chance to get a pastry during the break, didn't you?

So you may notice some other responses. You may have a little bit of salivation, you might even have a little rumbling in your tummy, if you didn't have much at the break. Importantly, you might have a brief but manageable desire for chocolate.

The next slide, however, is probably not nearly as evocative for you. You probably don't find your heart pounding when you see these curious little plastic vials with white pellets in them, you probably don't have your ears ringing or your head buzzing and light, you probably don't taste cocaine in the back of your throat, and most likely, you're not gripped on an overwhelming desire to leave the room, run into downtown Dallas, and try to buy some cocaine. If any of you feel the desire to leave the room in this case, we'll blame last night's dessert and say you're going to look for chocolate.

Now desire states such as these are often daily events for the addicted individual, and they, in fact, have been the focus of my clinical and research efforts for the past decade and a half. So this morning, what I would like to try

29

to dois give you an overview of our work in Philadelphia to better understand these states, which is sort of a cardinal feature, excuse the term cardinal, our work of addictive disorders, and, to treat them, and most recently, to even try to peek inside the brain and see what goes on when our patients are in these states of compelling desire.

Now we became interested in these states not just because they are colorful. Not just because they're colorful but because they seem to be an important part of what shackles our patients to their preferred drug, pulling them back into a cycle of relapse often long after they have become drug free. So many different things can lead to relapse. I'm sure some of the prior speakers yesterday talked about some of the predisposing conditions for relapse. But our patients often credit these craving episodes with some peculiar and powerful trigger power in leading to relapse.

Now this issue of relapse is a difficult one. It's a frustrating one for clinicians, for caretakers, for families, for religious caretakers, for the patients themselves. Let's look a moment at the addiction cycle.

Patients go through a cycle of use, but very often, either with or without our help, they will manage to stop using, for at least a while, and become drug free. But what's frustrating for them and for families, and for the people who care for them, is that there's often a strong tendency to return to the drug at some point, after withdrawal has passed, after the drug has left the body. For a very long time, withdrawal was given important status in the understanding of addiction and people talked about withdrawal as being the push that would drive people back to use. But I'm really talking about a relapse here that occurs after withdrawal has passed, well after the drug has left the body. In fact, detoxification is not really a very tough thing. We can send people for a quick detoxification, a time to dry out from alcohol or drugs, but the difficulty is there's a tendency to return to the drug long after withdrawal has passed. So our efforts have focused on trying to understand the return to drug use that can occur long after the discomfort of withdrawal.

We should treat withdrawal as an important feature of addictions, but the difficulty is that long after the people get over the hump of withdrawal, there is this vulnerability to return that persists, the inexorable pull back to the drug.

So for a long time, withdrawal was equated with addiction, I'm going to try to put that in a different context today so that it's just the very early stage, and what I'm trying to talk about and understand better are the mechanisms that lead to relapse long after withdrawal has passed.

The point is that we have very effective treatments for withdrawal—you know about some of them. We have the nicotine patch for smoking, and yet people relapse even on the patch, because even though they're not in withdrawal discomfort, there's still the desire for the cigarette. We have opiate substitution treatments for opiate addition, and yet, there's still the desire for opiates, even for patients who are maintained on methadone. We have very effective treatments for withdrawal in many cases, but relapse still occurs. So this relapse, this pull back, is a big, big clinical issue in the care of the addicted individual.

So today when I talk about this word "craving," and I'm going to use this word regularly, not just because I'm the craving lady but because I can't stop using this word. When I talk about the word "craving," it's not going to be so much in reference to the kind of craving that arises out of discomfort or dysphoria or withdrawal, but rather the kind of craving that is associated with the desire for the positive, pleasurable, rewarding, euphorigenic effects of the drug. That kind of craving can be described by me, but I think it might be interesting for you to hear a patient describe this state in its full blown form. He's more eloquent than I, so let's take a couple of moments and listen to the description of this state that we're trying so hard to find better treatments for.

MALE VOICE: Yeah, what you call craving is what I can feel before I use. Actually, it's something that just pulsates through my body, it pulsates in anticipation. It goes, I guess it's in reminiscence of several highs that I've had on cocaine, of where it just, the point right before death, where it just pulsates throughout your whole body, you feel like you're being lifted up into the heavens.

DR. CHILDRESS: Is it a familiar feeling?

MALE VOICE: No way.

DR. CHILDRESS: Okay.

MALE VOICE: I think it is a total brain rush, then it rushes to your toes, just through your body.

DR. CHILDRESS: This is just the prior state, not even the drug yet.

MALE VOICE: You feel it go down and it runs into your toes and it comes back up, and it's rushing, pulsating through your body like some enormous wave.

DR. CHILDRESS: And then even before that.

MALE VOICE: Oh, yes, you feel ...

DR. CHILDRESS: So this is, if you can remember ...

MALE VOICE: This is what you are trying to achieve, this is where you're going, this is what you have on your mind, this is what I have on my mind in order to, in trying to achieve, and if I don't achieve that, then it's real bummy; I got to go back for more. And I do achieve it, I go back for more and it's always ... just a simple thing like seeing a person who you know uses or has used. You're walking down the street or driving down the street and you see that person is high. I'll say, "Well, you know," and then all of a sudden it hits you. I don't know if it's a desire to be that person or a desire to outdo that person, that you can get stoned more than he is or she is, or just more like a dare, can you keep it together and still be stoned out of your mind?

31

DR. CHILDRESS: Right.

MALE VOICE: My heart flutters, my fingertips get cold, I think I have sweats, I know they get cold, the chills, oh, the anticipation is just amazing, just ... it's pulsating, and you think that, why do I have to do it if I feel it already? It pulsates through my body. It's like whoom whoom whoom.

DR. CHILDRESS: Whoom! Pretty compelling this description of this state. And the point to review is that this kind of state can occur at any point in this addiction cycle, it can occur early while use is still going on, can occur even while a person is in the discomfort of withdrawal, and can occur as we heard descriptions earlier, at many points long after drug use has ceased.

How did we begin to study this state and learn more about it? We need to know something about the conditions under which it occurs, that was the first step for us. And so what we did is talk to patients.

In Philadelphia, the cocaine epidemic really began in earnest in the mid 1980s; that's when it became cheap and available. Before that, my work was mostly with patients who were heroin addicted. Many of our patients who were sworn heroin preferers, when cocaine became widely available, added it to their heroin, in the form of what's called a speed ball, injecting both things together. They're a very potent and rewarding combination.

So we began to talk with our patients about the conditions under which this kind of state could occur, that would be most reliably triggered, and we got a long list, some of the things very individualized, but I'm going to give you a sense of the long laundry list that can actually trigger cravings.

One thing is the little vials, just the sight of paraphernalia along the street. In Philadelphia, between the center where I work, just about four or five blocks from the Veteran's Hospital, you used to see these little plastic vials, and that was the main mode of packaging for cocaine, sort of like a Hansel and Gretel trail of rice between the packaging centers and the distribution centers and, unfortunately, the treatment centers. So you would have evidence of the drug use problem all around you. In fact, our center is right in a very heavy drug-using area in West Philadelphia. The site of that paraphernalia, even empty paraphernalia on the ground would be enough to trigger this state. Certainly the trigger would be the sight, as our patients described, of someone that they had used the drug with on a regular basis. In Philadelphia, as in any large city, there are places that are known to be drug distributing addresses. So if someone in Philadelphia says 40th and Market, for our patients, that would be enough to get their tummy rumbling and to get this state going. So people, places, and things are all triggers, which is why the many self-help groups have recommended to avoid people, places and things associated with drugs, if at all possible.

Money is a big trigger for our patients, unfortunately, because we want them hopefully to return to being productive members of society, holding a job and earning wages. But very often, the first paycheck after getting out of detox or rehab is the occasion of the first relapse. The money has become closely associated with a certain amount of drug, with cocaine, such that it acquires this interesting trigger power.

Alcohol or other drug use is another trigger. For many of our cocaine patients—and this is not just true for cocaine but other drugs as well—they're used in combination with other substances that patients may not consider to be problematic. So a patient may come in and say, "My problem is cocaine. Yes, I use a little alcohol to come down, it's not really a problem." They don't feel that the alcohol is out of control for them, but what is often the case is that very much like coffee in one hand and cigarette in the other for many people, the two have become associated such that now when they stop cocaine, if they use alcohol, it's reminiscent of the cocaine and has become a link, and triggers desire for it, in this very interesting fashion.

It doesn't have to be something external. We all walk around with our memories of powerful experiences. These drug highs are probably among the most powerful experiences that people can have. So sometimes a patient would wake up from a dream about cocaine or just be visited by a memory of what the high was like, and that certainly would be sufficient to get this state going. So even if you're very good at avoiding a lot of the externals, you're still the companion of your memories, and it makes it very difficult.

Music. Sometimes a patient has regularly used cocaine or other drugs in a certain musical setting. Later, out of detox, out of rehab with good intentions, they hear the music and it starts this cascade of responses.

Even smells. Smells, as we said earlier, can be very powerful, very evocative. If patients walk into a pharmacy and it smells sort of chemical, it reminds them, for example, of the smell of cocaine being cooked in the crack pipes and smoked—so smells can be very powerful.

And even mood states. Patients may often have begun drug use in association with other psychiatric syndromes such an anxiety or depression. They may have begun in a self-medicating fashion—now they have a double whammy. They now have a disorder in its own right and these mood states, that are still problematic for them, seem to acquire the power to remind them of their drug. So now they know the mood can be briefly disrupted by the drug, and the mood itself acts as a trigger for desire for the drug because of the repeated association.

Our hypothesis, when we began to think about this sort of cascade of responses that occurred when patients encountered something reminiscent of the drug, is really a fairly simple one. Think back to your first year psychology course and Pavlovian conditioning. This is how we think it comes about. Very simply, many different things in the external environment and in the internal milieu over the natural course of the patient's addiction have been very, very good, reliable signals for the arrival of cocaine. So very much, as with Pavlov's dog—initially the meat powder elicits salivation, reliably. If you give the dog a tone or a light that comes on before the meat powder each time or think about the way your cat approaches at the sound of the can opener before you open the can of tuna, there is a signaling power that's acquired by these stimuli, these triggers, that proceed the important biologic event. So what we think here happens is that these many, many different stimuli out in the world and inside have now been linked, forced to link with the arrival of cocaine such that they now have this power, this ability, to trigger a number of interesting responses, and some that may be very clinically important. Physiological arousal, you've heard me describe this and we'll talk about this more in a moment, leads to the desire to seek out drugs.

How do we set about to study this in controlled conditions, because one of the things we want to try to do is develop better treatments. Very often— and this has been true sometimes in traditional treatment communities—the word "craving" is sort of an uncomfortable word. Patients, and sometimes even counselors would prefer to let the craving dog lie, they'd rather not talk about it. They'd rather sort of say, "You're not craving anymore, are you?" Because it was sometimes taken as a sign of lack of commitment or some failing, somehow the patient wasn't in the right stage or the right mind. We're really going to try to counter that with education and understanding, but we need, in order to do that, to understand more about how this thing comes about and how to better focus treatments on it; we wanted to try to do this under controlled conditions.

So we talked to our patients about ways that we might be able to do this. They said, why not simulate some of the things that they experience every day in the real world in our laboratory and measure, see what happens. So we did, we brought things into the laboratory that would remind them of their real world that they encountered on their way into the laboratory each day, and basically we brought in video tapes that were reminiscent of cocaine use, that had patients kind of re-enacting things that were related to cocaine: paraphernalia, having them hear a tape or a snippet of a drug talk; or in one case, watching someone adding a bit of baking soda to a little bit of cocaine hydrochloride, putting the two together in water, dissolving it, heating it, putting some cold water in, precipitating a little crack pellet. That was in the days when you had to make your own before the drug dealers decided to make it easier for everyone—McDonald's style—so there are crack pellets available for everyone now, whether it's in little vials or little plastic bags. We brought this into the laboratory and measured, under protective conditions, meaning that the patients are always talking with a counselor or a clinician afterward to make sure that they're comfortable before they go back to the ward, back to their homes.

How did we measure these? In the early days, it was with our venerable old polygraph. Many of you are familiar with polygraphs which measure the arousal that occurs when someone is not telling the truth. In this case, we were letting the body tell the truth of its arousal when it sees these drug-related paraphernalia, tapes, sounds; and then recording it.

So we wondered if we would see the kind of arousal that you heard that patient describe. Whether, in fact, the fingertips would get cool and the heart would pound, and whether we'd be able to reliably show this as a group phenomenon, not just one colorful, eloquent speaker among hundreds, but that it would be common. And we had patients also being asked at various points during their exposure to these cues, how they were feeling. Are you experiencing desire? Are you feeling a little bit as though you've used the drug already, a little bit of a high state? And sure enough, when we checked, you'd have a drop in skin temperature. That was common, lower skin temperature, and it was basically an arousal response. It's nonspecific, so your skin temperature would drop if you were running from a bear or running to your cocaine or running to you chocolate or running to your lover. Heart rate tends to go up, other indices of arousal also tend to increase. And subjectively, and this is an important one, most patients endorse a feeling of increased desire when they see these things, consistent with what we expected clinically.

And we basically also see an increase in the sensation of euphoric feeling, a little bit as though you've used cocaine. Just seeing these triggers can sometimes make you feel a little bit high. How can this be? Well, one thought is that basically you are having a brain state that may be similar to what happens with the drug itself, that has become learned or conditioned and which can be triggered by these various stimuli.

So we set about to try to develop treatments. Now that we had a measure, we wanted to see if we could actually try to reduce patients' responses to these triggers. And by the way, I should mention that all of this work on craving is always done in the context of a full service treatment program. That often includes professional psychotherapy, particularly with people who have experience with psychiatric disorders, and attendance at self help groups—all the kinds of anonymous groups that you're familiar with—and medications when necessary; so there's a full bank of services.

So our first attempt was based on fairly straightforward approach, à la Pavlov; let's call it the tuna and the can opener idea. Think about what happens when your cat first hears the can opener and thinks that the tuna is surely coming. There's a lot of arousal, there's approach, there's anticipation, there's excitement. But if you give the sound of the can opener over and over and over again—and no tuna—after a while, the cat looks up and doesn't approach, it has less of a response. So our first approach was essentially a classic passive cue exposure approach. We said, "What if we bring in a lot of cues and in a protected setting, give our patients lot of exposure, where they know they can't use, they're going to be on the inpatient unit, and maybe that will transfer out to the real world so that when they walk out there, they won't have as much reactivity, as much response, they won't feel as much pull. Let's try that."

So we dutifully put together large groups of cues, brought them on the inpatient unit, gave patients hour-long sessions over two weekends. And what do you think? They actually did reduce their reactivity to many of our cues and when we looked at what happened when they left the hospital, the people who had that cue exposure did have more cocaine-free urines for a time than the people who had had equal amounts of treatment but not the cue exposure.

But interestingly enough, the people with the cue exposure initially have an advantage, but there's a precipitous decline, with both groups showing some relapse by the end of the eight weeks, a return to cocaine use, and fewer cocaine free urines.

When we talked to patients, what they said was, "Yes, your tapes in there are pretty boring. But when I go around the corner and I see my dealer, I know it still means cocaine." So there had been an incomplete transfer. We knew this was a risk, but we had unwittingly set up sort of a perfect, what's called in the literatures discrimination learning. These patients knew my tapes and that Anna Rosa was never going to give them cocaine here in this setting, and they'd quickly learn that these cues in this context were no longer predictive of cocaine. They still had some reactivity, but it was reduced; however, this passive approach was never going to transfer completely to the outside. They knew that those outside cues were going to lead to cocaine.

In England, they do *in vivo* cue exposure. Like bridge phobia therapy here, or snake phobia therapy, where you can actually bring people and expose them to the real thing until they get past the arousal. They can do that in England because their drug scene is not quite so violent. We didn't feel we could take our life into our hands, go to the crack houses of the patients, show them the cues, and see what happened. We thought that would be ill-advised. So we did not go in the direction of passive cue exposure for this approach, we thought: "We've got to get clinically smarter. We've got to get clinically informed. Let's beg, borrow, and steal for our patients the best techniques that the people who have done well would prescribe. What do they do? What works for them in terms of managing these craving states? Let's package that, and let's try to bottle that and make it available to our patients, use it as a set of clinical tools that can be added into standard treatment." And so we did.

So what we have done, and I actually have this manual available, it's written at a level that is intended for those who are not necessarily at the master's or doctorate level, but people who are counselors, working with addicted patients. If any of you would like a copy, they're free, it's grant supported work. We put together a package of strategies that patients might be able to use whenever and wherever this state was triggered. We taught them these strategies in the context of a clinical setting. They would come in, we would ask them their state at the moment and ask them to describe for us a recent craving episode which in and of itself will create a little bit of this state, and then we taught them the tool of the day.

The tools began with things that were very simple. A deep relaxation response. You could use meditation, you could use prayer as a counter to this arousal in its very earliest form for some patients: their thoughts begin to shift toward cocaine, but their heart not yet pounding, the snowball not yet rolling down the hill, but they're in Wednesday night, thinking about the fact that the paycheck arrives Friday morning, and they notice this and they can begin to address it in an active way. Right there in the session, they are asked to recreate a little bit of this feeling by recounting an episode of craving, and then with the therapist, to do a deep relaxation or meditative type of response.

Another approach is "delay." Delay would be when the patient would bargain with himself not to act on this impulse for at least five minutes, and to always have a behavioral alternative, a Plan B, so that essentially, the patient is learning to use the craving state as a signal to do something else. So just as the state itself is signaled by drug use or drug thoughts, now they say, "Ah, this state, all right, my plan when I have this state is to take a walk, work out, pray— whatever would be the competing alternative response. This is very effective for many patients.

Recording negative and positive consequences: having been in the presence of the therapist, the individual writes down the three most negative consequences of acting on this craving and going through and using the drug.

Negative consequences, by the way, are very different from patient to patient. For some patients, you might think, "well, the loss of a spouse, the loss of a job, the loss of his home." Now for one patient, a male patient, it was the loss of his chest size. "I've shrunken, I'm no longer myself." But for many patients the consequences are fairly abstract: "I feel as though I've lost myself or that when I use, I'm not myself." "It has an impact on my family, on my community, on my children, that I don't like." "I don't like myself, I don't recognize myself." These would be followed by, in that same session, three positive consequences of how things can go when they don't use. So for them it might be writing down, "I will be able to feel good about myself." "I will be able to buy my children their holiday presents." "I will be able to function in a way that my wife and I can continue in our relationship."

The next tool, for patients who are able, builds on this idea of negative and positive consequences but uses imagery. So instead of writing down concrete consequences of what are the three things that are most important to me that are negative, that are going to happen if I use, and are positive if I don't use, the person has at hand a very negative, visceral image of what things were like at a very low point in cocaine use that he can pull up at any time. So when he's beginning to feel this tingle of craving, the rosy glow of, "oh, what the high was like," they say, "Wait a minute. Remember that time in the hotel when I hadn't had a shower for five days? I had no money, no clean sheets and no food. That's me when I'm on cocaine. I want to hold that right out in front of me. What happens Monday morning when you don't go in to the job and, in fact, you lose it because you were abusing cocaine all weekend long? So to bring those consequences into a visual form, we ask to patient to mentally form a positive image, of what things can be like when, in fact, the person is not using cocaine, not acting on the desire. It could be them at a family holiday table surrounded by friends, family, connecting.

Mastery imagery enables them to make this craving into something that they can actually do battle with. If you're on the West Coast, it might be a surfing image: the craving is a huge, unmanageable wave coming in to you and you are trying to manage the wave, to get inside the tube in just the right away and bring it in until it's just a trickle of foam and it disappears.

Many of our veteran patients like combat images they would be imaging "blowing away" a craving with their favorite automatic weapon. So we have a number of different approaches and they would always be fitted to the individual. In each case it is something that you can manage and that you can beat and that you do have responsibility for trying to manage. That's very important. It makes you an active participant. You're not simply the victim that's visited by the state of craving, but you must, in fact, deal with it, counter it.

And finally, there is reflection, having them really examine their thoughts when they're in this state. Usually they have the thought and move quickly into action. But having them look at permissive thoughts such as, "I haven't used in six weeks, just this time a little bit won't matter. I can use $10 and stop on Friday night; it's not going to take me all the way through my paycheck this time." And having them begin to throw up the flag when they hear those thoughts, to recognize them as being bad indicators in the past.

So we do that over a period of eight outpatient weeks and find that, in fact, it does confer an advantage. The people who have this sort of active training and learn to struggle with this state, to engage it and to use these strategies have fewer cocaine-positive urines.

So that's the way that we've been going at this clinically.

Another path has been, in addition to these behavioral strategies, to find a medication that would make things a little bit more manageable, that would sort of keep these desires within a more manageable range. And we've had, at our center and it's been true across the country, an intensive effort over the past decade, NIH funded efforts, to look for medications that might be helpful in these addictions, more broadly than cocaine, but particularly cocaine.

What we've done in our cue work is to paste our cue reactivity assessments onto these medication trials. So when someone was trying to see if medication A would work, we'd say, "Let's see if it will blunt the reactions to the cues. Does it take away the cravings, does it reduce the heart rate, what about the arousal?" And what I can tell you at this point is there's this perfect correspondence between our laboratory findings and the clinical ones that nothing has really worked yet.

We have a number of medications, and I won't drag you through the whole hospital formulary that have been tried, many of them in the category of medications that were intended to manipulate the limbic brain systems, either in an attempt to repress those systems during the early withdrawal phases, or to simply block them in an attempt to blunt the rewarding or reinforcing effects of the drug.

There's been one trial out in California with a dopamine-blocking drug in a cue reactivity paradigm that seemed to suggest some blunting, but these dopamine-blocking drugs are the things that we commonly know as neuroleptics, as antipsychotic medications. They have a lot of nasty side effects, and because of them it's something that probably doesn't offer a great deal of promise as a first line medication for cocaine dependents. And it's not even clear that it would be the first route to take anyway.

For example, we have schizophrenic patients, and I'm sure you've seen them before, who are on these medications for their schizophrenia, and what do you think they do with their disability check the first of the month? They go around the corner and still buy stimulants so they can still feel the effect, clearly they're willing to pay for it, of a stimulant drug like cocaine or amphetamine, even though they're on the dopamine-blocking drugs. So we have some conundrums still with regard to medications development. This is the way we've done it, but I'm not going to drag you through the results because they're pretty much, as I said, all consistent. We basically test the cue rate activity at the beginning of a medication or placebo and then test again later, when they're on it, to see if it reduces craving.

There is another sort of basic research that complements the treatment research. We were thinking that maybe the reason that we're not having such good luck in coming up with a medication to complement our behavioral strategies is that we don't know exactly what it is that we're trying to treat. What is the nature of this beast? Can we peek inside the brain and see what goes on during this state? And in the last few years, this has actually become possible.

So what we have done in the last few years, through brain imaging, is ask what the brain substrates of these craving states are. We've begun to get pieces, though not a complete answer, and just asking where the acting is in the brain takes us to these neuroanatomical substrates. And what did we think were the culprits? What did we think were the candidate for the brain regions that might be important?

Others here will speak about the limbic reward circuitry, the loop in the brain that's involved with motivation, with affect and mood, with our most powerful motivations..These drives are vital to stay alive as individuals, for example, the drive for food, and alive as species, such as reproductive behavior. We suspected that these circuits were important because of really good animal research, preclinical research, showing that animals giving themselves cocaine increase neurotransmitter activity in many of these limbic regions, and that in fact, as you heard described earlier by the patient, the state of desire itself is very much like the effect of the drug. So if we know where the drug itself is acting, the desire state, at least in part, will be evidenced in those same brain regions.

So we're interested in limbic brain regions, and especially with a pair of little almond shaped structures in the brain called the amygdala. And these structures have long been known to be important in emotional behavior, very important in learning about rewarding or pleasurable events or dangerous ones.

If you have an animal or a person that gets some damage to their amygdala and they look at something that's signaling a wonderful reward or a very dangerous event, the response is blunted. They're no longer able to appreciate the significance of stimuli. So we thought conversely, that's what's going on, perhaps in part, when people see these stimuli; their amygdala should be hot and activated. And we looked at some other associated limbic structures that the amygdala talks to, and we thought, "Let's see." So without reading this and getting scared by the dopamine, we thought that we should be able to see in response to these cues an increase in regions in the brain involved in motivation and affect, these limbic structures. And we looked at cocaine patients who were good cravers, these are people who had been around for a long time and who could talk about having this state. We used a technology called PET scanning which is essentially taking, in this case, a picture of brain blood flow activity. The blood flows where nerve cells are more active in releasing their chemical messengers, so you can use it as a marker of where things are more active. So we're imaging a picture of where the brain's blood is flowing more.

A PET scanner is a big doughnut-shaped device that is set up to detect minute amounts of radio tracers, of radioactive measures.

Basically what we did was show patients neutral videos while they were in the PET camera, and then our cocaine videos that we knew from our previous work in the polygraph room, could cause craving. And the first question was, "when someone's got their head in a huge doughnut-shaped scanner and got people walking around in white coats and taking blood samples and doing all the things that go along with the PET scan, including saying, 'Don't move,' and having their head in a head holder, could they still crave?" Could we study this state realistically in a PET setting?

We could and did. The subjective response to the cocaine video and the cocaine patients was craving which appeared only during the cocaine video experience, not during the neutral ones.

Did we see limbic activity? Did we have hot amygdala? Yes, we did. The anterior singulate up in the forebrain was also reliably activated in cocaine patients viewing these cocaine videos, but not in controls.

I hope from this brief survey that you can see that we're trying to get on the path to a fuller understanding of these desire states, trying to distinguish between states that represent an abiding appreciation of good things in life, that help us get up in the morning and that make life worthwhile, from the disorders of desire, which cause our patients, our neighbors, our families, our caretakers, so much pain. And I think a better understanding of these biological underpinnings, these disorders, should lead both to additional treatment tools—these are tools that we desperately need—and hopefully to increased compassion for those afflicted.

I'd like to note that I think identifying these biological substrates, trying to understand their mechanisms, is not— at least in my mind—at odds with patients taking individual responsibility for their behavior, for its impact on others, for reaching out to treatment. We know that treatment can be of great benefit and that to go untreated causes much more pain and hardship. Educating patients and caretakers and families about the power of these addictions, however, and the biological systems which basically fuel them, does not absolve any of us of the responsibility, but hopefully, it helps us better recognize the challenges that we're up against.

THE ROLE OF COERCION IN TREATING AND CURING ADDICTIONS

SALLY SATEL, M.D.

Introduction: Why Coercion?

To judge by the character of the present debate over national drug control policy, an observer would never guess how completely the participants agree about some very important things. The debate is dominated by its extremes, opposing camps that deride each other's arguments. On one side, the "drug warriors," as their critics label them, want to stamp out drug use altogether: They advance strict controls on drug production and harsh punishments for trafficking. At the other end of the continuum, drug legalizers condemn the abolitionist strategy as costly, punitive, and unrealistic, promoting in its place a regime of relaxed controls plus regulation for some or all drugs.

Yet all assent to two crucial points. First, many drug addicts need drug treatment if they are to lead productive and satisfying lives. Second, the more treatment available to each of these addicts, the better. The White House's Office of National Drug Control Policy estimates that the nation's present treatment capacity can accommodate only half the country's 3.5 million addicts, and there is need to narrow the gap.

These agreed-on propositions have not been acknowledged for what they are: starting points from which to work towards a policy consensus. The rea-

---

N.B.: A longer version of this article appeared as a monograph: *Drug Treatment: The Case for Coercion*. 1999. American Enterprise Institute Press. Washington, D.C.—S.S.

son for this avoidance is a large, uncomfortable fact: even if we close the so-called treatment gap, the most promising way —perhaps the only way— to put enough addicts into treatment for long enough to make a difference entails a considerable measure of coercion. This is a proposition massively supported by the empirical data on drug treatment programs, yet it runs counter to some of today's most powerful political and cultural currents.

Data consistently show that treatment, when completed, is quite effective. Indeed, during even brief exposures to treatment, almost all addicts will use fewer drugs and commit less crime than they otherwise would, which means that almost any treatment produces benefits in excess of its cost. But most addicts, given a choice, will not enter a treatment program at all. Those addicts who do enter a program rarely complete it. About half drop out in the first three months, and 80 to 90 percent have left by the end of the first year. Among such dropouts, relapse within a year is the rule.

In short, if treatment is to fulfill its considerable promise as a key component of drug control policy, whether strict or permissive, addicts must not only enter treatment but stay the course and "graduate." If they are to do so, most will need some incentives that can properly be considered coercion.

In the context of treatment, the term coercion—used more or less interchangeably with "compulsory treatment," "mandated treatment," "involuntary treatment," "legal pressure into treatment," "involuntary treatment," and "criminal justice referral to treatment"— refers to an array of strategies that shape behavior by responding to specific actions with external pressure and predictable consequences. Coercive drug treatment strategies are already common. Both the criminal justice system and the workplace, for example, have proved to be excellent venues for identifying individuals with drug problems, then exerting leverage, from risk of jail to threat of job loss, to provide powerful incentives to start and stay in treatment.

Moreover, evidence shows that addicts who get treatment through court order or employer mandates benefit as much as, and sometimes more than, their counterparts who enter treatment voluntarily.

This essay presents the case for employing coercion to increase the efficacy of treatment for drug addicts. With the aid of coercion, substance abusers can be rescued earlier in their "careers" of abuse, at a time when intervention can produce greater lifetime benefits. With coercion, more substance abusers will enter treatment than would enroll voluntarily, and those that enroll will enjoy an increased likelihood of success.

The argument will begin by recounting the story of early formal efforts to rehabilitate drug addicts and by drawing the lessons of those efforts. It will proceed to explore modern approaches to coercive treatment and examine the effectiveness of those approaches. It will then lay out the sources of current resistance to coercive strategies and, finally, suggest ways in which to integrate the theory and practice of coercive treatment into current policy.

The aim of the examination is to make the case that unless we acknowledge the necessity for coercive strategies, we will lose the best chance we have for treating addicts in ways that will bring about a significant increase in the quality of their lives and that of the society they inhabit.

A Brief History of Coercion in Drug Treatment

The Rise of Coercive Treatment

The nation had a perceived drug problem for some fifty years before coercive strategies arose in response. The first wave of cocaine, heroin, and morphine addicts was inadvertently created from the 1880s through the early1900s, first by well meaning physicians, later by hawkers of patent remedies. Most of the resulting "medical addicts," as they were called, were genteel women, personified by the heroin-addicted mother Mary Tyrone in Eugene O'Neill's *Long Day's Journey into Night.* They did not evoke moral censure.

Very different were the addicts who emerged over the first two decades of the 20th century. These were poor male "pleasure" addicts, harshly condemned as a social menace. In response, the Treasury Department, in 1919, cracked down on physicians who prescribed cocaine, heroin, and morphine. States imposed and enforced criminal penalties for use. Officials in big cities, fearing that the hundreds of male addicts thus deprived of their prescriptions would turn in desperation to violent crime, established opiate clinics to dispense morphine and heroin. By 1920, some forty such clinics were established.

Some of the clinics were worse than ineffective. The most notorious, like the Worth Street Clinic in New York City, were corrupted by diversion of drugs and presented the spectacle of bedraggled dope fiends, as they were portrayed, loitering around the neighborhood.

The best-run of these facilities, like those in New Haven, Connecticut, Los Angeles, California and Shreveport, Louisiana, did reduce drug-related crime and illicit trafficking but were still unable to point to addicts whom the clinics had cured of their addiction. The Shreveport clinic, however, did keep a close eye on its 198 patients, maintained meticulous records, and required that its addicts hold jobs and keep up their physical appearance or be cut off from the clinic. This requirement, historian Jill Jonnes notes, "probably weeded out most of the 'sporting' addicts and other unsavory types who so frustrated the New York doctors."

In time the federal government extended its policy of total drug abstinence to the clinics, which had all closed their doors by 1925 when the medical staffs were threatened with indictment by federal authorities. With the end of this short-lived clinical era, treatment for opiate dependence was largely unavailable between the early 1920s and the end of the Second World War. Though relatively few new addicts were created during this period, those who had

45

become afflicted in the early 1900s tended to remain opiate-dependent. In particular, a growing population of aging addicts came to inhabit federal prisons, to which addicts convicted of selling or possessing drugs were routinely sent.

Narcotics Farms

As early as 1919, when governments began reining in physician prescribing of opiates, the Narcotics Unit of the Treasury Department urged Congress to set up a series of federal narcotics farms where users could be confined and treated. It was only in 1935, though, in response to the problem of aging addicts, that the U.S. Public Health Service opened a facility in Lexington, Kentucky. Three years later, another federal farm was established in Fort Worth, Texas. These facilities received both criminal violators and addicts who enrolled in treatment voluntarily.

The Lexington facility was a hospital-prison-sanitarium in which medical and moral approaches to treatment converged. It was located, as Jonnes has described it,

> on 1,100 acres of rolling bluegrass ... an Art Deco campus-like affair with barred windows. In its early years, Lexington was literally a working farm operated by patient-inmates with chicken hatcheries, slaughter houses, four large dairy barns, a green house and a utility barn. When not farming, inmates could work in sewing, printing or wood working shops.

The facilities did not, however, succeed in providing a wholesome and salutary rural respite. According to Jonnes, the "effect of going to Ky (as patient-inmates called the Lexington farm) for most addicts was to expand their network of addict pals." The doctors were dedicated but frustrated, often noting that their patients would likely relapse upon returning to the inner cities from which they came.

The data confirmed the doctors' impressions. According to a report by the U.S. Comptroller General, approximately 70 percent of the hospital's voluntary patients signed out against medical advice before completing the six-to-twelve-month treatment program; and within a few years, 90 percent had relapsed. Most who remained in treatment did so under legal pressure from a court.

Still, though the farms are generally considered to have been failures, they generated useful clinical information. Most important, several follow-up studies of the participants indicated that addicts who after treatment were supervised under legal coercion had better outcomes than those not so supervised. A follow-up of over 4,000 addicts six months after discharge from treatment found that those on probation or parole were more than twice as likely to remain abstinent as voluntary patients, probably because the former had compulsory post-hospital supervision. A longer-term followup of the same population confirmed the critical role of post-hospital surveillance: It found that of those serving more than twelve months of parole, 67 percent remained drug-free a year after discharge, while the figure for voluntary patients was only 4 percent.

The data showed, in sum, that some kind of post-discharge supervision was needed. The information also yielded the lessons that (a) a six-to-twelve-month treatment stay was too brief; (b) the need was for intensive vocational services rather than psychological services aimed at personality change; (c) the threat of reinstitutionalization had to have teeth.

Therapeutic Communities

After World War II, organized crime was able to reactivate the old heroin trafficking routes disrupted by the war, and inner-city physicians began to encounter the next generation of heroin addicts. Therefore the 1950s saw a resurgence of interest in the treatment of addiction—and, in particular, the emergence of the notion of the self-regulating therapeutic community (TC), an idea enthusiastically welcomed by clinicians and policymakers who were heartened by early TC success stories and demoralized by the gloomy results of previous treatment efforts.

The idea of a therapeutic community was exemplified by Synanon, a residential facility established by former alcoholic Charles Dederich in Santa Monica, California, to treat both alcohol and heroin addicts. Synanon was followed by the establishment in New York City of Daytop Lodge and, in 1967, Phoenix House. The latter, a residential center on the Upper West Side, was founded by psychiatrist Mitchell Rosenthal, inspired by the efforts of six former addicts who were trying to keep themselves clean and enlisted his help.

Modern therapeutic communities immerse patients in a comprehensive 18–24-month treatment regimen built around the philosophy that the addict's primary problem is not the drug he abuses but the addict himself. Though psychiatric orthodoxy holds that addiction is a discrete, self-contained "disease," the therapeutic community's approach recognizes drug abuse as a symptom of a deeper personal disturbance. The strategy for rehabilitation is to transform the destructive patterns of feeling, thinking, and acting that predispose a person to use drugs.

In this effort, the primary "therapist" is the community itself, not only peers but staff members, some of whom are graduates of a program themselves and can serve as role models. The dynamic is mutual self-help; residents continually reinforce, for each other, the expectations and rules of the community. For meeting community expectations, residents win rewards—privileges like weekend passes or increasing responsibility, culminating in leadership roles. If a resident defies the rules, he or she loses privileges and must perform the least desirable chores. All residents must work—above all so that they learn to accept authority and supervision, an ability vital to their future success in the work force.

Researcher George De Leon has identified three stages in a resident's attitude towards such communities:

(1) compliance: adherence to rules simply to avoid negative consequences such as disciplinary action, discharge from the program, or reincarceration;

(2) conformity: adherence to the recovery community's norms in order to avoid loss of approval or disaffiliation;

(3) commitment: development of a personal determination to change destructive attitudes and behaviors

Those who negotiate the commitment stage have excellent outcomes. De Leon, in a long-term follow-up study of addicts admitted to Phoenix House, found that after five to seven years, 90 percent of those who had graduated were employed and crime-free, while 70 percent were drug-free.

But the graduates constituted only 20 percent of De Leon's sample. Generally, half of voluntarily committed patients leave therapeutic communities prematurely within days, generally considered to be the threshold at which individuals form an independent commitment to a treatment program. Perhaps one in five to ten fully completes a program.

These dropout rates are not hard to understand. In the early months of a program, residents of a therapeutic community often rebel against the rigid structure, loss of status they enjoyed on the street, and deprivation of getting high. Ambivalence about relinquishing drugs is a powerful psychological force pulling patients back to the street. Even patients with strong motivation experience flagging resolve, momentary disillusionment, or intense cravings. If a patient succumbs to these pressures, he or she may have gained some benefit from even the brief exposure to treatment but is at high risk for relapse into drug use and crime.

De Leon therefore sees legal pressure as the initial force that can literally get patients through the door into treatment and keep them there until they internalize the values and goals of recovery. Coercion alone can not do the job: One researcher put it that "if contact with therapy does not bring its own rewards, the potency of coercion will decline precipitously, and could ultimately work against treatment goals." But the threat of consequences like incarceration, the loss of a job, or some other aversive event can sustain an ambivalent or flatly resistant patient during the early months of treatment until those rewards—newly learned skills, a transformed self-concept, social maturation, and optimism about the future—ultimately inspire him or her to change.

Thus it is of interest that in De Leon's Phoenix House sample, it did not matter statistically to a patient's chances of "graduating" whether he or she had enrolled voluntarily or been mandated to treatment. This similarity did not mean, in De Leon's view, that compelled treatment made no difference; it was the opposite. The compelled patients began with worse prognoses, because of their legal involvement and their higher incidence of antisocial personality disorder and low motivation. Counteracting these disadvantages, though, was the fact that individuals who had court cases pending or had been legally referred to the community spent, on average, more days in treatment than voluntary patients did. The relatively bad prognosis was made up for by more treatment days. "Retention in treatment," De Leon therefore concluded, "is the best predictor of outcome, and legal referral is a consistent predictor of retention."

Methadone

The postwar period also saw, in the early 1960s, a renewed receptiveness to the idea of drug maintenance. The number of heroin users was increasing, and the treatment available to New York City's 100,000 heroin addicts, half of those in the nation, remained limited to hospital-based detoxification and the Daytop Lodge therapeutic community. A few years earlier, a joint committee of the American Bar Association and the American Medical Association had called for restoring physicians' freedom to prescribe heroin and for the establishment of an experimental clinic for this purpose. In 1963, both the New York Academy of Medicine and President John F. Kennedy's Presidential Commission on Narcotic and Drug Abuse (the Prettyman Commission) made similar recommendations.

Marie Nyswander and Vincent Dole, physicians at New York's Rockefeller Institute, set out to develop new pharmacological approaches to treating heroin addiction. They hypothesized that suppressing the physiological craving for the drug was the key to treating the addiction, and they sought a replacement or "substitution" drug that would, unlike heroin and morphine, not wear off within a few hours. Ideally, a long-acting medication would stabilize individuals so that they could hold down a job and function normally.

Nyswander and Dole chose methadone, a long-acting synthetic opiate developed by German chemists searching for an inexpensive morphine-like medicine during World War II. Addicts could take methadone orally and needed to do so only once a day in order to prevent withdrawal and craving. Moreover, because methadone worked by blocking opiate receptors, patients would not experience euphoria even if they took heroin in addition.

Dole started six patients on methadone in 1965. Around the same time, the U.S. experienced an influx of heroin from the Golden Triangle of Burma, Laos, and Thailand, fueling an epidemic that peaked in most American cities between 1969 and 1972. By 1969, almost 2,000 New York City addicts were enrolled in Dole's maintenance clinic, and by 1970 the city had expanded the clinic system to serve 20,000 voluntary patients.

There are not many studies of the relationship between compelled treatment and methadone therapy because, though methadone is one of the best-studied anti-addiction therapies to date, few patients are legally mandated to maintenance treatment. The major source of compelled treatment, the criminal justice system, prefers rehabilitation that aims for total abstinence rather than substitution of one dependence-producing agent for another.

However, over twenty years ago, M. Douglas Anglin of UCLA conducted an important study of whether addicts coerced into drug treatment differed from voluntary patients in their responses to treatment. Anglin divided some 600 methadone-maintenance patients according to whether they were subject to high, moderate, or low levels of coercion. The 19 percent in the "high level" category were under official legal supervision, including required urine testing, and perceived their entry into treatment as motivated primarily by the legal system. Another 19 percent, moderately coerced, were under active legal supervision and either were having urine tests or perceived coercion as the reason for their entry into treatment. Finally, 62 percent of the sample, under a low level of coercion, were not under legal supervision and not subject to monitoring via probation or parole. The majority of these reported feeling no legal pressure, even as minor as a fear of arrest, impelling them towards treatment.

When Anglin compared the three groups, he found that all of them showed substantial improvement when measured on narcotics use, crime, and social functioning. Once again, compelling patients to accept treatment did not bar clinical progress and, given the relatively poor prognoses of those involved, probably aided such progress.

The same lesson emerged from a more recent experience with methadone treatment at the Southeast Baltimore Drug Treatment Program. A research team led by psychologist Michael Kidorf of Johns Hopkins University noted that unemployment was a common problem among inner city drug users and lamented that "standard drug abuse treatment services appear to have only small effects on employment." In response, the Baltimore clinic, like its predecessor clinic in Shreveport some 70 years before, instituted the once-again-innovative requirement that its methadone patients be employed for at least twenty hours a week in order to receive methadone and related services. Patients were given two months to find employment or enroll in job training or community service programs. If they did not, they received five weeks of intensive counseling; those who did not obtain employment after counseling were tapered off methadone.

Because these patients had been enrolled in the same clinic before the requirement went into effect, their performance prior to the new rule could be compared with the same population's performance afterwards. Before the requirement, despite enhanced counseling with vocational training, none had managed to secure either paying or volunteer employment. By two months after the imposition of the requirement, however, 75 percent of the sample had secured and maintained verified paid employment, volunteer work, or education.

Civil commitment

Compelled treatment showed its potential in the California Civil Addict Program, created in 1961 as the first-implemented statewide civil commitment program in the country. Serving mostly heroin addicts, the program flourished during the 1960s. The California Department of Corrections ran the program, providing high-quality treatment by specifically recruited and specially trained corrections personnel.

During the program's most active years, its protocol included an average of eighteen months of inpatient treatment out of a total commitment period of seven years. After eighteen to twenty-four months in residential treatment, patients spent up to five years being closely supervised by specially trained parole officers with small caseloads who monitored patients closely and administered weekly urine toxicology tests. For any narcotics use violation discovered by these tests, the officers had authority to take action up to returning patients for treatment to the institutions from which they had been discharged.

This program became the venue for an unfortunate natural experiment: During the program's first two years, judges and other officials unfamiliar with its procedures mistakenly released about half of the committed population after only minimal exposure to the inpatient part of the program. Dr. Anglin's research team took advantage of this circumstance, selecting a sample of individuals who had participated in the program's inpatient treatment for a sustained length of time and comparing it with a matched sample of individuals who had been erroneously released. The team compared the two groups on their self-reported percentages of time spent on drug use and criminal activity, then verified the data through arrest records and urine specimens taken at follow-up interviews.

By one year after the premature release of half the study population, the two groups had sharply diverged. Individuals who had been prematurely released were more than twice as likely as those who had completed 18 months as inpatients to use narcotics. During the subsequent years of outpatient supervision, narcotics use declined for both groups; but the decline for those who had been kept as inpatients averaged 22 percent, while the figure for the discharged group was only seven percent.

Criminal activity followed a similar pattern. Before commitment, both groups had devoted about 60 percent of their time to such activity. A year after one group had been prematurely discharged, the figure for the treated group was 20 percent while the figure for the discharged group was 48 percent. At the end of seven years, criminal activity among the treated group had undergone a further reduction of 19 percent, but the reduction figure for the discharged group was only seven percent.

New York followed California's model, with a crucial and deleterious difference. Prompted by California's success, New York began its own civil commitment program in 1966. New York had the advantage of that year's federal Narcotic Addict Rehabilitation Act, which aimed to link criminal justice agencies to community-based treatment programs. The Act provided for compulsory treatment for addicts charged with certain nonviolent federal crimes; for treatment instead of sentencing for those convicted of such crimes, and for voluntary commitment of drug users not involved in criminal proceedings. The Act also began what was to become, in the 1970s, massive federal funding of treatment programs.

However, New York—unlike California, which mandated addicts to rehabilitation—allowed addicts to choose between treatment and incarceration. Those who chose the former were treated in residential settings developed during those years by the state Narcotics Addiction Control Commission, but this phase of treatment lasted only about nine months. Inpatient treatment was followed by parole-like supervision for another two to four years. Unfortunately, supervision was loose, and a high percentage of patients went AWOL. Governor Nelson Rockefeller was, not surprisingly, discouraged. "Let's be frank," he said in his 1973 Address to the Legislature; "we have achieved very little permanent rehabilitation, we have found no cure."

Modern Evaluations of the Effectiveness Of Compelled Treatment

Through the 1960s, the heroin epidemic continued, along with increasing rates of compounded national anxiety about the drug problem, raising the specter of a country inundated with returning soldiers hooked on narcotics. There were long waiting lists for treatment, and politicians were forced to confront the inadequacy of the system.

In June, 1971, President Nixon declared the first "war on drugs." He created the Special Action Office for Drug Abuse Prevention (SAODAP), precursor of the office of today's "drug czar." The new director of SAODAP, Jerome Jaffe, emphasized that "its implication as a landmark in the area of treatment should not be minimized. For the first time in the history of the Nation there was an explicit commitment to make treatment readily available."

Federal treatment resources expanded rapidly. In 1969, six community / mental health-drug treatment centers were in operation. Four years later, there were 300 such programs, and by 1977 there were more than 3,000. The programs were of four types:

(1) inpatient: This term describes programs in which a patient enters a hospital or free- standing facility for a few days to a few weeks, often beginning with several days to a week, depending on the abused drug, for detoxification. The aim is to break the cycle of use physiologically, to stabilize the patient psychiatrically, and to arrange for longer-term outpatient or residential treatment.

(2) outpatient (drug-free): This treatment ranges from one or two counseling visits per week, or several weekly visits including group therapy, to intensive versions offering daily sessions.

Patients learn how to identify and avoid triggers for drug craving and use and to handle drug cravings. They are typically referred to community agencies for health, mental health, educational, vocational, legal, and other needed services.

(3) methadone maintenance: This treatment foresees extended dependence on heroin and other opiates. A daily oral dose of methadone, a long-acting narcotic, acts as a heroin substitute, blocking the physical withdrawal and craving associated with abrupt discontinuation of heroin. Patients may be maintained on methadone for many years, depending on individual needs. High-quality programs offer rehabilitative services. Some use newer maintenance medications, such as LAAM (levo-alpha acetylnethadol), which has the advantage of being longer-acting than methadone, or buprenorphine, which has the advantage of being less addictive.

(4) therapeutic communities: These residential programs involve stays of six to 24 months, phasing into more independent residential living. The programs are highly structured: Patients progress through a hierarchy of occupational training and community responsibilities. The goals are to resocialize patients and enable them to develop stable relationships.

National Outcome Studies

The first evaluation of this network of community-based programs began in 1968 when the National Institute of Mental Health funded a proposal by Saul B. Selis, director of the Institute of Behavioral Research at Texas Christian University, for the Drug Abuse Reporting Project (DARP). Data collection began in 1969 and lasted four years, following about 44,000 patients enrolled in 52 federally funded programs. The project followed subgroups for five and twelve years following discharge from treatment.

In 1974, the Institute transferred control of the project to the newly created National Institute on Drug Abuse (NIDA). NIDA subsequently funded two more large studies, the Treatment Outcome Prospective Study (TOPS), which followed 12,000 patients who entered treatment between 1979 and 1981, and the Drug Abuse Treatment Outcome Study (DATOS), which followed 11,000 patients who entered between 1991 and 1993. More recently another federal agency, the Center for Substance Abuse Treatment, undertook the National Treatment Improvement and Evaluation Study, of 4,400 patients who entered the project between 1993 and 1995.

Taken together, these studies assessed roughly 70,000 patients, of whom 40 to 50 percent were court-referred or otherwise mandated to residential and outpatient treatment programs.

Two major findings emerged from these huge evaluations. The first was that the length of time a patient spent in treatment was a reliable predictor of his or her post-treatment performance. Beyond a ninety-day threshold, treatment outcomes improved in direct relationship to the length of time spent in treatment, with one year generally found to be the minimum effective duration of treatment.

The second major finding was that coerced patients tended to stay longer. (On this second point, DARP was an exception, finding no correlation between criminal justice status and either time spent in treatment or improvement. One can say only that DARP's compelled patients stayed as long as, and did no worse than, voluntary patients.)

To evaluate these findings, it is important to know whether addicts who entered treatment under legal coercion were meaningfully different from other patients. The findings from these studies are mixed. Some show that legally coerced addicts had a relatively unfavorable pre-admission profile—more crime and gang involvement, more drug use, worse employment records—that their noncoerced counterparts. Other studies detected little difference other than the particular offense that triggered the mandate to treatment.

In the DARP study, the baseline characteristics of voluntary and legally referred patients were similar. Because the subjects were relatively homogeneous on these dimensions, being primarily young, male, inner-city "street addicts," more than 80 percent with at least one previous arrest and over half previously incarcerated, the authors speculate that legal status was unlikely to have been a very discriminating variable.

The TOPS study, by contrast, discovered some differences. True, legally mandated and voluntary patients had similar drug use patterns, previous criminal justice involvement, and number of prior treatment episodes. But the legally mandated patients were younger than their voluntary counterparts and more likely to be male. When researchers looked specifically at patients who reported that the criminal justice system was the primary source of their referral to treatment, they found that these legal referrals were not only younger but used mainly alcohol and marijuana rather than "harder" drugs. The authors speculate that the legally mandated patients were "caught" earlier in their careers, that they were incarcerated too recently to have reestablished their habits, or both.

Though the studies do not present a consistent picture of pretreatment characteristics of legally mandated patients, they make it reasonable to conclude that even legally coerced addicts having relatively unfavorable prognoses can benefit from treatment as much as voluntary patients do, since the latter often remain in treatment for a shorter period.

A 1990 report from the Institute of Medicine summarized that "contrary to earlier fears among clinicians, criminal justice pressure does not seem to vitiate treatment effectiveness, and it probably improves retention." Thus, while there is conflicting evidence on whether a legal mandate brings individuals into treatment earlier, coercion can be almost surely be credited with derailing many an addiction career once individuals have been brought into treatment.

Of special significance, in light of the importance of length of treatment, is the fact that all four national outcomes studies showed high rates of attrition among patients, with half dropping out within ninety days. For these early dropouts, the benefits of treatment disappeared within the year. With substantial, durable change rarely occurring in less than a year or two of treatment, the high dropout rate makes retaining patients in treatment a pressing challenge.

Some researchers have hypothesized that the key to retention is to match each individual patient with the proper type of treatment. Though in principle such matching makes clinical and economic sense, there is surprisingly little tested information about such attempts. Two prospective studies by A. Thomas McLellan of the University of Pennsylvania suggest that tailoring patient care can indeed make a difference. McLellan assigned patients to programs according to particular psychiatric, medical, or family needs and found better outcomes for these patients than for those without such treatment. One of the national outcomes studies, DATOS, similarly found that even severely drug dependent patients were more likely to be abstinent at their one-year follow-up if they had received support services targeted to specific needs.

However, these findings are not uniform. The American Society for Addiction Medicine has developed widely used criteria for placing patients in specific treatment modalities; but the few studies assessing the validity of these criteria have not found an effect on outcomes.

Thus far, it appears that "patient matching," while it may be one means of assigning patients to treatment, is no substitute for length of treatment. It is length of exposure to treatment that powerfully predicts patient success, no matter what the treatment setting. The federal Center for Substance Abuse Treatment, in a recent study examining the relationship between these two variables, compared one sample of addicts who had 10 months of residential care followed by two months of outpatient care with another sample that had six months of residential care followed by another six months of outpatient care. Regardless of the treatment scheme to which patients were assigned, those who completed the entire twelve-month treatment period had the best outcomes. Further, those most likely to complete the course of treatment were patients under probation, parole, or pre-trial supervision.

Treatment Alternatives to Street Crime

TASC, established as a federal program in 1972 as one of the first initiatives of the Nixon administration's war on drugs, was moderately successful in cutting the number of street crimes committed by addicts. TASC was meant to serve as a bridge between the criminal justice and treatment systems. It functioned as a diversion program for drug abusers, diverting them from jail or prison by identifying nonviolent addicted criminals and referring them to treatment in the community. TASC assigned arrestees to case managers who were to get them into treatment and send progress reports back to the courts. The program, now supported primarily by state and local governments, subsequently expanded to supervising probationers and to post-sentencing disposition.

TASC has been the subject of a number of evaluations. Most are positive; others are partly so. In one such study, the TOPS project compared a subgroup of TASC-referred patients with a group of voluntary, unmonitored patients involved in the criminal justice system. Comparing patients' drug use one year before treatment to their drug use after the first three to six months of treatment, the TOPS researchers found that the TASC patients' use had declined by 81 percent; the comparable figure for the control group was 74 percent. Predatory illegal acts had declined by 96 percent for the TASC group but only 71 percent for the control group.

The Education and Assistance Corporation analyzed results from the Brooklyn, New York TASC program. Of 173 felons placed in treatment in 1992, 71 percent remained in the program for at least two years. At 29 months after completion of the program, the group's rearrest rate was nine per cent. This was much lower than either the 25 percent re-arrest rate among offenders from a control program or the 28 percent re-arrest rate among the general inmate population in New York State correctional facilities.

In Texas, a study found that seven percent of TASC-referred offenders were incarcerated during an 18-month observation period, compared with 28 percent of offenders who did not enter treatment or who stayed less than three months.

Finally, researchers at UCLA and RAND studying five regional sites compared TASC offenders mandated to treatment or to surveillance, including urine testing and case management, with a control group of offenders who received standard probation with little supervision. The TASC and control groups were similar on most demographic, drug, and criminal-record variables. At six months after patients' entry into the study, the researchers measured police-confirmed new arrests and technical violations and unverified self-reports of drug use.

The findings varied across the sites. In three places, TASC patients showed greater reductions in all three outcomes. In some places there was no difference on one or another outcome. At two sites, Birmingham, Alabama and Portland, Oregon, the researchers actually found more criminal involvement and technical violations among TASC patients—but the authors attributed this phenomenon to the fact that the TASC offenders were being watched gasingestmass{}

more closely and were thus more likely to get caught. (The authors also thought that the figures on self-reported drug use among TASC patients might be artificially low because heavily monitored groups may be more likely to minimize their reporting of punishable behavior.)

Coercion of Criminals

An estimated 60 percent of the cocaine and heroin used in the United States is consumed by the five million Americans who are supervised by or incarcerated within the criminal justice system. Moreover, offenders who abuse drugs are more likely than non-abusing offenders to return to crime following release from incarceration. Therefore there is considerable potential within the criminal justice system for reducing drug abuse and related crime by mandated treatment. Evidence indicates that diversionary and in-prison treatment programs, though currently available to only some 15 percent of offenders, have a benefit beyond the crime-reducing effects of incarceration or probation as usual. Results from several categories of criminal commitment show that treated offenders have lower rates of recidivism. Though these studies do not always directly measure post-treatment drug use, crime itself can reasonably be used as indirect evidence of drug involvement, since the two activities are so highly correlated. Conversely, declines in drug use are accompanied by declines in crime, particularly income-generating crime.

Drug Courts

One major category of coerced treatment of criminals occurs in drug courts, which offer nonviolent offenders, usually recidivists, the prospect of dismissed charges if they plead guilty and agree to be diverted to a heavily monitored drug treatment and testing program overseen by a judge. While in the TASC model judges do not have direct contact with treatment personnel, a drug court is a hub from which services such as treatment, case management, and vocational training radiate.

Drug courts originated in southern Florida in the late 1980s, when the area was hit hard by cocaine-related arrests that flooded courtrooms and overwhelmed jails. Addicts out on probation were quickly rearrested for new drug-related crimes, and the revolving door to the justice system seemed to be spinning out of control. Drug courts promised a way to break the cycle by "reserving" jail and prison beds for dangerous offenders while sending criminally involved addicts to treatment. The first one opened in Miami in 1989.

Enthusiasm about drug courts has spawned a drug court movement. Today, according to the National Association of Drug Court Professionals, there are almost 300 drug courts in operation, up from about 20 in 1994. An estimated 90,000 individuals have been enrolled. As of spring, 1998, every state but Rhode Island had at least one drug court in operation. California, where nearly a quarter of all state prisoners are incarcerated because of a drug offense, has over 70.

Though the accumulated evidence of drug courts' effectiveness has yet to reach a critical threshold, because there has been only a handful of independently evaluated studies, the early data look promising. Over 70 percent of drug court participants have been incarcerated at least once previously, almost three times more than have been in drug treatment; thus for many offenders, drug court is the route of entry into rehabilitation. In almost all drug courts, retention in court-ordered drug treatment is consistently several times greater than in voluntary treatment.

A General Accounting Office report found that the average retention rate of drug court programs was a highly respectable 71 percent. Even the lowest retention rate that the GAO found in a drug court, 31 percent, exceeds the average one-year retention rate of some 15 percent for non-criminal addicts in public sector treatment programs; this comparison is even more impressive in light of the fact that the criminally involved addict is generally considered the hardest to treat in conventional settings.

The GAO report also found, like other studies, that the longer a participant stayed in drug court treatment, the better he or she fared.

A survey by the Drug Court Clearinghouse at American University found similar patterns. Survey results first emphasized the element of coercion in drug court participation. Though 80 percent of offenders offered the drug court option chose to take it, many saw it as simply an expeditious way to get their charges dropped. Indeed, some actually said they planned to return to drugs after they "went through the motions" in the program. Yet the survey also found that drug courts operational for eighteen months or more reported completion rates of 48 percent. Re-arrest rates, primarily for drug crimes, varied according to graduates' characteristics and degree of social dysfunction but averaged just 4 percent after one year from graduation. Even among those who failed to finish the program, re-arrest rates one year after enrollment ranged from 28 percent down to 5 percent. By contrast, the Bureau of Justice Statistics reports a 26 to 40 percent rearrest rate for individuals convicted of drug possession who are traditionally adjudicated.

Evaluations of particular drug courts also show good results. The Portland, Oregon drug court was evaluated in 1998 by the State Justice Institute (49), which made careful efforts to match drug court participants with other arrestees with similar demographic characteristics and criminal histories who either had refused drug court or were ineligible for administrative reasons. Two years after adjudication or leaving the program, on outcomes measures such as rearrest and conviction, those who did not enter drug court were at least as likely to be rearrested for felonies as those who did. Among those who did enroll, those who finished less than three months in the program were twice as likely as graduates to be re-arrested. Even among individuals who did not finish, those who completed at least three months had significantly fewer arrests than those who did not.

Maricopa, Arizona's drug court, was the subject of a 1997 evaluation by RAND, which found that among a sample randomly assigned to the drug court, rates of rearrest for any crime were significantly lower than for those randomly assigned to probation alone.

A recent review of the Broward County, Florida, drug court found that drug court graduates were half as likely to be re-arrested for a felony, and one-third as likely to be re-arrested for a drug felony, as demographically similar offenders who were eligible for drug court but had instead chosen and completed probation.

An independent evaluation found the Dade County, Florida drug court superior to disposition as usual. Between June, 1989 and March, 1993, the Dade County program enrolled 4,500 defendants, 20 percent of all arrestees in the county who were charged with drug-related offenses. During that same period, 60 percent of the enrollees graduated or remained in the program. A year after graduation, only 11 percent were rearrested in Dade County on any criminal charge. By contrast, the rearrest rate was some 60 percent for a matched sample of drug offenders in 1987, two years before institution of the drug court. Furthermore, the time that elapsed between graduation and first re-offense was two to three times longer in the drug court group than in the nondrug court group.

In the most mixed evaluation of results in a drug court, the Urban Institute found that participants randomly assigned to the District of Columbia Drug Court from 1993 to 1995 were twice as likely to be drug free in the month before sentencing as those assigned to probation as usual; the figures were 27 percent versus 12 percent. However, six months after sentencing, re-arrest rates for any crime averaged four percent for the treatment track versus six percent for the control track, not a statistically significant difference.

Prison-Based Programs:

According to a 1997 survey of state departments of corrections sponsored by the Corrections Program Office, approximately 70 percent of all state prison inmates are in need of substance abuse treatment. Reporting states indicated, however, that only 15 percent complete a prescribed substance abuse treatment program before their release from confinement.

About 12 percent of prisons have intensive treatment programs based on therapeutic community principles, lasting from six to fifteen months and open to nonviolent offenders who are within eighteen months of eligibility for work release or parole. Within the prison, these offenders are segregated from the rest of the inmate population, in order to maintain the integrity of the program and to protect participants from other prisoners.

In a comprehensive review of the prison-based programs of the 1970s and 1980s, Falkin and coauthors concluded that in-prison therapeutic communities are effective. Examining programs such as New York's Stay'n Out (which they praised as a national model), Oregon's Cornerstone Program, and others, the authors found that the treatment experience, optimally for nine to twelve months, was strongly correlated with successful subsequent parole. For example, violations of parole occurred among 50 percent of the offenders who stayed less than three months in Stay'n Out, among 39 percent of those who stayed longer than three months, and among only 15 percent of those who completed the program. Reincarceration rates within three years of release from prison were significantly lower for Stay'n Out participants, no matter how long they participated, than for matched offenders who had expressed interest in being treated but did not meet technical eligibility requirements.

Similarly, Cornerstone graduates had a 36 percent reincarceration rate over a three-year follow-up period, while the figure was 63 percent for parolees-as-usual. The graduates' relative success occurred despite the fact that they had begun with more severe criminal and substance abuse histories than the control group.

Work Release

In 1987, the Delaware Department of Corrections established the Crest program, the first therapeutic community work-release center in the U.S. Offenders who had been released from prison after participating in the Key program, a prison-based therapeutic community for drug-involved offenders at a maximum security prison, entered the Crest Center for three months of on-site treatment, three months of additional treatment, and job training, also within a therapeutic community.

Led by the Center's director, James Inciardi, researchers from the University of Delaware's Center for Drug and Alcohol Studies compared four groups of mostly male participants: Key participants who did not go on to Crest, Crest participants who had not gone through the Key program, Key and Crest combined, and a control group that had been incarcerated without treatment, then gone on to conventional work release. The Key and Key-Crest groups had begun with higher levels of drug abuse and longer criminal histories. The Key-only group was older and less likely to be white.

The study found that the longer one's tenure in treatment and the closer to time of release the treatment was received, the better the post-release outcome. Overall, the therapeutic element of the prison-parole combination appears to reside more heavily in the parole phase than in the incarceration.

At an early follow-up, in-prison treatment was found somewhat more beneficial than no treatment. By eighteen months, however, there was no significant difference between the Key and control groups in rearrest rates and urinalysis-confirmed drug use. By contrast, at eighteen months Crest-only participants maintained an advantage over the control group. In addition, at the six-month follow-up, the Crest group was as successful as the Key-Crest group; but by 18 months, the Key-Crest group was superior, with 77 percent arrest-free and 47 percent drug-free among Key-Crest participants, while the figures were only 57 percent arrest-free and 31 percent drug-free among the Crest group.

The Key-Crest combination outranked all the others, with nearly half the individuals drug-free at 18 months, three times the figure for the control group, while Crest-only participants had an intermediate likelihood of being drug free.

Diversion from Prison:

In 1990, the office of the Kings County (Brooklyn) District Attorney developed the Drug Treatment Alternative to Prison program in response to the increasing pressure of drug-related commitments on the state prison system (by the mid-1990s, drug offenders would constitute nearly one-half of admissions to state prisons). The program diverts nonviolent drug felons to long-term, community-based residential drug treatment at about two-thirds the cost of incarceration. Like drug court, the program offers dismissal of charges in return for an offender's completing treatment under close judicial supervision. Also like drug court, DTAP may be chosen by offenders for reasons having little to do with a desire to become drug-free. For some, the program is a way to avoid incarceration; for others, it promises an expunged criminal record.

The Vera Institute of Justice in New York City has conducted an independent evaluation of DTAP. Vera found that participants began with more severe pretreatment deficits—in education, employment, and legal involvement—than those of offenders placed in other diversion programs, Yet DTAP's overall retention rate at one year was 64 percent, two to four times higher than that of residential programs in general. At one year, 11 percent of DTAP participants had been rearrested, half for drug offenses; by comparison, drug offenders sent to prison are more than twice as likely to be rearrested within a year of release, with more than half those arrests drug-related. Fewer than five percent of ex-prisoners are re-arrested while in treatment, but dropouts have high rates of re-offense, ranging from 80 to 92 percent, with an average time before return to custody of only one week.

Coercion without Treatment

Practical experience suggests that simply diverting addicts to monitoring systems may be sufficient incentive to improved behavior for those with relatively low levels of drug involvement. This proposition has not, however, been rigorously tested. Whether drug testing and sanctions alone can lead to abstinence or near-abstinence in certain offenders is an important question for several reasons. First, some offenders will inevitably, if choice is available, opt for routine processing with a short, fixed period of incarceration over a diversionary program that requires long periods of supervision and threatens reincarceration if they backslide. Second, the supervision associated with standard probation, or even sometimes with parole, lasts for just months, as compared with the years-long average duration of a career of addiction, and is of only low intensity. Finally, even among offenders who do choose treatment or are mandated into it, some might be successfully managed with less expensive forms of monitoring.

A few jurisdictions, instead of specifically mandating treatment, are extending the heightened supervision typical of diversionary programs to larger numbers of offenders for longer periods of time. This approach is called coerced abstinence.

As outlined by its major proponent, Mark A.R. Kleiman of the UCLA School of Public Policy and Social Research, coerced abstinence focuses on reduced drug consumption rather than on the intermediate goals of entry into treatment, retention, and compliance. According to Kleiman, a functional coerced abstinence program would do the following:

(1)   screen probationers and parolees for drugs;

(2)   subject identified users to twice-weekly urine tests;

(3)   impose a brief, perhaps two-day, period of incarceration for every positive test;

(4)   impose sanctions immediately; and

(5)   permit less frequent testing after a period, perhaps six months, of continuously clean tests.

Of course, if some individuals are unable or unwilling to abstain under this pressure alone, it will be necessary to mandate treatment, with adverse consequences for failure. Yet, considering that only one-quarter of probationers report ever having been tested for drug use and that half the people who commit new crimes while on parole or probation are under the influence of drugs or alcohol, there can be little doubt that more consistent application of surveillance would yield benefits.

The District of Columbia conducted an experiment in coerced abstinence as part of a drug demonstration project funded by the federal Center for Substance Abuse Treatment through the National Institute of Justice. Between 1992 and 1995, the District's Pretrial Services Agency randomly assigned arrestees to three different presentencing tracks. In the "sanctions track," urine samples were obtained twice weekly, and arrestees were subject to increasingly severe penalties for missing or dirty urine samples. No formal treatment was provided, though individuals could seek it or could go voluntarily to Narcotics Anonymous.

The second, "treatment track" was an intensive, day-long treatment program. The judge was kept informed about participants' performance but did not impose sanctions frequently or reliably. Finally, for the control group on the "standard track," urine samples were collected twice a week, but there were no predictable consequences for missed or dirty samples.

The Urban Institute analyzed the first 850 of 1,223 defendants to reach sentencing. They found that "treatment track" participants were twice as likely to be drug free in the month before sentencing as those in the "standard track," by 27 percent versus 12 percent. But "sanctions track" participants, subject to frequent urine testing and known consequences for violations, were three times as likely as "standard track" participants to be drug free during the same month, by 37 percent versus 12 percent. At six months after sentencing, re-arrest rates for crimes of any kind were two percent for "sanctions track" participants, four percent for the "treatment track," and six percent for "standard track" participants.

Thus the researchers found that certainty of consequences was psychologically powerful. "The reason the sanctions track people did so well," said senior researcher Adele Harrell, who conducted focus groups with study participants, "is because they knew what the judge would do. And he did it." Harrell also credited the "swiftness of the penalties—they had to report to court immediately for a test failure— and their fairness." One participant summed up to Harrell, "[Y]ou get a dirty-urine, man, you're going to jail. They're letting you know ... you know the chances."

At least a dozen similar pilot programs and initiatives are in place, in cities in Arizona, California, Colorado, Connecticut, Michigan, and New York. Maryland's "Break the Cycle" program requires clinics to report to probation or parole officers within twenty-four hours after an addict has failed or skipped a drug test (63). Project Sentry in Lansing, Michigan, in operation for 25 years, provides comparable testing, mostly short-term, for drug-involved offenders on probation or pre-sentencing release. Offenders are tested three times a week, and drug use results in progressively more severe sanctions, beginning with three days in jail for the first positive or missed urine test, ten days for the second such failure, twenty for the third, and one month for each thereafter.

An evaluation of 5,000 participating offenders by the Michigan Office of Drug Control Policy found that 75 percent remained drug free and were not arrested during the six-to-twelve-month observation period.

In Coos County, Oregon, probationers' positive drug tests have dropped since the Drug Reduction of Probationers program, began in 1988. This program, too, is built around certain, swift responses to positive tests—immediate arrest and two days in jail for the first violation, 10 days for the second, and 30 days for the third. Oregon officials found that prior to implementation of the program, 43 percent of all probationers tested positive for drugs. Within about six months after implementation, the figure was down to 10 percent.

Resistance to Coercion

Coercive strategies for drug treatment range from the least intrusive— social contracting, in which individuals are simply given incentives to behave in certain ways-to the most restrictive, as with forced treatment and confine-ment in the case of life-threatening behavior. No matter where on this con-tinuum a particular coercive strategy lies, however, it has met with significant resistance.

(1) One source of this resistance is the healthy reluctance we all feel to curtail anyone's personal autonomy. Political scientist James Q. Wilson has observed that this reluctance sometimes leads us to insist on the same freedom for others that we would for ourselves, even when the others in question have great difficulty in making use of such freedom.

(2) Many clinicians voice another objection to coercive strategies: They believe, mistakenly, that a patient must desire drug treatment in order to benefit from it.

(3) Another source of resistance is the current medicalization of addic-tion, the most recent round in the century-long debate over whether drug abuse should be treated on the "medical model" or the "moral model." Thus the National Institute on Drug Abuse of the National Institutes of Health now dubs addiction a "chronic and relapsing brain disease," as part of the Institute's attempt to define addiction as simply another long-term medical condition like asthma or high blood pressure. This view, instead of challenging the inevita-bility of relapse by holding patients accountable for their choices, suggests the need for biological remedies for addiction. It also discounts the therapeu-tic potential of the coercion that the criminal justice system can exercise.

However, contrary to what this medicated view would predict, the com-pulsion to take drugs does not necessarily dominate an addict's minute-to-minute or even day-today existence. The temporal architecture of his or her routine reveals that he is capable of reflection and purposeful behavior for some, perhaps a good deal, of the time. During the course of a heroin addict's day, for example, he may feel calm and his thoughts may be lucid as long as he is confident of access to drugs and he is using them in doses adequate to prevent withdrawal but not large enough to be sedating. Likewise, there are periods in a cocaine addict's week when he is neither engaged in a binge nor wracked with intense craving for the drug. At these moments, he is not a victim controlled by brain disease. He might even choose to change his behavior—depending on what he thinks is at stake.

This potential for self-control permits society to entertain and enforce expectations of addicts that would never be possible with someone who had, say, a brain tumor. Making such demands is of course no guarantee that they will be met. But confidence in the legitimacy of such demands would encour-age a range of policy and therapeutic options, using consequences and coer-cion, that are incompatible with the idea of an exclusively no-fault brain dis-ease.

(4) A final source of resistance to coercion in this therapeutic age is the belief that self-improvement is more successful and admirable when under-

taken for one's self and one's self alone, not for anyone else or for the larger good. In this view, betterment achieved as a result of intrinsic motivation is more durable, and even more worthy, than is personal gain that is externally compelled.

But, as we know, addicts are notoriously poor self-disciplinarians. They are also extremely ambivalent about giving up drugs, in spite of all the damage that drugs have caused them. Addicts' problems of self-governance demand that a rehabilitative regime for them include limit-setting, consistency, and sometimes physical containment

Social Contracting

Contracting confers advantages on individuals when they manifest a desired behavior and penalizes them for violating expectations. For instance, addiction-impaired doctors, nurses, lawyers, and pilots may be allowed to keep their jobs or licenses "in exchange" for abstaining from illicit drugs or problem alcohol use under the close monitoring of a state professional society. Recall the public service announcement, "Help an Addict: Threaten to Fire Him," made popular in the late 1980s by the Partnership for a Drug Free America. Employers who follow that directive have established Employee Assistance Programs providing treatment for workers. With good effect, the military threatens drug and alcohol abusing soldiers with dishonorable discharges unless they abstain.

Most addicts admit being pressured into treatment by external forces such as health, employment, social relationships, financial conflicts, and emotional disturbances. Researchers estimate that only a small minority of addicts in treatment enrolled solely on personal initiative, unpressured by others. Thus the therapeutic potential of contracting, for job security or other social opportunities, is considerable.

Employee Assistance Programs:

These programs were first established as early as the 1940s by employers concerned about the impact of employee alcoholism on workplace safety and productivity. The Drug Free Workplace Act of 1988 encouraged further expansion; and now, according to the Employee Assistance Professionals Association, there are some 20,000 EAPs nationwide. Four out of five Fortune 500 companies have one. From 20 to 60 percent of the EAP caseload is provided by mandatory referrals to treatment as an alternative to dismissal from work.

Evidence suggests that individuals mandated to treatment via EAPs are as likely as voluntary participants, perhaps more likely, to profit from workplace-centered drug and alcohol treatment. In a study of industrial alcohol policy, Beaumont and Allsop found that workers mandated to treatment had better outcomes than those who were self-referred. The authors note that workers' age and length of service were positively correlated with both mandatory referral and improvement, interpreting these connections to mean that older workers felt a greater personal professional investment in their jobs and thus responded more powerfully to the threat of job loss.

Walsh and colleagues conducted a randomized trial of treatment options for alcohol-abusing workers. They assigned workers to one of three rehabilitation regimes: compulsory three-week inpatient treatment, compulsory attendance at Alcoholics Anonymous for a year, and a choice among options.

During a two-year follow-up period, all groups showed comparable improvement in job performance. However, individuals participating in the most restrictive option, inpatient treatment, were significantly less likely than the others to relapse.

Researchers at the University of Pennsylvania made a similar study of 304 transportation and city service union members in Philadelphia. One group, of 111 individuals, was referred to the union's EAP because of positive urine tests during random screening at the worksite; another group of 103 was self-referred. For the first, coerced, group, failure to abide by the terms of the evaluation and referral procedures was grounds for dismissal. Though most of these coerced individuals were "resistant to entering any treatment setting," all attended treatment. The level of verification in the study was high: There were urine tests, self-reports of earnings were checked against pay stubs, and self-reported criminal convictions were checked against arrest records.

The researchers found that coerced individuals were more likely to complete a course of treatment than were self-referred workers. Seventy-seven percent of the coerced workers in inpatient care and 74 percent of coerced workers in outpatient counseling finished. Comparable figures for voluntary workers were 61 percent and 60 percent. At a six-month follow-up, 92 percent of all participating workers were re-interviewed; coerced and voluntary patients showed similar levels of improvement. "This is interesting," the authors note, "in that many clinicians feel strongly that intrinsic motivation is a prerequisite for engagement and improvement ... [F]or the participants in the study, the coercive referral condition did not hinder the chances for successful treatment."

However, the American Civil Liberties Union has condemned the workplace drug testing that serves as an element of this strategy. "Employers need to kick the drug test habit," said ACLU legislative counsel Solange Bitol in testimony before the House Small Business Subcommittee on Empowerment on a proposal to provide $10 million to small businesses for drug testing. The ACLU objected not merely to using taxpayer money for this purpose but to the activity of employer testing per se.

Public Agencies

Increasingly, public agencies are fighting to adopt a quid pro quo strategy towards drug abuse. In 1996, a federal judge ruled in favor of the New York City Housing Authority's efforts to obtain expedited court-ordered evictions in cases involving drugs and other threatening behavior. Previously, such evictions had taken two years or more to carry out. The Legal Aid Society of New York City argued against the new eviction procedure, filing court papers on behalf of tenants despite overwhelming tenant support for the Authority's plan.

In Dallas, Alphonso Jackson, president of the city's Housing Authority from 1989 to 1996, asked tenants to agree to undergo drug testing as a condition of living in the special Self Sufficiency Program within Dallas public housing. He was made a defendant in numerous lawsuits on the issue filed by the ACLU and legal aid organizations (F35). The Doe Foundation in New York City, which operates the Ready, Willing and Able training program, became the target of a similar lawsuit after it took over a Harlem men's shelter in 1996. The shelter, at the time of the takeover, was described as a "lawless crack den" (76). The foundation began requiring applicants to the shelter to be drug-free as a condition of acceptance and, once enrolled as trainees, to be drug tested routinely. In addition, the foundation required that residents work in street cleaning and house painting operations. Initially, 62 percent of the residents tested positive in scheduled, pre-announced tests. Nine months later, only two percent were testing positive in random tests.

In 1997, the Coalition for the Homeless and Legal Aid sued the foundation. What raised these advocates' ire was the requirement that residents work as a condition of participation. Even though the programs pay each participant, the Coalition denounced them as "tools for slave masters."

These plaintiffs could look for a precedent to a 1995 trial court opinion by Justice Helen Freedman in Manhattan. She ruled that residents of public family shelters could not be obligated to follow rules and regulations such as drug testing, curfews, and job training.

The fight over drug testing has engaged other public bodies as well. The ACLU has fought efforts by public high schools to perform random drug tests on students, even those that would first require consent from parents. This controversy went all the way to the Supreme Court, which ruled such policies constitutionally permissible.

Despite the challenges, many not-for-profit homeless shelters and churches require abstinence as a condition of receiving services. As we have seen, there is even a state-funded methadone clinic, in Baltimore, that requires patients to be employed and drug-free as a condition of remaining in the program.

Courts, too, are experimenting with various forms of social contracting. Over the years, judges have noted that a high percentage of child abuse and neglect cases involve substance abuse by parents; a 1996 report by the National Committee to Prevent Child Abuse puts the figure at up to 80 percent. Accordingly, a few cities—Pensacola, Florida; Kalamazoo, Michigan; Kansas City, Missouri; Reno, Nevada, and New York City—have recently established

Family Drug Courts. Though little information is as yet available on outcomes, these new institutions are notable because they are determined to use incentives such as child custody, visitation privileges, and the removal of children from homes as leverage to compel parents to comply with drug treatment and remain drug free.

Welfare reform legislation, too, has stimulated many states and localities to revise their procedures for awarding benefits. For example, Montgomery County, Maryland, now denies benefits to applicants who refuse to undergo drug testing.

With estimates of problem substance abuse among welfare recipients estimated to be between 15 and 30 percent (though, according to the Legal Action Center, some states put the figure as high as 50 percent), the efficiency of surveillance and sanctioning procedures will be put to the test. Although social services organizations do not yet capitalize on their built-in potential for leverage, more will be doing so as the public demands more civic responsibility from beneficiaries.

Contingency Management

The goal of this technique is to intervene in an addict's life with an arrangement of environmental consequences—rewards, punishments, or both—to systematically weaken drug use and strengthen the skills necessary for abstinence. The underlying behavioral theory, operant conditioning, holds that the act of using drugs can be modified by its consequences.

The earliest CM studies were conducted with alcoholics. Miller and colleagues, for example, examined the question of whether CM could be used to reduce public drunkenness. They selected twenty alcoholic men from the city jail in Jackson, Mississippi and randomly assigned them to an experimental or control group. Men in the experimental group, if they reduced their drinking, could earn housing, employment, food, and medical care through cooperating local social service agencies. Men in the control group, by contrast, received these services whether they were drunk or sober. The researchers assessed the men's alcohol intake objectively, via breath alcohol levels or observation of gross intoxication.

Over the course of the two-month study, arrests in the experimental group decreased by 85 percent. In the control group, they did not decline at all.

In the past decade, researchers have begun studying CM in depth. Though sample sizes tend to be small and follow-up limited in duration, the findings are so consistently promising that CM merits close review. Stephen Higgins and colleagues at the University of Vermont have produced a detailed summary of CM studies involving abusers of heroin and cocaine; a few representative studies are described below Higgins and his colleagues conducted numerous CM trials with cocaine addicts.

In a 1994 study, forty patients were randomly assigned to either ordinary treatment or treatment plus vouchers. The vouchers, assigned a monetary value and exchangeable for retail items, were awarded on a schedule of increasing value with each consecutive clean urine sample submitted; conversely, a cocaine-positive sample would reset the value of the vouchers at their initial low level.

At the end of twenty-four weeks, 75 percent of the voucher group remained active, compared with only 40 percent of the no-voucher group. For the voucher group, the average duration of continuous cocaine abstinence, documented by urine tests, was twelve weeks; for the non-voucher group it was six weeks. At nine and twelve months after entry into the study, self-reported cocaine use remained significantly lower in the voucher group.

A similar study took place in Baltimore, conducted by Ken Silverman and colleagues at Johns Hopkins University and involving thirty-seven inner city methadone maintenance patients who concurrently abused cocaine. During the twelve-week study, all patients received standard counseling. A group of nineteen received vouchers contingent on cocaine-negative urine tests, while eighteen received vouchers on a schedule linked to that of the experimental group but dispensed independently of urine test results. The parallel dispensing of vouchers to the two groups was meant to uncouple the effects of voucher receipt itself from its meaning as a reward predictably dependent on urine test results.

At the end of the three-month study, the experimental group had substantially reduced cocaine use, but the comparison group remained largely unchanged. About half the patients exposed to the contingent vouchers had achieved between seven and 12 weeks of continuous abstinence; by contrast, less than five percent of the control group had attained as much as three consecutive weeks of abstinence.

Though there was a rebound resumption of drug use after the contingent vouchers were discontinued, as in most other CM studies, the experimental group performed significantly better at all stages of follow-up.

Intensified CM techniques have had results even for subgroups resistant to voucher incentives. To examine such populations, Silverman and his colleagues chose a sample of intravenous cocaine-abusing patients, many of them also HIV-positive, who had failed a standard CM voucher experiment. The researchers ran these individuals, in randomized order, through three different nine-week voucher regimes—one in which the total redeemable value of vouchers that could be earned was high, one in which it was low, and one in which it was zero.

The findings were dramatic. Not a single patient in the zero-value voucher program achieved more than two weeks of abstinence. Only one person did so in the low-value program. But in the high-value voucher program, 45 percent attained at least four weeks of sustained abstinence.

The major drawback of these CM studies—patients' tendency to resume drug use, albeit at a lower level, when the contract is withdrawn—also reveals the major potential of CM for entitlement reform. The backsliding of patients in the studies was probably due in part to the short duration of these research projects: A mere few months is not enough time to enable a patient to learn the new skills, secure the employment, and attain the measure of personal growth needed to live drug-free. Entitlement reform need not be limited by such constraints.

Contingency Management in Real-World Conditions

Jesse Milby of the University of Alabama sought to apply CM in a situation that approximated real-world conditions. He randomized 176 homeless, crack-addicted individuals to receive ordinary or enhanced care. Members of the enhanced group, after two months of daily intensive therapy, were eligible to participate in a work-therapy program refurbishing condemned housing and, for a modest rental fee, to live in this housing. Participation was contingent on submitting twice-weekly clean urine tests.

After six months, this group had achieved significantly greater improvement in employment status, days of homelessness, and cocaine use than the usual-care group.

At Seattle's Harborview Medical Center, psychiatrist Richard K. Ries directs a clinic for mentally ill substance abusers. Clinic patients are asked to sign over their Supplemental Security Income checks to the outpatient clinic, which then acts as the patients' "representative payee," managing bank accounts on their behalf. The clinic covers rent and other basics. Patients, by complying with treatment, are allowed to "earn back" discretionary funds and ultimately, when they demonstrate ability to manage money responsibly, to control the passbooks to their bank accounts.

Ries and his colleagues compared treatment outcomes between patients in the incentive program and those attending the clinic as usual. Over a three-month period, sicker patients were significantly more likely to attend treatment sessions as their healthier counterparts and were just as likely to participate in job training sessions and stay out of the hospital and jail.

Studies such as these suggest that with drug abusing individuals, manipulating benefits to reinforce positive social behavior could provide a partial solution to the perverse incentives that entitlements often provide. Street ethnographers have long known that addicts routinely purchase drugs with welfare payments and food stamps; more recent quantitative reports have described a persistent temporal pattern in which receipt of monthly benefits is linked to increases in emergency room visits for intoxication and overdoses and in hospitalizations for psychosis among cocaine-abusing schizophrenics.

Thus the Veterans Administration has instituted a CM project that would distribute veterans' service-connected benefits contingently to mentally ill substance abusers. Conceivably, federal disability payments, welfare benefits, and other forms of cash entitlement could be dispensed in accordance with CM principles

Coercion of Pregnant Addicts

The clash between the need for coercion and resistance to coercive strategies has been especially marked when the subjects have been drug-addicted pregnant women. Pregnant women have in fact been subjects of CM trials. Using incentives such as goods-redeemable vouchers or baby supplies donated by neighborhood businesses, researchers have succeeded in increasing attendance at prenatal clinics while reducing drug use.

The criminal justice system has also embarked on even more coercive strategies for pregnant addicts, arousing intense controversy in the process. Prosecutors in many states have gone so far as to bring criminal charges against pregnant women who abuse drugs. Some prosecutors have used child-endangerment statutes; others have charged delivery of drugs to a minor (via the umbilical cord). The assumption, a reasonable one, has been that a pregnant woman who cannot bring herself to stop abusing drugs or alcohol, either directly, through self-imposed "cold turkey" withdrawal or through treatment, is either so profoundly addicted, in a physiological sense, that she is not competent to protect her unborn child or, if not physiologically addicted, so irresponsible as to be unfit for unsupervised parenthood. The primary goal of bringing charges, accordingly, has been to protect the baby by coercing the woman into residential treatment as an alternative to trial or incarceration.

The most publicized cases of such coercion occurred in Charleston, South Carolina. Staff at the Medical University of South Carolina became concerned about the increasing numbers of cocaine-related complications of late-term pregnancy. Nurses and doctors tried unsuccessfully to convince women at risk to enter drug treatment.

In 1989, the hospital adopted a policy of required urine screening if a woman met any of several criteria: no prenatal care, detached placenta, stillbirth, pre-term labor, intrauterine growth retardation, mother's previously known drug or alcohol abuse. Of women who screened positive, none kept her assigned appointment at the medical center's substance abuse clinic. When these women returned to the hospital in pre-term labor, their urine screens were again uniformly positive. After delivery, each woman again refused an appointment for drug treatment.

In late 1989, the Charleston Police Department and the state's Office of the Solicitor became involved, and policy became more restrictive: Any woman testing positive who refused an appointment with the substance abuse or prenatal clinic was arrested and charged with either possession of an illegal drug or, if her urine or her infant's drug test was positive at the time of delivery, distribution of drugs to a minor. In early 1990, the policy was modified to allow a woman to avoid arrest by successfully completing treatment. Women who declined such treatment were placed on probation.

A report on the operation of this policy, published in the *Journal of the South Carolina Medical Association,* indicates that the incidence of positive urine screens for cocaine dropped dramatically after the restrictive policy was implemented, from over 20 per month to five or six per month (Horger et al.).

Authors of the report acknowledged that the program was controversial. "Critics of our protocol," they wrote, "point out that the threat of legal problems may have driven obstetric patients away." They noted, though, that "delivery rates remained constant, and the Medical University remains the only facility within a fifty mile radius which offers obstetric care for indigent and Medicaid patients. Consequently it is unlikely that these patients could have delivered at neighboring facilities." Nor did the number of home births increase during the year after the policy went into effect.

The South Carolina experience suggests that mandatory treatment of pregnant addicts who have previously rejected voluntary treatment leads to the birth of healthier babies and does not deter women from giving birth in hospitals. Nevertheless, the issue has galvanized women's advocacy groups. The Center for Reproductive Law and Policy, condemning the South Carolina program as an excuse to "punish women for their behavior during pregnancy," is pursuing a lawsuit against the state.

This suit is a continuation of a campaign against the Medical University of South Carolina that began in 1992, when the Office of Civil Rights in the U.S. Department of Health and Human Services sent investigators to the hospital to determine whether racial discrimination had occurred. The next year, the Center for Reproductive Law and Policy filed a civil action against the medical center, also alleging racial discrimination. In 1997, U.S. District Judge C. Weston Houck ruled that there was no basis for the charge. "The catalyst for targeting these individuals [African-American plaintiffs] was a policy designed to prevent cocaine abuse in pregnant women," the judge wrote, opining that " plaintiffs have not shown a statistically significant disparate impact on black women in this case."

The medical center, despite its legal victory, closed its program in 1994 in response to a threat by HHS to cut the hospital's federal funding.

Civil Commitment

Perhaps the greatest controversy about coercive strategies has arisen over the issue of civil commitment. When an addict has sustained significant temporary brain damage from compulsive drug-taking, then this ultimate intrusion is warranted. Such time-limited, often life-saving suspension of autonomy allows for urgent medical attention to suicidal impulses, severe depression, or psychosis.

Over half the states now have statutes that allow judges to commit an addicted person to treatment without his or her consent in much the same way that they can mandate a gravely disabled mentally ill person to undergo treatment in a psychiatric hospital. The process is appropriate for addicted individuals considered incompetent to attend to their own welfare and safety; the standard for this form of coercion is helplessness, not necessarily dangerousness to society.

As early as 1870, the American Association for the Cure of Inebriety tried to persuade states to create institutions in which doctors could treat and confine alcoholics and drug "habitues" rather than send them to jail. In the 1930s, narcotics farms were able, in a similar way, to accommodate some so-called civil addicts whose severe addiction made them dysfunctional but who were not involved in crime.

As we have seen, California and New York used civil commitment extensively in the 1960s and 1970s. Unsurprisingly, the Constitutionality of the process has been challenged; but the Supreme Court has upheld the process. Since then, the California Supreme Court and the New York State Court of Appeals have also upheld civil commitment, reasoning that life-threatening developments—the college student so heavily addicted to cocaine that she drops out of school to work as a prostitute in a crack house, or the homeless addict who refuses to see a doctor for a gangrenous foot—can justify the intrusion into personal autonomy.

Nevertheless, civil commitment of addicts now occurs only occasionally, usually when a desperate loved one or concerned physician brings an addicted individual to the attention of a judge.

Conclusion

Coercion has been applied in the service of rehabilitating addicts for over seventy years. The experience has yielded a powerful clinical lesson: Addicts need not be internally motivated at the outset of drug treatment in order to benefit by it. Indeed, addicts who are legally pressured into treatment may outperform voluntary patients, because they are likely to stay in treatment longer and are more likely to graduate. Without formal coercive mechanisms, the treatment system would not attract many of the most dysfunctional addicts and surely could not retain them.

But, though official bodies, especially criminal justice organizations, are accustomed to wielding such leverage, they do not do so systematically enough to yield maximum benefit. Some judges will forgo referral to treatment altogether if they perceive an offender not to be motivated towards rehabilitation. Other judges express disappointment with the laxity of supervision addicts receive in treatment, citing failure to follow up with the court, verify patient participation, and perform drug testing—the very surveillance mechanisms that are necessary to retain unmotivated addicts.

Ironically, it appears that among current programs, with their various mixes of treatment and coercion, the treatment component has relatively less clout than other forces in shaping addicts' behavior. That is why examples of combining treatment with external monitoring, as in Employee Assistance Programs and drug courts, are so encouraging. If more institutions, like public housing or even disability programs, adopted principles of contingency management, individuals would be likely to remain in treatment longer and enjoy greater improvement. Such behavioral gains would serve both addicts and the communities whose resources they presently strain.

A coordinated effort by social service agencies to track and monitor drug use and enforce consequences for that use will be costly in the short run. In addition, it will also require the creation of a certain amount of new bureaucracy. Those facts make coercive strategies unattractive even to those who are not moved by criticisms based on radical notions of individual autonomy. It remains true, however, that as a clinical strategy, coercion is solidly promising. What is more, increasing our capacity to leverage addicts into treatment will be important whether we maintain our present policy of drug prohibition, decide on a policy of outright legalization, or choose anything in between, since any one of these policies will depend on drug treatment to rehabilitate addicts.

Addiction impairs participation in a free society. It interferes with the ability to ensure one's own welfare, respect the safety of others, and discharge responsibilities as apparent, spouse, worker, neighbor, or citizen. Addiction is a behavioral condition for which the prescription of choice is the imposition of reliable consequences and rewards, often combined with coercion that keeps the addicted individual from fleeing. To say this is not punitive; it is clinically sound and empirically justified.

Every day, all people respond to contingencies, incentives, and consequences. If we do not work, we do not get paid. If rent is not paid, we are evicted. If children are mistreated, they can be taken away. Meeting obligations in these circumstances is not the antithesis of freedom but a prerequisite to it. No less is this true of individuals with drug problems, though it is our job to structure the contingencies before them in creative ways to help them regain their freedom.

References

Anglin, M. D. "The Efficacy of Civil Commitment in Treating Narcotic Addiction." In C. G. Leukefeld and F.M. Tims, eds. 1988. *Compulsory Treatment of Drug Abuse: Research and Clinical Practice.* Washing-

ton, D.C.: U.S. Government Printing Office. NIDA Research Monograph 86, DHHS Publication No. ADM 89-1578.

_____. 1988. "Efficacy of Civil Commitment in Treating Narcotics
Addiction." *Journal of Drug Issues* 18, 527–45.

Beaumont, P.B., and S.J. Allsop. 1984. "An Industrial Alcohol Policy: The
Characteristics of Worker Success." *British Journal of Addiction* 79,
315–18.

De Leon, G. "Legal Pressure in Therapeutic Communities." In C. G.
Leukefeld and F.M. Tims, eds. 1988. *Compulsory Treatment of Drug
Abuse: Research and Clinical Practice.* Washington, D.C.: U.S.
Government Printing Office.

De Leon, G., G. Melnick, and D. Kressel. "Motivation and Readiness for
Therapeutic Community Treatment among Cocaine and Other Drugs
Abusers." *American Journal of Drug and Alcohol Abuse* 23: 169–89.

DeLeon, G., H.K. Wexler, and N. Jainchill. 1982. "The Therapeutic Community: Success and Improvement Rates Five Years after Treatment." *The
International Journal of Addictions* 17: 4, 703–47.

Education and Assistance Corporation. 1995. "Brooklyn TASC Predicate
Program: A Program Briefing." Carle Place, New York, Education and
Assistance Corporation, Criminal Justice Division.

Falkin, G.P., H.K. Wexler, and D.S. Lipton. "Drug Treatment in State Prisons."
In D.R. Gerstein and H.J Harwood, eds. 1990. *Treating Drug Problems,*
vol. 2. Washington, D.C.: National Academy Press, Institute of
Medicine.

Gerstein, D. R., and H.J. Harwood, eds. 1990. *Treating Drug Problems,* vol.
1. Washington, D.C.: National Academy Press, Institute of Medicine.

Higgins, S.T., J.W. Tidey, and M.L. Stitzer. "Community Reinforcement and
Contingency Management in the Treatment of Alcohol, Cocaine, and
Opioid Dependence." In A.W. Graham and T.K. Schultz, eds. 1998.
American Society of Addiction Medicine Principles of Addiction

Medicine, 2d ed. Chevy Chase, MD: American Society of Addiction Medicine, Inc., 675–90.

Horger, E.O, S.B. Brown, and C.M. Condon. 1990. "Cocaine in Pregnancy: Confronting the Problem." *Journal of the South Carolina Medical Association* 86, 527–31.

Inciardi, J.A., et al. 1997. "An Effective Model of Prison-Based Treatment for Drug-Involved Offenders." *Journal of Drug Issues* 27: 2, 261–78.

Jaffe, J. H. "The Swinging Pendulum: The Treatment of Drug Users in America." In R. Dupont, R. Goldstein, and S. O'Donnell, eds. 1979. *Handbook on Drug Abuse.* Washington, D.C.: U.S. Government Printing Office.

Jonnes, J. 1996. *Hep-Cats, Narcs, and Pipe Dreams: A History of America's Romance with Illegal Drugs.* New York: Scribner.

Kidorf, M., et al. 1998. "Increasing Employment of Opioid Dependent Outpatients: An Intensive Behavioral Intervention." *Drug and Alcohol Dependence* 50: 73–80.

Kleiman, M.A.R. "Coerced Abstinence: A Neo-Paternalistic Drug Policy Initiative." In L. M. Mead, ed. 1997. *The New Paternalism: Supervisory Approaches to Poverty.* Washington, D.C.: Brookings Institution Press.

McLellan, A.T., et al. 1993. "The Effects of Psychosocial Services in Substance Abuse Treatment." *Journal of the American Medical Association* 269: 15, 1953–1959.

McLellan, A.T., et al. 1997. "Problem-Service 'Matching' in Addiction Treatment: A Prospective Study in Four Programs." *Archives of General Psychiatry* 54: 8, 730–35.

Milby, J.B., et al. 1996. "Sufficient Conditions for Effective Treatment of Substance-Abusing Homeless Persons." *Drug and Alcohol Dependence* 43, 23–38.

Miller, P.M. 1975. "A Behavioral Intervention Program for Chronic Public Drunkenness Offenders." *Archives of General Psychiatry* 32, 915–18.

Rockefeller, Nelson. Jan. 3, 1973. Annual address, Message to the Legislature, State of New York.

Silverman, K., et al. 1996. "Sustained Cocaine Abstinence in Methadone Maintenance Patients through Voucher-Based Reinforcement Therapy." *Archives of General Psychiatry* 53, 409–415.

Silverman, K., et al. In L.S. Harris, ed. 1996. *College on the Problems of Drug Dependence.* NIDA Research Monograph no. 174, NIH Pub. No. 97-4236, p. 74. Washington, D.C.: U.S. Government Printing Office.

COMPULSIVE SEXUAL BEHAVIORS

FRED S. BERLIN, M.D., PH.D.

I am going to talk about the concept of sexual compulsion. To start, I want to point out that a variety of terms that have been used: compulsion, addiction. I prefer the expression "being sexually driven" for reasons that will become clear shortly. Let me give you a brief overview of how I am going to try to present this discussion this morning and then I will go back in detail into each of the sections that I have outlined.

First of all, I want to talk about how we would evaluate people with respect to the issue of sexual compulsion, introducing some of the concepts that I think are important. So evaluation is number one.

Second, I want to talk a little bit about the etiology, or cause, of these problems, and in fact I am going to try to broaden the discussion and talk about the etiology of sexual drive in general. What are the factors that we know about that cause the intensity of sexual drive that people might experience? Also what factors are we now able to identify about qualitative differences in sexual makeup? So a little discussion on cause is second.

Third, I want to talk about the rationale for treatment. I think this is important, because I am going to use medical terms such as diagnosis and treatment in an area in which many might argue that we are simply talking about bad people misbehaving. I think there are people of sound mind who simply do misbehave. Therefore, if I am going to use medical terms such as diagnosis and treatment, I think it is incumbent upon me to explain briefly why that makes sense

Finally I will talk a little bit about what we do to try to treat these kinds of conditions: the compulsions and, as was discussed in a previous session, some of the sexual disorders that exist. I do not want to steal Patrick Carnes' thunder very much here, though, so I will try to speak briefly just to some of the biological treatments that have been used to treat the kinds of conditions that I will talk about.

Evaluation of Sexual Compulsion

Let me start, then, with the issue of how we would evaluate someone to determine whether or not there is some problem in their sexual makeup: a compulsion, some aberration that needs to be recognized and possibly treated.

The first point I want to make is that there are many people who engage in improper sexual conduct who do not have a compulsion or do not have an aberration of their sexual makeup. It is important that we recognize that. We see it all too frequently: the person who, for example, decides to commit a sexual assault, a criminal who breaks into a home and decides to rape a woman. There are many, many instances where the problem is just that somebody simply lacks a sense of conscience and moral responsibility, rather than that there is some compulsion or drive that is pushing him or her. One should not assume that everybody who engages in sexual misconduct is acting out of some sort of compulsive or sexual disorder.

One of the areas we have worked on quite a bit at Johns Hopkins is to try to help mentally retarded people deal with their sexual needs. I suppose most of us do not take much time to think about it, but imagine for a moment what it is like to have the mental age of an eight-year-old with the intensity of sexual drive that most of us experience as adults.

Furthermore, if one has the mental age of an eight-year-old, how can one find an acceptable sexual partner? Adults are not going to want to be involved with someone who has that kind of limit intellectually.

It is for that reason, not because they have a sexual compulsion, but because they have a drive that perhaps exceeds their ability to cope, that some mentally retarded people get into difficulty. We usually do not treat that as a compulsion.

I simply want to emphasize, before talking now about compulsive or driven behaviors, that there are plenty of times when people misbehave sexually for other reasons.

There are individuals who do seem to get into difficulty because there is something abnormal or different about their sexual makeup. So, I want to talk about how people can differ from one another sexually. I am going to name four ways in which people can differ and then I will discuss each in more detail.

First of all, people can differ regarding the kinds of *behaviors* that they do or do not desire sexually. So that is number one. Secondly, people can differ regarding the kinds of *partners* that they are or are not attracted to sexually. Third, people can differ in the *intensity* of their sexual drive. The preceding were qualitative differences in sexual makeup. There are also differences in intensity. Finally, people can differ in their *attitudes* about their own sexual desires.

Now, let me talk about why the knowledge of each of the above is important clinically to someone who is evaluating a person either for a sexual compulsion or some sort of aberration in sexual makeup.

Types of Sexual Behaviors

The first way in which I said people differed was the kinds of behaviors that they crave or desire sexually. A clear example of that is a psychiatric disorder known as transvestitic fetishism. To translate that jargon, it is a condition, usually in men, in which the individual is sexually aroused by dressing in women's clothing.

Now, I think it is obvious that any man is capable of doing that. But to argue that the average man has recurrent, intense, erotically arousing fantasies and urges about behaving in that way would be preposterous. Yet there are some people, because of this aberration of their sexual makeup, who recurrently crave sex in that fashion and may do so with such intensity that it becomes a compulsion that is difficult for them to manage.

The psychiatric name for a sexual disorder is the term *paraphilia*. A sexual disorder is called a paraphiliac disorder. In the *Diagnostic and Statistical Manual of Mental Disorders*, the book that spells out for the profession the nature of various psychiatric conditions, the definition of a paraphiliac disorder is that the person experiences intense, recurrent, erotically arousing fantasies and urges about something. In transvestitic fetishism, it is about dressing up in clothing of the opposite gender.

A second example of a psychiatric disorder that is a craving for an abnormal kind of sexual behavior is exhibitionism. Again, the average man is capable of exposing himself, but it is ridiculous to say that the average man experiences intense, recurrent, erotically arousing fantasies and urges about doing so to the point where it may be a daily struggle to prevent himself from acting.

So the first point in terms of sexual makeup is that some people have abnormalities in the kinds of behaviors they crave, and if those cravings are intense enough this can become a compulsion.

Types of Partners

Now, the second way in which I said people differ from one another is regarding the types of partners that they are or are not attracted to sexually. An example that was one of the most serious and dangerous of sex offenders that I have ever seen based on this observation was a man named Jeffrey

Dahmer. Dahmer was in no way whatsoever attracted to people who were alive. And yet he was recurrently drawn, in a very compulsive way, towards human corpses, towards people who were dead. His abnormal sexual makeup regarding the kinds of partners he was attracted to was so intense that it had become compulsive, resulting in the deaths of seventeen young men and eventually the incarceration and murder of Dahmer himself. This is a very dramatic example of how a clear aberration in sexual makeup of strong intensity can cause tremendous problems for society and for individuals who are so afflicted.

The second example of people who are attracted to unusual kinds of partners is one that is, I think, endemic now in our population and is a major mental health as well as criminal justice problem, and that is *pedophilia*. There are some people who are not at all attracted sexually to adults, whether male or female. Yet they recurrently crave sex with a child.

When an individual has no attraction at all to adults sexually and is recurrently craving sex with children, that is referred to as the exclusive form of pedophilia. If a man is attracted exclusively to little boys, it is homosexual pedophilia. If it is exclusively to girls, it is heterosexual pedophilia. And if it is exclusively to both boys and girls, it is the exclusive form of bisexual pedophilia.

Because I do not have space here, I am not going to go into as much detail about pedophilia as I often do. But as many of you know, this has been a problem for society in general and it has been a problem for the church as well, although no more of a problem for the church than for any other part of the community. We have all been struggling with it, and certainly it has been a privilege for me to work with a group of wonderful people in the Ad Hoc Committee on Sexual Abuse set up by the National Conference of Catholic Bishops to try to learn how to deal more effectively with it. The Church may now be able to provide some leadership in this country about how we can help society manage an affliction that is causing tremendous difficulties.

Intensity of Craving

Now, the third way in which I said people differ was in intensity of sexual drive. The intensity dimension is, I think, what determines whether or not we call something a compulsion.

In other words, someone might be privately aware that he or she may have some attraction to children or certain kinds of unusual sexual desires, but it is not so intense that it cannot be managed. These persons are aware of it, but through their willpower and their efforts and their moral convictions, they are able to control themselves.

On the other hand, if a person is unfortunate enough to have some abnormality in the kinds of behaviors or kinds of partners sexually desired, and that is paired with a very strong drive, then he or she may really have great difficulty, like the alcoholic, who has cravings that he may not be able to walk away from, unaided. Such an individual may need professional treatment to assist in dealing with the kinds of cravings that he or she is experiencing.

Attitude toward Sexual Makeup

The last way in which I said people differed is in their attitude about their own sexual makeup. There are some people, for example, who are attracted to children, who have desires to cross-dress, and who have other kinds of abnormal sexual cravings, where those cravings do not conflict with their personal sense of what is morally right or wrong. If the sexual desires that a person experiences are not in conflict with their personal sense of morality, those sexual desires are said to be *egosyntonic.*

There actually is a group of pedophiles, men who are attracted to children, who argue that they do not think there is anything wrong with this. There is a group in New York City called NAMBLA, North American Man-Boy Love Association. These are people who are attracted to children. There is no conflict with their personal sense of morality. They argue that it is society that ought to change its values and that it is not they who need to change.

Trying to work with or treat somebody who has a sexual aberration or a sexual compulsion and an attitude that there is nothing wrong and that treatment is not needed is exceedingly difficult. It is like trying to treat an alcoholic who denies having a drinking problem. We often feel little confidence in trying to work with such people.

Now, there are other people who are sexually attracted to children, and they may have strong attractions that they are having a difficult time coping with, but these attractions are very much in conflict with their personal sense of morality. If they could somehow cut out the part of their brain that is causing them to have those attractions, they presumably would do that in a moment.

In the work that I've done I have met a number of individuals, including priests, who have been struggling with sexual attractions towards children. I will have to tell you, I had some concerns about the attitude of some of them. In some cases I doubted whether it was even a compulsion, but instead just a lack of moral conviction. So that happens.

In other cases, though, I have seen people who I felt were truly tortured. They were having very strong desires that were difficult to cope with. Morally they did not want to act on them. They were struggling and conflicted people, decent people trying to do right, but needing help because of the compulsivity or aberration tied to their sexual makeup.

I have stayed away from jargon, but now I will give you a little to show that I am being specific. Let me present a patient that I am treating and say to you the diagnosis is egodystonic homosexual pedophilia, of the exclusive type. We assume we are talking about a man. It is homosexual pedophilia, so it is a man attracted to little boys, and not to little girls. It is the exclusive form of homosexual pedophilia. So it is only little boys. He has no attraction to adults. It is egodystonic, so we know something about his attitude. Even though he is experiencing these desires and having difficulty resisting, such temptations are in conflict with his personal sense of morality. Because of that, he is likely quite motivated to seek help and treatment that will enable him, like the alcoholic, to learn how to resist these cravings and not give in to unacceptable temptations.

Now, I ask a question—if I tell you that there is an aberration in someone's sexual makeup, either in the nature of the sexual cravings they are having or in the intensity of their desires, what does that tell you about his or her character, temperament, personality, conscience and so on?

It does not tell you anything. In other words, if I were to diagnose myself sexually, and to say that my diagnosis is heterosexual, what would that tell you?

What it would tell you is that as a man, that I am a man attracted to women, and at my age you would probably be safe to assume I have acted on those attractions. But it would not tell you if I am kind or cruel, caring or not caring, generally a person of conscience or lacking in conscience. That has to be evaluated entirely in its own right.

For some people we see, the problem is simply that there is an abnormality in sexual makeup, in the kinds of cravings they have and/or in the intensity of their desires, and that is the problem and we have to treat it as such. At other times, in addition, they may also have some characterological problems. They may have some moral weaknesses. They may have some other aspect of their makeup that also needs fixing, if I can put it that way. If that is the case, we have to address that, as well.

I am simply making the point that one should not assume that because someone is struggling sexually, that it necessarily means that they are flawed in some other way. Fundamentally decent people sometimes can need help in dealing with sexual cravings in the same way that sometimes fundamentally decent people who want to stop drinking may need help.

Etiology of Sexual Abnormalities

Let me move on to the etiology of sexual abnormalities, or, even more broadly, the etiology of sex drive in general, and then just briefly I will talk about rationale for treatment and discuss treatment.

What is the cause of somebody having an abnormal attraction, let us say an abnormal attraction to children, such as pedophilia? What is the cause of somebody recurrently wanting to dress up in women's clothing because for him it is an extremely powerful sexual turn-on? Or, to broaden it even more, what is the cause of any of us experiencing sexual desire? Why am I attracted to women? What determines the nature of that attraction, the fact that it is women rather than men? What determines the intensity of my sexual desire?

First of all, there is a lot that we do not know yet and that we need to better understand. But I do want to make three points about the cause of the kinds of sexual desires that people experience. The first point, I think, is an important one to understand, and that is what sexual desire is not due to. Sexual desire, both in its intensity and in its quality, the nature of that desire, is not due to a volitional or voluntary choice.

Now, what do I mean by that? When I was a little boy, did I sit down and say to myself, look, when you grow up, do you want to grow up to be attracted to women or to men or to boys or to girls? Do you want to grow up to have a desire sexually to dress up in women's clothing? Let me think about all this. What do I want to be like in my sexual makeup when I grow up?

Is there any child that ever sits down and says to himself, "Let me decide what is going to be the nature of the sexual feelings that I have when I grow up"? I didn't decide in growing up to be attracted to women. I discovered in growing up that I am attracted to women, and that is a very fortunate discovery to have been able to make. It makes my life immeasurably simpler.

The man who is attracted exclusively to little boys is not that way because he was a bad little child who sat down and weighed his options, and then, because he was a bad kid, decided to be different. He discovered in growing up that he is afflicted with that abnormal sexual orientation, and it is one of the saddest and most tragic of afflictions, both for the individual and society in general. Nobody in their right mind, in my opinion, would decide, if we had the choice—which we do not— to grow up to be sexually attracted to little boys. Some grow up discovering themselves to be so afflicted.

Suppose I am one such person. Now, I am going to talk, because I understand the delicacy of this issue, about the fact that it is not my fault that I am attracted to little boys. It is, though, going to be my responsibility to do something about it. There is going to be a moral responsibility — even though it is not my fault I have these attractions— to not act on them. So I am not disregarding moral imperatives. I am simply making the point that the fact that I have these attractions is not something I decided to do. What I do about those attractions will then get into some of the moral issues.

The point I have made is also related to the debate regarding whether pedophilia, or even homosexuality, is caused by biological or environmental factors. In one sense, that does not matter. The point is that, whether it is due to biology or whether it is due to environment, the attractions are not volitional. Whether I learned to be attracted to children, whether my genes caused me to be attracted to children, whether it is some interaction of the two factors is something science needs to better understand. But either way, it is not there because I decided to be different. I am not simply choosing to experience an alternative lifestyle.

All right. There is now some quite persuasive evidence for some of the sexual aberrations that in some cases environment plays a role and in some cases biology. Many people who are sexually attracted to children, for example, were themselves victims when they were children. It appears that in some cases being victimized warped their subsequent sexual development in a way that predisposed them to have pedophilia.

Thank God, many kids who are abused are not damaged in that way, but the fact that some were not so damaged does not mean that a percentage were not, indeed, scarred by the experience. So often when we see an adult with pedophilia we see a former victim grown older.

There is evidence now in some cases about biology. I will not have time to go into it, but some of these disorders have been associated in some, certainly not all instances, with chromosomal abnormalities, hormonal abnormalities, and so on.

What about the rationale for treatment? As I said earlier, we can look at this as simply a moral issue alone. If you are doing something wrong, you just need to stop it. I would remind all of us that at one time, that is, for example, how we looked at alcoholism. If we talked about alcoholism perhaps 150 years ago, the man who was an alcoholic was simply the bum in the gutter. The woman with a drinking problem was held in even more contempt. It was simply a moral issue.

Rationale for Treatment

We know there are still important moral issues when it comes to alcoholism. We never want to forget the importance of looking at things from the moral perspective. But we also have today, for example, the Betty Ford Clinic, which says that in addition to the moral problems there are important medical and scientific issues that also have to be factored into the equation.

I would argue, and I think Patrick Carnes has done a terrific job in making this point, that the same historical evolution of thinking about alcoholism is now needed with regard to some of the struggles that people are having with sex, a very powerful biological force. Some people may need help with that as well.

What are some of the reasons they need help? First, many people who have these problems, do not even recognize them initially. It is just like the alcoholic. How often does someone with an alcohol problem raise his or her hand and say, "I need help"? When people are experiencing strong cravings and satisfying those cravings is pleasurable, whether for alcohol, for abnormal sex, or whatever, people often rationalize and deny. That is the way the human mind works. They minimize. They have a hard time looking themselves in the mirror and saying to themselves, I should not do that which I crave so strongly and which will give me so much pleasure. So often we have to sit them down

86

and force them to begin to look more objectively. You are causing problems. You are embarrassing the community. You are impairing your thinking. You are acting immorally. You need to sit down, take yourself to task, look at yourself, and see it. If we are dealing with someone who is fundamentally a decent person and we force them to begin to look at it more objectively, then he begins to develop some insight and can begin to work on dealing with the problem that he had been trying to minimize.

A second reason, though, that we need to try to treat people is that we have to understand the impact that something as powerful as the sex drive can have on a person's volitional capabilities. What kind of power does a biological drive have? How does it effect behavior? We all assume that most people can do whatever they want just by putting their minds to it. If we did not make that assumption we would have absolute chaos. How could we hold one another morally accountable? If we do not assume that people have willpower and can control themselves, how can we hold anyone responsible for his or her own actions?

Is it the case, though, that people invariably can control their behavior through their own actions? Let me put on my white coat as a physician for a moment to address that issue. There are millions of Americans right now struggling to take off weight, by dieting. These individuals, in my judgment, in most cases are very sincere.

As a doctor, I can tell you that I can give these people a diet with a 100 percent guarantee. Doctors have done that. We have got the Pritikin diet, we have all sorts of diets. So I am going to tell you my, Dr. Berlin's, absolute, guaranteed way to lose weight. The way is just this: eat a little bit less every day. If you just do that, you are going to lose weight.

But the power of a biological drive is such that millions of decent people struggling just to make that simple change in behavior are having a difficult time doing it.

Now, what is the phenomenology, the mental phenomenon that someone can describe when he or she is trying to diet? You probably all know this, but I just want to drive the point home with an example. It is New Year's Eve, 1999. It is time to make the resolutions. You just had a big meal, so you are not at all hungry. And you decide, this is it, I am taking off twenty pounds. You mean it, and because you're not hungry, and because it is a resolution, you are absolutely sure you can do it.

What then happens? You gradually begin to be discomforted by your cravings, by your appetite, by your hunger, and you begin to rationalize. "Well, you know, that one little Coke will not matter. A few pretzels won't make much difference." Now, no refrigerator ever walked up the stairs to the bedroom. And you have told your friends, you have told everyone, about your resolution to lose weight. It is another embarrassing situation. So you premeditatedly and sneakily go to get the food, and you eat it.

As soon as you have had it, you are sorry. You are really sorry. You want to kick yourself. You promise never again. You mean it. And yet, as soon as the hunger reoccurs you want to eat again.

Patrick Carnes, in his book *"The Sexual Addict,"* really points out how the same phenomenon can occur with another biological drive, the sex drive.

I have often heard it said, well, you have to eat. If you do not eat, you are not alive. That is true. Then they will say, well, you do not have to have sex.

Well, God put the sex drive in each and every one of us for a very important reason. That is for the human race to continue. Yes, it is true, if I do not eat I die. But if I do not have sex, metaphorically speaking, the human race dies. If that powerful drive that is within us gets aimed in the wrong direction, let us say towards children, for example, towards cross-dressing, towards exposing, it still recurrently craves satisfaction. It still wants repeatedly to be satisfied. But now it is aimed in a direction that can cause great harm, if satisfied. Therefore people may need professional assistance so that harm does not occur. That is why treatment should be given.

Some people use the word "compulsion." I mentioned that I prefer the word "driven." The individual is driven by a powerful biological force, and therefore, like the overeater, like the alcoholic, like the drug addict. He or she may need professional assistance.

The person is still morally responsible, and has moral obligations in the sexual area. But let me point out in terms of the concept of free will that, as with alcoholism, sometimes the first thing the person has to do is acknowledge, "I have to admit that through my willpower alone I am not able to control this. But with the help of a Higher Power, with the help of proper professionals, I will exercise my responsibility to get the kind of help that now will enable me to control myself so I can lead my life in a proper moral fashion."

So I do believe that free will can be impaired. That does not mean that people who are so impaired cannot get the proper help so that they can again live their lives in a proper and moral fashion. Despite the attached stigma, much greater in the case of struggling with sexual temptations than with something like alcoholism, in my judgment, I think we have to move beyond that and recognize that decent people can be struggling sexually. They need help so that they can begin to lead their lives in a more moral and disciplined fashion.
Types of Treatment

Now, what about treatment? The four kinds that have been used traditionally are insight-oriented psychotherapy— that's number one. Number two is behavior therapy. Number three is surgery: I am talking about castration. Then finally there is medication plus counseling.

Insight-oriented psychotherapy is based on the idea that if everything goes well during early psychological maturation, we will all grow up to be attracted to age-comparable members of the opposite gender. The theory then says that some people develop sexual aberrations because something goes wrong during their early psychological development. Through therapy and introspection you can figure out what went wrong in your early development and then, having figured it out, and with the sort of emotional catharsis that goes along with figuring it out, you will be able to make things better. Things were broken, you figured out why, and you are going to fix it.

I know there are some who do not entirely agree with it but I am going to give you my viewpoint on sexual abnormalities. I do not think there is good evidence that insight-oriented therapies work. First of all, I think I could spend forever on a psychiatrist's couch and not figure out why I am attracted to women rather than men. I do not know that I can necessarily figure it out. Furthermore, even if one can find out why he or she is experiencing certain sexual attractions, it does not change those attractions.

I don't mean this to be too cynical, but if we are treating a pedophile, for example, someone who is sexually attracted to children, the goal is not to have a more well-adjusted pedophile who now better understands those attractions, but is still out there acting on them. The goal is to stop. It is like alcoholism. I do not care if you understand why you are an alcoholic or not. What I care about is that you stop drinking.

If you are hurting other people, if you are behaving in ways that are unacceptable, the treatment that is going to be necessary is to stop that conduct, not simply to better understand why it developed in the first place.

Behavior therapy has been based on the idea of trying to recondition a person's erotic arousal patterns. Again, I am not saying that that can be done. You can teach people how not to give in to unacceptable temptations, but I am not sure you can teach people to change their sexual makeup.

I ask myself, for example, could someone do something that would erase my attraction to women and replace it with an attraction to little boys? Could somebody really recondition me that way? I doubt that. If we wanted to treat the man suffering from homosexual pedophilia that way, we would have to just do that, albeit in reverse. We would have to help erase an attraction that has been natural for him all of his life, an attraction to little boys, and instill in him an attraction to women, something that may never have been there. Again, there are some therapists who believe they can do that, but I am not convinced. I am not going to talk here about castration. I do not think that's necessary. Let me finish with the approach that we do use: medication and counseling. Let me start with counseling.

We can think of the child being to the person with pedophilia what the bottle of alcohol is to the alcoholic. In other words, there are many reasons why people drink. But the final common pathway is that the alcoholic gives in to his or her cravings to drink, gets into a car, kills an innocent child, ruins his or her own life in the process. Again, there may be many factors that determine whether people who are craving sexually for children act on those cravings.

But if they do, an innocent child can be injured, and they can destroy their own lives in the process.

What have we learned about how we can help people with craving disorders? I mentioned the Betty Ford Clinic earlier. I mentioned Patrick Carnes' work. We have learned a good deal about some of the things we can do for people who are having unacceptable cravings.

One of the things we can do is group therapy. Now, I do not want to suggest that as magic, but how can it help?

One thing that happens in group therapy is therapeutic confrontation. You can confront the denial, the rationalizations that I mentioned earlier are present, and force the person to begin to look more objectively at the implications of his or her actions.

A second thing you can do in group therapy is almost the opposite of confrontation. That is therapeutic support. You could not put a guy who is having abnormal sexual cravings, particularly for children, for example, in a group of middle-age people talking about marriage problems. In going around the circle, when it gets to him, is he going to say, "Well, my problem is I've been craving sex with kids for years?" If you put him in such a group, he is afraid he is going to be injured rather than helped. But if you put people who are having difficulties struggling sexually into groups of other people who are having similar problems, they get the sense that someone is listening out of a desire to be helpful. You cannot have therapy unless people feel good about speaking openly and honestly. So if you can create an environment where people can speak openly and honestly, you are more likely to have effective therapy.

There are relapse prevention strategies. We teach alcoholics the changes in lifestyle they need to make to minimize the temptations that they are going to experience. You do the same thing with people who are experiencing unacceptable sexual temptations. They need to make profound changes in lifestyle. They may have to get pornography out of their life. They may have to stop associating with people who are sexually promiscuous. Because the temptations are powerful, we need to teach them the changes in life they need to make to get these behaviors under control.

Finally, where does medication fit into this? We do not have enough knowledge, and maybe we never will, about the biological differences that can contribute to qualitative differences in sexual makeup. I do not know how to take someone who is not attracted to adults and is attracted to children, and do something biological to turn around that attraction. If we knew enough about that, that would be a cure. We would have helped such people become a normal heterosexual. We would have erased their pedophilic desires. That would be a cure. We do not know enough about qualitative differences in sexual makeup biologically to do that.

We do know a lot about the intensity dimension, though. So if I am hungering for unacceptable sexual activities—whether I am just hungering to be promiscuous, or for children, or for something unusual such as cross-dressing —if we can at least make you less hungry, that should make it easier for you if you are a moral person who is trying to resist those temptations.

If I was trying to diet and we had an effective appetite suppressant, it would not be a guarantee or a cure. I would still have to try. But it should be easier for me if my appetite has been suppressed to be able to change my behavior.

We know that the hormone testosterone produced by the human testes fuels the intensity of sexual drive. And therefore, by lowering that hormone, testosterone, through various medications, we can give a man what would be the equivalent of a sexual appetite suppressant. There are drugs, such as Depo-Provera and Depo-Lupron, which do that and which now, I believe, have a role to play in helping people resist these compulsions and to bring their behavior under control.

In summary, there are many people who engage in sexually improper behaviors who do not have a compulsion. They are doing this for other reasons, perhaps a lack of a proper moral commitment and so on. So there are a group of people who misbehave sexually who do not have compulsions, who are not sexually driven, who do not have sexual addictions, and we want to recognize that and not excuse someone for sinning by saying that they have a sexual problem.

On the other hand, there are some fundamentally decent people who are trying very hard to live a moral life, but because of the abnormal nature of their sexual makeup or the intensity of their makeup they indeed need professional help, as with the alcoholic. Their problem is like an addiction; they do have sexual compulsions. We need to have ways of trying to help them, and I have tried to spell out a few ways of doing that.

SEXUAL COMPULSION: CHALLENGE FOR CHURCH LEADERS

PATRICK J. CARNES, PH.D., C.A.S.

With greater awareness of sexual exploitation, more cases of sexual misconduct by clergy are being brought to the attention of diocesan authorities. A high probability exists that a significant percentage of these behaviors could be described as compulsive or addictive. The actual percentage will vary by the type of behavior. When church leaders are confronted by problematic sexual behavior and it fits the parameters of addictive/compulsive illness, they should know what that means in order to make appropriate management decisions and to evaluate clinical approaches. The purpose of this paper is to summarize the nature of the problem, the typical course of treatment and recovery, and critical factors for monitoring progress.

Nature of the Sexual Addiction Problem

During the last three decades professionals have acknowledged that some people use sex to manage their internal distress. Similar to compulsive gamblers, compulsive overeaters, or alcoholics, they are not able to contain their impulses with destructive results. Depending on your professional framework, you have heard the words addiction or compulsion used to describe the disorder. In my field of addiction medicine, one of the signs of addiction is compulsive use. Some professionals at times may make distinctions between the two words. Others use them interchangeably. There is however a growing common understanding of the problem and how it occurs. Great progress is also being made in treatment. Advances in neurochemistry may soon redefine our terminology as we understand more clearly the biology of the disorder.

The first problem that all church decision makers face is identifying a case of possible sexual compulsivity. Typically clergy who are in trouble for their sexual behavior are not candid with those in authority about whatever incident has come to light. Nor are they likely to reveal that the specific behavior is actually a part of a consistent self-destructive pattern. It is the nature of this illness to cause the clergy person to hide the severity of the problem from others, to delude himself about his ability to control his behavior, and to minimize the impact on others. The expectation of other that they are to be models of moral behavior adds to their shame and fear, compounding the problem.

The most likely scenario is that if there is an incident it will present itself as a one-time event or simply as a moral lapse. In the past such events have resulted in suggestions for intensive prayer or a geographic change. If however there is a sexual compulsion, the problem will not disappear without further intervention. Further there is a wide range of behaviors which can be problematic, including compulsive masturbation, affairs, pornography use, prostitution, voyeurism, exhibitionism, sexual harassment, and sex offending. Seldom do these patients engage in just one form of sexual behavior; a collection of behaviors is more likely. For example, in addition to multiple affairs, there might also be problems of prostitution, pornography, cybersex, and masturbation. The following are situations which should prompt a decision maker to require an assessment:

I. **If the decision maker has evidence that there is a pattern of behavior**. For example, if the bishop knows there is an affair and hears reports or complaints of the clergy person using a massage parlor or prostitute, a pattern starts to emerge. A history of sexual issues over time would also indicate a problem.

II. **If there is a sexual incident and the decision maker knows that other excessive behaviors such as alcoholism, compulsive eating, compulsive working, or compulsive gambling also exist (or a history of those behaviors exists) in addition to evidence of a sexual problem.** Most often addictive and compulsive behaviors occur together and amplify each other. Or these behaviors can replace each other. For example, a recovering alcoholic may maintain alcohol sobriety but start sexually bingeing.

III. **If the behavior involves the abuse of power, including sex with children, congregants, parish staff, or other persons under the authority of that clergy person.** Any exploitation of power or complaint of exploitation should immediately trigger an assessment of the situation and temporary removal from duties.

IV. **If there are unexplained problems coupled with a sexual incident.** Unexplained absences, failure to perform expected tasks, and the disappearance of large sums of money could all be part of a compulsive pattern.

Remember that the discovery of sexual activity does not necessarily mean that there is addictive illness. To have a long term affair, for example, would be a problem for a celibate clergyman, but clinically that is not in itself a compulsive pattern. Nor does exploitative or even violent behavior mean addictive illness. According to a recent study of sex offenders, only 72% and 38% of rapists or pedophiles fit the criteria of addictive illness.

Finally it is important to note that women as well as men can have the problem, in fact, for every three men there is one woman. The ratio parallels gender ratios in compulsive gambling and alcoholism. Our experience with religious women who are also sexually compulsive is that the condition is much more hidden. The expectation of many church leaders that women, and certainly religious women, would not have the problem helps to keep the problem secret.

Sexual compulsion therefore can be very diverse. The following examples illustrate the diversity and complexity of sexual addiction among clergy:

A parish pastor had a one-thousand-dollar-a-week prostitution habit. After depleting his family inheritance he started to use parish funds by removing loose cash in the parish collections and making out false payroll checks for staff who did not exist. He fancied himself as having a "ministry" to the prostitutes he used. He also did not see himself as violating his vow of celibacy since he was an "emotional virgin" with no relationship entanglements.

A woman religious was the principal of a parish school. She was having an affair with a married man who had a child in the school. Simultaneously she was sexually involved with the pastor of the parish. Also she was having an intense sexual relationship with a woman in her order. Her self-imposed "cure" was to become a missionary, but the same pattern emerged overseas. She called her superior from a hospital after cutting crosses in her thighs as a way to stop her behavior.

A young monk had access to the internet in a part of the monastic library which was quite isolated. He started out of curiosity to explore sexually explicit websites. Soon he found himself hooked on pornography, chat rooms, and phone sex. He found himself unable to perform his duties and started to drink heavily. His superior eventually confronted him on his out-of-control drinking. Then the monk owned the real problem.

An order priest teaching at a college and graduate level was, over time, involved sexually with students. He also would have high risk anonymous sex with men in parks and rest rooms. Simultaneously he developed a significant compulsive overeating problem, weighing in excess of 330 pounds on a six-foot frame. His life came apart when he was arrested in a park by a vice officer.

While these examples represent diverse behaviors, the common theme is sexually compulsive behavior. These are people who have reached a level of

Table 1

Sexual Addiction Criteria	Initial	Long-Term
1. Recurrent failure (pattern) to resist sexual impulses to engage in specific sexual behavior.	73%	(94%)
2. Frequent engaging in those behaviors to a greater extent or over a longer period of time than intended.	66%	(93%)
3. Persistent desire or unsuccessful efforts to stop, reduce, or control these behaviors.	67%	(88%)
4. Inordinate amount of time spent in obtaining sex, being sexual, or recovering from sexual experiences.	58%	(94%)
5. Preoccupation with the behavior or preparatory activities.	37%	(77%)
6. Frequent engaging in the behavior when expected to fulfill occupational, academic, domestic, or social obligations.	52%	(87%)
7. Continuation of the behavior, despite knowledge of having a persistent or recurrent social, financial, psychological, or physical problem that is exacerbated by the behavior.	63%	(85%)
8. Need to increase the intensity, frequency, number, or risk of behaviors to achieve the desired effect, or diminished effect with continued behaviors at the same level of intensity, frequency, number, or risk.	36%	(74%)
9. Giving up or limiting social, occupational, or recreational activities because of the behavior.	51%	(87%)
10. Distress, anxiety, restlessness, or irritability if unable to engage in the behavior.	55%	(98%)

sexual frequency and loss of control that is self-destructive. Like compulsive gambling or compulsive overeating or alcoholism, they will make repeated unsuccessful efforts to stop. They know that disaster will follow, yet they proceed anyway, and may even continue to lead exemplary lives in every other aspect. Table 1 summarizes criteria clinicians use to diagnose this condition. In the table are statistics describing the percentages of clients who see themselves as fitting the criteria upon admission to treatment. There are also statistics from clients who have been in long-term treatment (average of 2.5 years). You will note a denial factor: individuals who have been in recovery longer see more clearly how they fit the criteria.

Profiles of Compulsive Behavior

The essentials of the treatment process is best understood by reviewing characteristics of those affected by compulsive sexual behavior. The emerging profile will help church leaders understand the requirements of treatment. All data listed in specific traits come from a study of over one thousand sex addicts published in 1991(Carnes). Other sources are noted separately. Critical characteristics are:

1. Distrust of Authority — Most of these patients come from dysfunctional families who have a significant problem with addictive disorders. Only 13% of the families of origin have no addictions reported. Children who grow up in these families are severely affected by parents with addictive disorders. Most important, 77% of the families are extremely rigid and controlling. Children from this type of family do not develop normal abilities of self-limitation and responsibility. To comply with authority meant an essential loss of self. As a result as adults they are comfortable hiding things from those in authority and resistant to accountability.

2. Intimacy Deficit — Over 87% of these patients come from a disengaged family, which means a family environment in which members are detached, uninvolved, or emotionally absent. All compulsive and addictive behaviors are signs of significant intimacy disorder and the inability to get needs met in healthy ways.

3. Post-Traumatic Stress Disorder — Common to all addictive/ compulsive behaviors is a history of trauma and abuse. Sexually compulsive patients have a history of sexual abuse (81%), physical abuse (72%), and emotional abuse (97%). Addictions and compulsions become a way to manage stress-disordered affect and may include repeating the trauma compulsively.

4. Extreme eroticization — One of the effects of abusive families and childhood sexual abuse is that as adults, survivors sexualize all interactions. They often sense that most people do not take the same approach to sexuality as they do, which adds to their shame.

5. Shame-based sense of self — Shame stems from a failure to achieve a positive sense of self with a profound belief in one's lack of worth. The constant failure to stop hated behavior confirms the belief that the person is fundamentally flawed and unlovable.

6. Compartmentalization — A survival mechanism for abused children is to compartmentalize, so as to avoid reality. As an adult this means dividing up life into compartments. This explains behavior in which a person lives as though no one would find out the truth, or tells outright lies without distress. Robert Louis Stevenson's use of the metaphor of Jekyll and Hyde to describe alcoholism illustrates this type of internal fragmentation.

7. Compulsive Cycles — Most addicts (72%) binge and then feel despair, like a bulimic bingeing and purging. Some clergymen preach against promiscuity or some sexual behavior only to be discovered or even arrested for that behavior. In their public pronouncements they are purging, while privately they were clearly bingeing. These cycles add to both shame and compartmentalizing.

8. Self-Destructive Behavior — Many report high-risk behavior which resulted in severe consequences. Children who are sexually abused often integrate fear into their arousal templates. Adult sex then requires a fear component, which results in risk-seeking sex. Frequently these patients report knowing that there was a 100% probability their behavior would be disastrous and did it anyway.

9. Other Addictions — Seldom do these patients have only a sexual problem. Most (83%) have other addictive/compulsive disorders as well. For example, 41% have problems with alcohol or drugs and 38% have some eating disorder. Other issues include gambling, financial disorders, and nicotine. Usually compulsive sexual behavior is part of an intricate weave of behaviors to manage internal distress. Sometimes addictions are "fused." For example, studies are emerging that show a close connection between cocaine use and sexual acting out (reports range from 50 to 70%) (Washton). Many of these patients would never use cocaine without sex and vice versa. Various reports also document "switching," or replacing one set of addictive/compulsive behaviors with another set.

10. Concomitant Mental Health Disorders — Dual-diagnosis issues with these patients are common. As with all addictive and compulsive disorders, there often is acute depression, which is constantly intensified by the failure to control sexual behavior. Other issues include bipolar swings, narcissism, and sociopathy, further complicating treatment planning.

The treatment challenge is to provide a therapeutic environment which gains the trust of the patient but also holds the patient accountable. Further, sufficient containment must occur to stop self-destructive behavior. Then the core issues of family control, dysfunction, and abuse can be addressed. Tools for managing stress, shame reduction, and relapse prevention are critical. Information about sex and sexual addiction along with cognitive behavioral interventions will break up cognitive distortions and dysfunctional beliefs. Other addictions and mental health issues also must be addressed as part of treatment planning.

Profiles of Sexually Compulsive Clergy

This profile would not be complete without addressing those characteristics specific to clergy who are sexually compulsive. Most of the empirical data available target populations of clergy who have committed sexual misconduct. Very little hard data exists on clergy sexual problems such as prostitution use or compulsive masturbation, although those issues are frequently reported. What we do know comes from studies of clergy who have been exploitative. Irons and Laaser describe a population of clergy who have committed sexual misconduct in which a little over half fit the criteria for sex addiction. This parallels studies of sex addiction in sex offenders (55%) (Blanchard) in general or in sexual misconduct in other professions such as physicians (55%) (Irons and Schneider). In general, a little over half of those evaluated for some form of sexual misconduct fit the criteria for sexual addiction. Those that do usually have other sexually compulsive behaviors like prostitution or affairs, which must then be part of the treatment process.

Other characteristics of clergy who are guilty of sexual misconduct are reported in the literature as well. Benson reports similar findings to those of Irons and Laaser, including reports in most cases of some recent narcissistic wounding, as in the death of a parent or some other loss. A summary of other characteristics include:

- About half also struggle with alcoholism (and these tend to have multiple victims).
- About one-third have other issues of compulsivity, including food, work, and spending.
- Chronic and pervasive lack of intimacy.
- A history of abandonment, abuse, and exploitation in their own childhood.
- Extreme shame about their behavior which alternates with acting-out cycle.
- A family of origin characterized by rigidity, dysfunction, and neglect.

- Grandiose care-taking of others (taking on too much responsibility in helping others as in a "suffering servant" or "prophet victim role").
- Sexual specialness or intrusion especially maternally.
- Extreme narcissism often to the point of personality disorder.

While many of these characteristics parallel the general sexual compulsive pattern, some are important to note as different. The extreme care taking that characterized their ministry provided justification or entitlement for their behavior. The narcissism created self-absorption, which limited awareness of their impact on others, especially their impact on their victims.

To summarize: these men were isolated, stressed, wounded from childhood, with poor relationship skills. They were quite successful at compartmentalizing and also unaware of large parts of themselves. The tasks of ministry became an overlay for basic cognitive distortions which allowed the behavior to continue. Because of this profile there are basic principles of treatment an administrator should make primary:

1. If sexual compulsion is involved, removing from active ministry immediately is important in order to break the compulsive cycle and minimize harm. Usually there is more than is being talked about, and nothing should continue until the extent of the behavior is fully understood.

2. A careful, multidisciplinary assessment team should work with the individual. This assessment team should not be connected with the facility that does the treatment. It is the nature of this illness to keep hidden what is unknown, and the assessment process will bring more clarity. Assessments by individual professionals simply do not break through those defenses as well.

3. Treatment must include participation in a treatment therapeutic community. Treatment works best if it is accompanied by a high degree of patient accountability with a high degree of compassion and care. Essential life deficits of the magnitude described in the above profile can only be addressed where those two elements are present.

4. If the ministry has been used to sexually exploit others, the administrator should be aware that a 44% probability exists that this person will not return to active ministry. Being in a power role would be too strong a trigger, insuring relapse. Those who can return to ministry must use contractual provisions similar to those developed for physicians, therapists, and other helping professionals. Usually that contract takes into account the

strengths of the individual, and matches those to doable tasks providing meaningful work with minimal risk to recovery. The monitoring of that contract as well as supporting the recovering person are critical tasks for the administrator. Therefore the selection of a treatment provider must include a willingness to work with that provider from the outset to support whatever outcome is determined. In that sense the administrator is part of the team.

5. Any contract must take into account the entire range of compulsive behavior. The assessment and treatment process will uncover much that is not part of the initial presenting problem. To focus for example on seduction of parishoners and ignore compulsive prostitution is asking for relapse in both. The administrator must select treatment resources which include the entire bandwidth of sexual patterns.

Given these parameters, the decision maker needs to understand the basic processes people in recovery go through.

The Recovery Process

A concentrated effort to understand how people successfully recovered from sexual addiction started in the mid-eighties. The study involved seven researchers, took five years, and focused on a thousand recovering people. The result was a book called *Don't Call It Love* (Bantam, 1991). To piece together the recovery process, we asked recovering sex addicts and their partners to complete a number of instruments, including an extensive life status inventory and a month-by-month history of their recovery. We also interviewed people with extended recovery in a stage-by-stage fashion and analyzed their responses. We then adopted two strategies to obtain a pattern of recovery. We developed a pattern from the retrospective information provided by the surveys and interviews, and we asked people with different periods of recovery (six months, one year, eighteen months, etc.) how things were going for them now. The two strategies yielded the same pattern. The following overview of a five-year recovery process is based on changes in classic quality of life indicators.

The First Five Years of Recovery

The First Year: There was no measurable improvement, and yet most addicts reported that life was definitely better. This apparent contradiction might be explained by one respondent's comment that "when you are hitting your head against the wall, even stopping the hitting helps." In fact, according to our assessments, some things got worse. Most slips, if any, will occur in the second six months of recovery. Further, all health indicators—accidents, sickness, and visits to physicians—show the second six months to be the worst over the five years. The first year appears to be characterized by extraordinary turmoil, which really tests the recovering person's resolve to change. Some of the consequences of addiction continue, and the change itself is difficult.

The Second and Third Years: Once through the first year, significant rebuilding starts. There is measurable improvement occurring in many areas including finances, ability to cope with stress, spirituality, self-image, career status, and friendships. Our survey documented improvement in finances, coping with stress, career status, and friendships continuing over the five-year period. These indicators reflect a period of intense personal work, which results in more productivity, stability, and a greater sense of well being.

Three to Five Years: Once the personal base of recovery was established, healing occurred in the addict's key relationships. Improvements, often-dramatic improvements, occurred in relationships with children, parents, siblings, and partners. There were some exceptions. About 13 percent found that a breach with their family of origin could not be healed because the family was abusive or was threatening to recovery. Also, some marriages were casualties to the recovery process. Most important, sex addicts reported a significant shift toward more healthy and satisfying sexual expression. With the healing of relationships, overall life satisfaction improved dramatically. Table 2 below summarizes our findings.

Table 2 Categories of Recovery over Time

Worst... Second 6 Months	Better... Year 2 and 3	Better... Year 3 Plus
S A Relapse	Financial Situations*	Healthy Sexuality
Health Status	Coping with Stress*	Primary Relationships
	Spirituality	Life Satisfaction
	Self Image	Relationship with
	Career Status*	Family of Origin
	Friendships*	Relationship with
		Children

*Continued to improve three years plus.

The question is asked: does it have to take three to five years to rebuild one's life? Probably not, given current technology. When the people in our survey went through recovery, the groups were generally small and inexperienced. Treatment programs were few, and therapists were learning as they went along. It is possible that, with more treatment options, the greater experience of therapists, and the growing maturity of the fellowships, recovery can move faster. Nonetheless, some aspects of recovery address core developmental issues, which take time to heal.

Stages of Recovery

In addition to our findings, we conducted a series of content analyses in which we were able to see six discernible phases or stages in which these changes occur. The stages are summarized as follows:

The Developing Stage (*Lasts up to two years*): During this period of time the addict's problems mount, creating an awareness that something must be done. The addict may even seek therapy or attend a Twelve Step group, but then drop out. We also noted that many therapists would fail to see the problem of sexual acting out, or if they did see it, failed to follow through on it. Even knowledgeable therapists would feel shame at this stage because the client dropped out of therapy. They would tell themselves that if they had been better therapists, the client might have gotten through.

Our research showed that no matter what therapists try at this stage, clients still might not be ready. Addicts have a growing appreciation of the reality of the problem but tend to counter this realization by minimizing the problem or thinking they can handle it by themselves. Some addicts temporarily curtail their behaviors or substitute other behaviors.

The Crisis/Decision Stage (*One day to three months*): At some point, the addict crosses over a line in which there is a fundamental commitment to change. Most often this is precipitated by a crisis, subterfuge, and duplicity, and loss of the care of the double life. This crisis may include events like arrests, sexually transmitted diseases, spouse or partner leaving, positive HIV test, sexual harassment suits, loss of professional license, car accidents involving death or injury, and suicide attempts. Sometimes a crisis is precipitated by a therapist or employer who refuses to continue enabling destructive behaviors. For some of our respondents, the commitment to change was not about crisis but rather about choice. They simply were no longer willing to exist in the old way. They reflected the old aphorism in Alcoholics Anonymous of "being sick and tired of being sick and tired" and become willing to go to "any lengths" to get better.

The Shock Stage (*First six to eight months*): Once they admit the problem, addicts enter a stage that parallels what happens to anyone who has experienced deep loss and change. Disbelief and numbness alternate with anger and feelings of separation. Addicts describe physical symptoms of withdrawal that are at times agonizing. They also report disorientation, confusion, numbness, and inability to focus or concentrate. Feelings of hopelessness and despair become more intense as their sense of reality grows. Addicts

103

become reactive to limits set by therapists, sponsors, or family members. When they join a recovery group, they experience a sense of belonging, along with the realization that recovery was the right decision for them. The time-honored Twelve Step wisdom, distilled in slogans like "Keep it simple" and "A day at a time," appears to be very appropriate at this point. Addicts do report feelings of relief and acceptance once the double life is over.

The Grief Stage (*Next six months*): As they come out of shock, the addicts become aware of their pain. This suffering has several components that interact at the same time. First, there is awareness of all the losses due to addiction, including jobs, relationships, children, time, money, and physical well-being. The wreckage is everywhere. Second, there is a sense of loss as the addiction ceases to serve as friend, comforter, and high. Third, the addiction has masked deeper hurts, usually stemming from child abuse and family-of-origin events. Without the cover of the addictive process, memories return and clarity about those early wounds emerges. Understanding the level of suffering at this point helps to explain why the relapse rate was so high during this time period. Similarly, the decline in the level of health in the second half of the first year parallels this painful period. High emotional stress impairs the immunological system, making addicts more vulnerable to illness, and reduces the ability to function normally, thereby increasing the vulnerability to accidents. These effects on health status provide a potent testimony to the power of pain.

The Repair Stage (*Next eighteen to thirty-six months*): Addicts who were successful in negotiating the rigors of the previous stage move from the pain into a deep internal restructuring. Belief systems about self, sex, family, and values are overhauled. New patterns of behavior develop. Systems theory would describe this phase as a "paradigm shift." It is a "second order" change in which the programming or internal rules are different, versus "first order" change, which is characterized by using the old solutions with greater energy, i.e., trying harder. Said in another way, by changing behavior one can make modest changes in condition. Change the paradigm and the results are dramatic. We were able to measure addicts taking responsibility for themselves in all areas of life including career, finances, and health. They reported a new ability to express their needs, to accept that they have needs, and to work to meet them. A common thread in our study was the deepening of new bonds with others. Addicts also reported efforts to complete things (degrees, projects, work, etc.) and to be dependable (being on time, following through, and responding to requests). In fact, addicts during this phase commented on learning not to live on the "edge" but rather choosing low-risk options over high-excitement options.

The Growth Stage (*Next two years plus*): As addicts achieve more balance in their lives and have a greater sense of themselves, they become more available to others. Relationships with partners, friends, children, and family go through a period of tremendous renewal. Here, too, is where life satisfaction measures really showed improvement. Addicts reported more compassion for themselves and others. They had a new trust for their own boundaries and integrity in relationships. A sense of achievement existed because of new milestones in love and sex. Addicts talked of a new ability to take care of and nurture relationships. Old relationships were transformed or ended.

Treatment Options

Participants in the study who had spent a significant amount of time in recovery were presented with a list of treatment and support resources and asked to indicate whether they had used them and if they were helpful. Further, they were asked to indicate anything else they had tried and whether or not that was useful. Table 3 summarizes the results of this part of our survey. Clearly a number of factors stood out as being helpful in recovery including:

- inpatient treatment experience
- a group experience
- long-term individual therapy
- Twelve Step work
- an active and knowledgeable sponsor
- an ongoing spiritual life
- the support of friends
- a period of celibacy
- regular exercise and balanced nutrition

Not everyone used all of these, but a pattern or recipe for success in recovery did emerge.

Some principles also became clear. *First, recovery is a long-term process.* Brief interventions, including therapy, medication, or limited hospital stay, did not produce the results wanted. This illness is the result of a combination of powerful family forces, neurochemical interactions, and trauma history which have impacted both developmental and internal processes. There is no quick fix. There is, however, a series of steps which, over a period of time, can make for predicable success.

Second, it became very clear that success was dependent on client follow-through and responsibility. If the client did not follow the recipe, success was marginal. This changes our perceptions of measuring outcomes. For example, completing steps one through three of a Twelve Step program in an inpatient facility, but never actively completing further steps or attending further therapy rapidly diminishes the chances of success, no matter how effective the program. Similarly, individual therapy without the support of the client's partner or a Twelve Step fellowship significantly reduces desired outcomes. Ultimately it was not one thing, but a series of interventions over time that maximized the probabilities of success.

Table 3 Treatment Choices

Type of Treatment	Helpful	Not Helpful
Inpatient Treatment	35%	2%
Outpatient Group	27%	7%
After Care (Hospital)	9%	5%
Individual Therapy	65%	12%
Family Therapy	11%	3%
Couples Therapy	21%	11%
Twelve Step Group (SA-based)	85%	4%
Twelve Step Group (Other)	55%	8%
Sponsor	61%	6%
Partner Support	36%	6%
Higher Power	87%	3%
Friends' Support	69%	4%
Celibacy Period	64%	10%
Exercise/Nutrition	58%	4%

Recovery for Catholic Clergy

While the pattern of recovery for people in general is helpful, it is important to note exceptions for clergy in general and Catholic clergy specifically. The statistics above indicated the importance of individual long-term therapy. For most, the long-term relationship with a therapist is fundamental. Yet, given the leadership roles of clergy and the profiles of sexual compulsion within the ranks of clergy some residential treatment experience is critical. Also clergy like other professionals fare best when there is a clear contract about return to work which is monitored. This contract assumes that a determination will be made about whether or not that individual can still return to active ministry. Finally, a contract assumes that meaningful work with appropriate setting and structure is available.

All church administrators face other issues as well. When sexual misconduct becomes public the congregation is traumatized as well. The work of Hopkins and Laaser has broken ground in helping wounded congregations. Similarly, church leadership must respond to the needs of victims. These efforts start the process of healing and model values important to the health of the whole church. From a clinical point of view, both of these initiatives have a profound impact on the actual recovery of the clergy person as well. To begin that work closes off potential areas of relapse since congregants and victims will be less likely to be reinvolved. Also, that process frequently provides information for the treatment process itself.

For Catholic clergy there are additional issues. Celibate clergy will explore healthy sexuality differently than most recovering people or clergy from other denominations. Yet they must learn about how their own backgrounds were factors in their sexual acting out. In fact, for some the spiritual benefits of celibacy were elusive because the abstinence triggered deep-seated responses to early trauma. In addition, they must now learn about sexuality and use it for the good of their priestly calling. One of the common themes in the literature is the general lack of training clergy have in sexuality, sexual abuse, domestic violence, addictive disorders, and healthy professional boundaries.

An additional issue is spirituality. The above statistics refer to the importance of a "higher power" in the recovery process for all recovering people. Survivors of abuse as well as addicts need to deal with the core problem of transforming suffering into meaning. It is the classic question, why do bad things happen to good people, or the problem of Job. Coming to terms with painful issues for most people means drawing on resources of their spiritual tradition.

When the original abuse, however, was perpetrated by a clergyman, the survivor is often blocked in accessing spiritual resources. A recent study of victims (McLaughlin) found that Protestants often switched to another denomination as a way to cope. The same study found that Catholics often simply stopped going to church altogether and became stuck in their process — usually in the anger phase. For Catholics there is something so fundamental in the betrayal by their priest they seem not to have the resiliency of Protestant victims. For priests who were victimized by priests the problem becomes exponential. First, as survivors they have the reaction of being betrayed by the church. But also being a priest who may have victimized others in the same way creates incredible suffering. A story heard over and over again is victimization within seminary or some church context being the start of the road to sexually compulsive behavior. The pastoral response to that issue is one of the most unattended challenges of this work in the church today.

Resources

Our resources to treat this problem have increased dramatically in the last decade. We now have the National Council on Sexual Addiction and Compulsion with a nationwide network of treatment facilities as well as individual therapists. Each week in North American and in some South American cities thousands of Twelve Step groups gather to support appropriate sexual behavior. Many of them meet in churches along with other Twelve Step meetings. In addition, there are now websites offering recovery information, clinical and resource information, and extensive bibliography. A medical journal dedicated to the problem also now exists.

One of the more recent advances is the formation of the Interfaith Sexual Trauma Institute (ISTI). With representatives from over nineteen different faith traditions, ISTI's mission is to serve as a clearing house and training facility for all denominations in prevention and responding to clergy sexual abuse. Founded by the Benedictine monks of St. John's University, Collegeville, Minnesota, ISTI each year holds an international conference to bring resources about these issues to all faith communities.

What follows summarizes some of the key resources available to administrators.

NCSAC
The National Office
90 Northchase Pkwy
Ste 200S
Marietta GA 30067
770-989-9754
www.ncsac.org

Sexaholics Anonymous
SAPO Box 111910
Nashville TN 37222-1910
615-331-6230

Sex and Love Addicts Anonymous
SLAA
PO Box 650010
West Newton MA 02165
781-255-8825

www.sexhelp.com
(Patrick Carnes' web site)

Future Prospects

Sexual misconduct by clergy is not a new phenomenon. There has long been a problem in Catholic as well as other traditions. What is different in these times is the level of accountability of church leaders and the options that are available to victims. Nor is the church alone in facing these issues. Confrontation of the sexual abuse of power is occurring in politics, education, business, and medicine. The opportunity here is for church leaders to use our new understanding of the impact of sexual exploitation in programs of spiritual renewal. This initiative must start with how clergy are trained and how they are treated if there is a problem. In part this means to treat separately moral problems and serious illness. Both tasks require dealing with the age-old problem of transforming suffering into meaning.

This article has outlined the basics of addictive/compulsive behavior and underlined the diversity of ways compulsive cycles can affect clergy functioning. It has also summarized the general path of recovery plus specified problems unique to recovering clergy. Part of what is different now is that we have new tools to help people who struggle with sexual compulsion. As clergy become more knowledgeable about them, they will be better able to help congregants as well as to meet the other sexual challenges of today.

References

Benson, Gordon. 1994. "Sexual Behavior by Male Clergy with Adult Female Counselees: Systemic and Situational Themes." *Sexual Addiction and Compulsivity: The Journal of Treatment and Prevention* 1:2, 103–118.

Blanchard, Gerald. 1990. "Differential Diagnosis of Sex Offenders: Distinguishing Characteristics of the Sex Addict." *American Journal of Preventive Psychiatry & Neurology* 2:3, 45–47.

Carnes, Patrick J. 1991. *Don't Call It Love.* New York: Bantam Books.

Hopkins and Laaser. 1995. *Healing the Soul of the Church.* Collegeville, MN: Liturgical Press.

Irons, Richard, and Mark Laaser. 1994. "The Abduction of Fidelity: Sexual Exploitation by Clergy—Experience with Inpatient Assessment." *Sexual Addiction & Compulsivity: The Journal of Treatment and Prevention* 1:2, 119–129.

Irons, Richard, and Jennifer Schneider. 1994. "Sexual Addiction: Significant Factor in Sexual Exploitation by Health Care Professionals." *Sexual*

Addiction & Compulsivity: The Journal of Treatment and Prevention 1:3, 198–214.

McLaughlin, Barbara. 1994. "Devastated Spirituality: The Impact of Clergy Sexual Abuse on the Survivor's Relationship with God and the Church." *Sexual Addiction & Compulsivity: The Journal of Treatment and Prevention* 1:2, 145–158.

Washton, Arnold. 1998. "Cruising and Using: Compulsive Sex and Substance Abuse." *Professional Counselor* 13:6.

Theological
Perspectives

FREE WILL, ADDICTION, AND MORAL CULPABILITY

REVEREND WOJCIECH GIERTYCH, O.P., M.A., S.T.D.

In a letter written to a fearful seminarian, St. Thérèse of Lisieux wrote in July 1897:

> I picture a father who has two children, mischievous and disobedient, and when he comes to punish them, he sees one of them who trembles and gets away from him in terror, having, however, in the bottom of his heart the feeling that he deserves to be punished; and his brother, on the contrary, throws himself into his father's arms, saying that he is sorry for having caused him any trouble, that he loves him, and to prove it he will be good from now on, and if this child asks his father *to punish* him with a *kiss*, I do not believe that the heart of the happy father could resist the filial confidence of his child, whose sincerity and love he knows. He realizes, however, that more than once his son will fall into the same faults, but he is prepared to pardon him always, if his son always takes him by his heart.[1]

St. Thérèse insists upon the importance of love and trust in the eternal Father. Moral difficulties stem from a distorted idea about God and our relationship with Him. St. Thérèse is trying to tell us that we should not focus excessively on sinfulness and punishment. It is the love of the Father, who can be taken by the heart, even from within the abyss of moral dysfunctioning, that is central in the message of the most recent Doctor of the Church.

I would like therefore to begin my presentation by affirming that moral culpability is not the main issue in a Christian reflection on morality. Moral culpability is important in a judicial perspective. A judge has to know whether the criminal was morally responsible for his actions, whether he deserves to be punished or whether he primarily requires medical treatment. This is not assessed easily, but some clarity is needed for the imposition of law and order; that is the social function of the judiciary. Within a religious perspective we are not faced with the same question. If we describe God as a judge, we do this only analogously. God has revealed Himself above all as a loving Father. When He judges, He separates evil from good, so that goodness may flourish. This is sometimes a painful process, but not one, as St. Thérèse teaches us, that is to be feared.

In the presentation of Christian moral teaching, as also in a Christian study of perplexing moral aberrations, the primacy of saving grace needs to be stressed. If our teaching fails to do this, then it generates the type of reaction that St. Thérèse describes in the first boy who remains locked in his culpability and terror. Is it not the case that an excessive and distorted emphasis placed upon moral culpability is one of the deepest causes of the neurotic stress that leads to addiction?

In many languages, it is common parlance to say that by nature we are endowed with reason and free will. This statement is not exactly precise. We are born with the spiritual faculties, but reason, certainly at birth, is undeveloped. We need many years of education before we learn how to be reasonable and wise. Similarly, we are born with the spiritual faculty of the will, which also needs to be developed and educated. There is room for growth during our lifetime in interior liberty. What exactly does this mean? Is freedom a natural quality of the will, or is it something that is acquired and developed?[2] If we will say that the will is enslaved, will not this mean that we deny the possibility of any moral responsibility? The suggestion that the will is hampered in its functioning, though it may be a useful excuse to explain away all forms of moral evil, is dangerous because it reduces man to the level of his animal nature. The insistence that we have a will that is capable of responsible action is a prerequisite for the defense of human dignity.

We need therefore to look into the nature of the will. How is it free? In what sense does the will need to mature so as to become more free? How does the will cooperate with reason? In what way is it subject to the influence of the emotions and of grace? In exploring these questions I will refer to the teaching of St. Thomas Aquinas, which is particularly clarifying. This teaching has not always been perceived in the Church, in particular since in late medieval philosophy the understanding of the nature of the will underwent an imperceptible yet decisive change that has tainted the further development of moral theology.

It is very rare that Aquinas uses the expression "free will." His preferred term to describe interior liberty is *liberum arbitrium*, which should best be translated as "free choice" and not as "free will." The modern understanding of the will, which goes back to the Nominalist philosophy of William of Ockham, suggests that the will is absolutely free. It was Ockham's conviction that the will is the most fundamental faculty, which has as its essential characteristic the capacity to direct itself at whim, to any orientation. Anything that would contradict the will in its indetermination, be it reason, be it a habitual disposition, be it a virtue, be it the dynamism of the body, or be it a superior power such as God, is experienced by the will, according to Ockham, as a limitation of its freedom. Ockham believed similarly that the will of God is absolutely arbitrary. If it were to be determined in any direction, this seemed to him to be incompatible with God's freedom and power. It follows from this theory, that first of all, the divine law is not sapiential but voluntarist, meaning that it could be changed, for example if God would suddenly decide that we are to hate Him instead of love Him. It follows that the human will is free up to the point that it meets the superior will of God which imposes an obligation, only because God wills to do so. The attribution of an indeterminate freedom to the will by Nominalist philosophy has led in consequence to the placing of obligation imposed by the arbitrary will of God at the center of moral reflection. This leads to a supposedly permanent conflict between the freedom of the human will and the freedom of the will of God. Ever since Ockham, and even more so under the later influence of the philosophy of Immanuel Kant, the will began to be understood as the power of execution. Either it executes its own indeterminate whims or it executes the obligations that have been imposed upon it from without. In this execution the will is in a state of constant conflict with the subvoluntary powers of appetites, that tend to encroach upon the freedom of the will. This theory of the will has led in consequence to a distortion of the attitude towards God—a distortion that St. Thérèse tries to manifest in her example.

St. Thomas Aquinas has a completely different understanding of the nature of the will. He saw in the will a spiritual faculty that is passively moved by the good. The will is not a power of pressure. It rather suffers the impression of the good that attracts it. This however is not a limitation of the freedom of the will, but its most profound expression. When recognized goodness moves it, the will elicits its inherent dynamism from within its wells.

Aquinas perceives in the will two levels.[3] The first and deepest level of the will is an imprint of the Creator. The will is endowed with a built-in finality that directs it to the ultimate end that is the source of happiness. This deepest orientation of the will to the supreme good is a determination. There is nothing wrong in saying that on this deepest level, the will is geared by its nature to that which is supremely good. It is not beneath the dignity and freedom of the will to will out of necessity goodness.[4] The second level of the will, is indeterminate. On this level, the will can move in various directions, because as a spiritual faculty it is open to all forms of goodness. This second level of the will has three movements: the liberty of specification, the liberty of exercise, and the tying of these two, to the ultimate end that is willed by the will in a determinate fashion.[5] These three second-level movements of the will are undertaken not by the will alone. They require the cooperation of the reason in acts of free choice. We can make this explanation clearer with an example. On the deepest level of the will, we desire in a determinate manner our goodness and supreme happiness. That goodness includes all the needs, both spiritual and material, of our human nature that we desire spontaneously. On the second level of the will, we desire specific goods. The question whether my thirst which is a natural movement in me will be satiated by tea or by coffee or by beer, is resolved on the second level of the willing by the liberty of *specification*. The question whether I want the beer now, at this very moment, is resolved by the liberty of exercise. The liberty of *exercise* turns the free choice on and off. The third movement of the second level resolves whether the beer that I want, now at this very moment, is compatible with the *ultimate end* that I desire.

Aquinas' description of the nature of the will retains both the inherent determinate finality of the will that attracts it towards supreme goodness, and it retains the indeterminate movement of the will as it makes its choices together with reason on the second level. It is important to note that the deepest movement of the will expresses that which is most fundamental in the will—its movement towards goodness. The essence of the will does not consist in its arbitrariness nor in the power of execution; it consists in the appetite for goodness. When the will is determined on its deepest level to love supreme goodness, it is in itself at its very best. It is in this context, that Aquinas prefers to use the expression "free will."[6] He says about the angels, who are permanently attached to God, that they are more free than we human beings, because our choice of evil is a sign of the defect in our liberty and not of its greatness.[7]

The deepest orientation of the will towards goodness, that is in accord with the final end of the will, is weakened, but not extinguished within us, as a result of original sin. When good choices are made on the second level of the will, the will experiences an interior satisfaction that flows from its deepest level. Why is it that nevertheless some choices are made that are evil?

Aquinas consistently gives a somewhat curious reason for this. The will sometimes moves towards that which is evil—because it is created out of nothing—*ex nihilo*.[8] The created status of the will in angels and men is the deepest cause of the occasional attraction towards the nothingness of evil.

When choices are made, always on the second level of the will, they are the fruit of the combined action of both the reason and the will. On this issue, there has been a series of misunderstandings.[9] The Franciscan critique of Aquinas in the thirteenth century understood his teaching in an intellectualist manner. It seemed that Aquinas had attributed the final choice to the reason and not to the will, which suggested that the will, in following blindly the judgments of reason, was deprived of moral responsibility. The commentators on Aquinas in modern times in turn understood him in a voluntarist way. They understood the relationship of the reason and the will in free choice to be sequential. It was felt that the reason, meaning the conscience, passes a judgment on the future moral act, and then the will passively executes the act. In this interpretation, the entire moral responsibility falls upon the will, which is either obedient or disobedient to the dictates of reason. Both these extreme interpretations are not in accord with the texts of Aquinas. The free choice as Aquinas explains it, is the fruit of the combined action of the reason and the will. This may seem to be a remote question of speculative philosophy, but in fact the way that reason and the will are understood to cooperate in action is important, because differences in interpretation generate a completely different moral climate.

If we accept that free choice is not an action only of the will, but the combined action of both the reason and the will,[10] it follows that there are in fact two moments of functioning in the reason. There is the moment preceding the act, when conscience passes a judgment about it, and then there is a second functioning of the reason within the act of free choice itself.[11] The moral act is not elicited solely by an obedient or disobedient will. The moral act is also rational, which means that within the free choice itself there is an inherent relationship to truth, and that the free choice is creative. In all the stages of the act, in the moment of intention, the occasional deliberation, the decision and in the execution, the reason is involved. As the reason and the will combine, there is an invention of the new act. That invention is creative.

It is true that there is no creativity of the reason vis-à-vis the moral norm. The conscience does not invent its own moral norms. But moral norms do not encompass the totality of the future act. The teaching of the norm is pedagogical; it points towards the truth and it warns against avenues that lead nowhere, but it does not describe the plenitude of the future act. There must therefore be creativity in respect to the act. The *liberum arbitrium*, free choice, expresses the inventiveness of the acting person in the choice of action that best manifests the true values that are incarnated in that particular moment. It is not surprising that Aquinas perceives in the free choice a particularly pertinent icon of the divine image. Only the free person acting out of interior liberty with the full creativity of virtuous action, manifests the divine image. Learning how to elicit persevering and creative acts of free choice within truth is a long process. People may encounter difficulties at various stages of the action. Some people have a difficulty with the intention; they are not very creative in the perception of what can be done. Others have good and colorful intentions, but they cannot pass on to make a decision. Some are first to have an intention, and last with the execution. The discovery that free choice is both rational and voluntary at the same time, and not an act, said to be "free" of the will alone, means that the development of the will does not consist in the boosting of willpower itself. It consists in the rich and inventive undertaking of acts of free choice.

In the creative eliciting of acts of free choice, even though reason and the will combined are the main actors, there is room also for the input of other forces. The sensibility of the person also plays a role. The imagination, the emotions, and the body influence the reason and the will at all stages of the act. These concomitant bodily forces should not be seen only as a danger that limits the freedom of the will and blinds the intellect, but also as a necessary support, which enables the free choice to be made in all its richness and playful diversity. In the case of the Christian, who is nourished by a personal relationship of love with the living God, the free choice is also conditioned by the gifts of the Holy Spirit, which inspire innovative acts of free choice to express charity. The gift of self, repeatedly made out of the love for God, that is, with a clear focusing upon God in the interiority of the act, strengthens the capacity for free choice. To grow in moral maturity we have to learn how to make personal creative choices. Of course, we know that the power of the emotions which is directed towards sensate goods, is not always in accord with what has been chosen by free choice. Attachments have to be purified, so that the free choices are carried through, but as they are made in a creative way and out of the love for God, interior liberty is strengthened.

This interior liberty, described by Fr. Pinckaers[12] as the *liberty of quality,* requires the practice of the virtues to mature. It profits from the light of the moral law and of the Word of God, but it is neither a blank copy of the moral law, nor is it in opposition to the moral law. It grows in an infinite number of ways, as various new and constructive acts of free choice are made. The understanding of liberty that was generated by the Nominalist understanding of the will, since it claimed that the will was arbitrary in its freedom, has been described by Fr. Pinckaers as the *liberty of indifference*—a liberty that is indifferent to value, that is closed in on itself, that is an innate given, which does not need to mature. When it meets obligation imposed by a superior liberty, the *liberty of indifference* does not know how to be creative. It can only either obey or sulk at its own weakness. We return to the metaphor given to us by St. Thérèse. The two boys in her parable have been formed in a different understanding of the nature of the will and of freedom, and this leads to different attitudes towards the heavenly Father.

Because the will is not to be interpreted as an arbitrary, indeterminate power, it follows that free choice can receive an interior strengthening of its orientation towards goodness from divine grace. Grace and the will are not in opposition. Since God has created the will, He can move the will from within (Phil. 2:13). Growth in the capacity for a gift of self takes place, therefore, as the primacy of grace is recognized within acts of love. St. Thérèse advises us to remain little.

> ...which means, that we are not to attribute to ourselves the virtues that we practice, believing that we can attain something, and that we are to recognize that the good God places his treasure in the hand of his little child so that He can make use of it whether He has the need.[13]

And again she says:

> If I would say to myself, for example: "I have acquired this virtue, I am certain that I can practice it," this would be the counting upon

one's own power, and when one does this, one risks to fall in the abyss. But I will have the right to make little stupidities up until my death, without offending the good God, if I am humble, if I remain very little.[14]

An openness to grace, which expresses itself in the trust and generosity of the child that loves, develops in a gentle way the interior liberty.

Neurotic Genesis of Addiction

It seems that the root of addictive behavior lies in an unhappiness that flows from an undeveloped capacity for the gift of self. An interior liberty which flowers in the creativity of multiple virtues grants a spiritual satisfaction. When good is done out of love for God and love for others, there is no need to search for compensation. The joy of service sufficiently satiates the soul. It is important however, that the goodness be undertaken out of personal liberty, and out of love. A spiritual and moral formation that fails to develop the interior liberty and views morality primarily through the prism of a cold obligation leaves a feeling of dissatisfaction. Works undertaken only out of a sense of duty and not out of an interior generosity may be socially acceptable and valuable, but they do not increase interior liberty nor do they grant spiritual satisfaction.

The voluntarist understanding of moral action, which mistakenly replaced the notion of *liberum arbitrium* with an arbitrary and indeterminate "free will," has placed too great a burden on the will. Since the reason and the will were said to function in a sequential pattern, it was seen that the will only is responsible for the moral action. It followed that in the case of moral failure, the entire responsibility was assumed by the will. If you failed, what you needed was a greater willpower. If the will is weak, then exert it as much as possible, so as to force it to obedience!

The will, however, is a spiritual faculty. It cannot be forced. It has to be attracted by goodness. The free choice is strengthened as goodness is perceived with greater clarity and fascination, and as it is chosen through the personal inventiveness of love. Creative acts of free choice grant a spiritual joy. "There is more happiness in giving than in receiving" (Act 20:35). If the senses are in accord with the truth that is the object of free choice, they increase the attraction for the good. The emotions, because they are directed to the here and now of a sensual good, supply a bodily dynamism for the free choice of the good which is perceived in all its concreteness. The emotions have within them an inherent disposition to follow the light of reason and the movement of the will.[15] The harmony of the senses with the spiritual faculties is not experienced by the senses as a painful burden, even though the habituation of the senses in the growth of virtue may require patient effort.

If however,because of a lack of understanding of the nature of the free choice, an excessive stress is placed upon the will alone, more often than not this leads to the erroneous mistaking of the will for the emotions. What is understood to be willpower is, in fact, the power of the emotions and not of the will. Classical philosophical psychology distinguished a group of emotions known as the *appetitus irascibilis*, the irascible or utility emotions. In this group we find the passions of audacity, ambition and anger. Their function is ancillary in the eliciting of acts of free choice. To get things done, you need at times to be able to be angry. When the energy released by these emotions comes as a consequence of free choice, it bolsters free choice. These emotions, however, should not be identified with the will, which is a spiritual faculty.

Since the emotions are carnal, they can be forced in a bodily way. When the energy of one emotion is used to stifle the movement of another emotion, there is no cooperation of the senses with the spiritual free choice. Emotional repression does not involve constructive action. It is destructive. In this psychic mechanism the reason and the will have no say, because the emotions themselves have managed in their mutual conflict to repress the undesired feeling. This mechanism seems to defend a moral order, but it is not liberating. It is neurotic. As we grow in virtues, the eliciting of good acts becomes pleasing, free, and easy. There is an understanding and a fascination with the spiritual good in free choice, together with an affirmation of concomitant feelings. If the emotions of the irascible appetite are mistaken for the will and they are used to eradicate undesirable feelings, the virtues do not grow, and the person does not acquire a greater interior freedom. A sudden boosting of the feeling of fear or of emotional energy in the face of temptation may prevent falling into sin in that particular moment, but it does not lead to interior peace and freedom. Neither scrupulous fear nor emotional energy but prudence and charity working through the spiritual free choice are to be the ultimate norm of action. The emotions of the irascible appetite are to serve free choice, aiding in the acquisition of the goods to which the emotions of the pleasure appetite strive. If they deny the feelings of the emotions of the pleasure appetite, they disable the reason and the will from directing the passions appropriately.

The exertion of repressive emotional energy in the place of true free choice grants the appearance of moral propriety, but it is only external. For the moment, neither the inventiveness of free choice nor the input of divine grace is needed, because the sheer emotional energy which is pretending to be the will seems to have ensured control. This is however a neurotic facade which causes interior stress that is then appeased by the occasional total collapse of all moral barriers. The emotions of the pleasure appetite in time demand some form of release to compensate for the unhappiness of a cramped interior liberty. It is in this hunger that addictions are born. The addictive behavior is generated by a repressed emotion, which at that particular moment acts in a chaotic and obsessive manner. Since the eruption of a repressed passion is beyond the control of the reason and the will, it follows that liberty and responsibility of action is temporarily diminished, although liberty in other fields may be retained. To attain moral equilibrium, therefore, it is the free choice in all its creativity and generosity of love that needs to be developed and not the emotions of energy, mistaken for sheer willpower. A practical living out of charity, in which childlike trust and friendship with God are maintained involves the flowering of grace within the generosity of free choice.

There are certainly also other and deeper causes of addictive behavior apart from emotional repression. If they evidently flow from serious mental disorders, they do not present an ethical problem, because they are obviously outside the realm of moral imputability. Neurotic reactions appear among perfectly free and responsible acts, and so they are perplexing. Both innate biological tendencies and cultural conditionings may contribute to the development of a particular form of addiction. I believe however that the underlying cause of addictive behavior lies in the lack of development of interior liberty, and therefore of charity. The psychiatric experience of Anna Terruwe and Conrad Baars[16], who cured neuroses on the basis of a Thomistic psychology of the passions, permitted the liberation from addictive behaviors including homosexual activity. They lacked a knowledge of the history of moral theology with its misguided emphasis on voluntarism, but they perceived from a clinical perspective the pernicious consequences of a faulty emotional, not sapiential, reception of true moral norms. In moral formation, it is not sufficient merely to present and explain moral norms. What is needed is an initiation into a spiritual encounter with God, which is expressed through mature free choices in faith and charity.

The Culpability of Addictive Behavior

Before we tackle the tricky question of moral culpability among addicts, we have to be clear about exactly what do we mean by culpability— in a theological perspective.

We find in Aquinas a distinction between the evil of fault and the evil of punishment—the *malum culpae* and *malum poenae*.[17] Fault is an evil that flows from within the will, and punishment is an evil that befalls the will.[18] *Culpa* therefore refers to a weakness of the will, which fails to strive towards goodness, and *poena* refers to a burdensome weight that falls upon the will from without. This distinction is primarily between that which is internal and that which is external to the will. In our modern thinking, which has become judicial, we are immediately tempted to tie these two concepts together. When we hear of culpability, we immediately think of punishment that is due. (For this reason we find it difficult to accept the theology of original sin, which says that we are born with a fault in our will that is removed by Baptism. What is in fact said in this theology, is not that we are born deserving immediate punishment, but that we are born with a will that is inherently weakened in its movement towards goodness. And we are born with disorder in all our faculties, which conditions the will from without. That is why the will needs to be magnetized, set straight towards God, and that happens at Baptism.)

Another distinction of Aquinas is that between *peccatum* and *culpa*.[19] A *peccatum*, which should best be translated as a misstep, denotes a human action which lacks the appropriate reference to reason. The qualification supplied by right reason is absent. The *culpa* refers to a misstep that was willed. In common parlance it is customary to identify sin with fault, *culpa*. When it is asked: "Is it a sin to do such and such an act?" the question refers to the objective rationality of the act. Does the act correspond with right reason? When it is asked: "Was it a sin, when I did such and such?", meaning "Am I at fault?", it is the presence of individual free choice that is questioned. It may be that the act was not chosen, or the involvement of the will was diminished or minute. This may be due to conditionings of the will that came from without (from outside the person, or from outside the will but from within the person, as is the case in the neurotic exclusion of the spiritual faculties). It is therefore possible that in a particular evil act there was a *peccatum* and there was no *culpa*. A teenage girl who was forced into an abortion by her impetuous mother may have no *culpa*. The pressure exerted upon her may have been so binding that there was no personal free choice on her part. The act, nevertheless, is still a *peccatum* because it is a disorder that carries with it destructive consequences.

In the light of these distinctions, it is clear that addictive behavior which is destructive is an objective *peccatum*. Is it a fault? Who are we to know? If the evil action has been recognized as such, and willed, meaning that free choice has chosen to ignore the truth of the matter as it is enlightened by the moral norm and has accepted the disordered action, there is full culpability. The *peccatum* is also then a *culpa*. If however, emotional tension (coming from neurotic pressure or from any other cause such as a sudden event) erupts prior to the act of free choice, the antecedent passion limits the scope of free choice, and therefore the moral imputability. Neurotic tension which builds up as a result of the mistaking of emotional power for the qualitative movement of the free choice tends to explode in an obsessive and compulsive way, outside the scope of free choice. In such addictive behavior, the *culpa* may be limited or even nonexistent. There may also be situations in which moral responsibility lies not in the addictive behavior itself (which was unfree), but in the fact that the capacity for free choice, for the generous gift of self (at the expense of various attachments) was not developed earlier, for whatever reasons.

In questioning the moral culpability of the addict, certainly within a theological context, which is most appropriate for the Church, we should not ask therefore whether the addict deserves to be punished (by society or by God). We should rather discern within him or her the weakening of the capacity for free choice, and we should then offer salvific means (both natural and supernatural) that can assist in the growth of personal freedom. In the interpretation of one's own addiction, the addict needs to be freed from a fearful position and led towards the heavenly Father in the attitude of the trustful boy of St. Thérèse's parable, which will allow for the development of free choice and of charity.

References

[1]LT 258.

[2]John Paul II writes in *Veritatis splendor*, m.103, that "Christ... has set our freedom free from the domination of concupiscence". Does not this mean that outside of faith in Christ our freedom is to a certain extent enslaved?

[3]*De Veritate*, q. 22, art. 5: Et ideo, quod voluntas de necessitate vult quasi naturali inclinatione in ipsum determinata, est finis ultimus, ut beatitudo, et ea quae in ipso includuntur, ut est cognitio veritatis et alia huiusmodi; ad alia vero non de necessitate determinatur naturali inclinatione, sed propria dispositione absque necessitate.

[4]*De* Veritate, q. 22, art. 5, ad sc. 2: Non pertinet ad impotentiam voluntatis, si naturali inclinatione de necessitate in aliquid feratur, sed ad eius virtutem.

[5]*De Veritate*, q. 22, art. 6: Invenitur autem indeterminatio voluntatis respectu trium: scil. respectu obiecti, respectu actus, et respectu ordinis ad finem.

[6]*De Veritate*, q. 24, art. 1, ad 20: In appetibilibus, de fine ultimo non judicamus judicio discussionis vel examinationis, sed naturaliter approbamus, propter quod de eo non est electio, sed voluntas. Habemus ergo respectu ejus liberam voluntatem... non autem liberum judicium, proprie loquendo, cum non cadat sub electione.

[7]*Ia*, q. 62, art. 8, ad 3: Quod liberum arbitrium... eligat aliquid divertendo ab ordine finis, quod est peccare, hoc pertinet ad defectum libertatis. Unde maior libertas arbitrii est in angelis, qui peccare non possunt, quam in nobis, qui peccare possumus.

[8]*De Veritate*, q. 22, art. 6, ad 3: Et tamen, quod voluntas sit flexibilis ad malum, non habet secundum quod est a Deo, sed secundum quod est de nihilo.

[9]Cf. Daniel Westberg. *Right Practical Reason. Aristotle, Action, and Prudence in Aquinas* (Oxford: Clarendon Press, 1994).

[10]*De Veritate*, q. 24, art. 4: Et ideo liberum arbitrium habitum non nominat, sed potentiam voluntatis vel rationis, unam siquidem per ordinem ad alteram.

[11]*De Veritate*, q. 17, art. 1, ad 4: ...iudicium conscientiae consistit in pura cognitione, iudicium autem liberi arbitrii in applicatione cognitionis ad affectione... Et ideo contingit quandoque quod iudicium liberi arbitrii pervertitur, non autem conscientiae... Et sic aliquis errat in eligendo, et non in conscientia.

[12]Servais Theodore Pinckaers, *The Sources of Christian Ethics* (Washington, D.C.: The Catholic University of America Press, 1995).

[13]CJ 6.8.8.

[14]CJ 7.8.4.

[15]*Summa Theologiae,* I-II, 74.3, reply 1: Appetitus sensitivus natus est obedire rationi.

[16] Anne A. Terruwe, and Conrad W. Baars, Psychic Wholeness and Healing (New York: Alba House, 1981); Baars, Conrad W. *The Homosexual's Search for Happiness* (Chicago: Fransciscan Herald Press, 1976).

[17]Beemer, Th. C. J. "Thomas Aquinas on the Extinction of Guilt", *Tibi Soli Peccavi, Thomas Aquinas on Guilt and Forgiveness*, ed. Henk J. M. Schoot, Leuven: Peeters, 1996, p. 47–58.

[18]*De Malo*, q. 1, art. 4: De ratione culpae est quod sit secundum voluntatem, de ratione autem poenae est quod sit contra voluntatem.

[19]*De Malo*, q. 2, art. 2: ...in quocumque enim, sive in subiecto sive in actu, sit privatio formae aut ordinis aut mensurae debitae, mali rationem habet. Sed peccatum dicitur aliquis actus debito ordine aut forma aut mensura carens... Sed rationem culpae non habet peccatum nisi ex eo quod est voluntarium.

SACRAMENTAL CONFESSION AND ADDICTIONS

REVEREND ROMANUS CESSARIO, O.P., S.T.D.

Introduction

In his recent encyclical on faith and reason (*Fides et ratio*, 1998), Pope John Paul II established the parameters for this afternoon's seminar discussion: "It should never be forgotten that the neglect of being inevitably leads to losing touch with objective truth and with the very ground of human dignity" (n. 90). Our aim, then, is to show that "neglect of being" can affect adversely discussion of how persons with addictions can benefit from receiving the sacraments. Why?

Like all the sacraments, Penance supplies a way to grow in the "new being" that belongs to us because of our union with Christ. Penance and Reconciliation especially helps us to move away from those patterns of human action that erode the good, and therefore the dignity, of the human person. As the New Testament makes plain, in order for this "new being" to flourish, the Christian must abide in the objective truth that divine revelation ultimately identifies with God Himself (see John 15: 26). But how does this mystery of the divine piety apply to the person who suffers from an addiction?

In order to answer this question, we must proceed in three steps by looking at: first, human action and the moral good; second, the origin of human freedom; and third, the applicable principles of sacramental theology.

Human Action and the Moral Good

Catholic theology has always appealed to the transcendentals—being, one, true, good—in order to locate human action within the larger framework of creation and providence. John Paul II has made this tradition his own, and so revealed his personal preference for Christian moral realism.[1] Take for example the 1984 post-synodal exhortation "On Reconciliation and Penance in the Mission of the Church Today." As the Pope stressed the intrinsic connection between truth and reconciliation, he reminded us that the "Church promotes reconciliation in the truth, knowing well that neither reconciliation nor unity is possible outside of or in opposition to the truth" (n. 9). So as early as the mid-80s, John Paul II anticipated a main theme of the 1998 encyclical. Perhaps the Pope first conceived "Fides et ratio" in the confessional, that sacred place where any penitent with the right dispositions can come forward and, in the person of the priest, meet the reconciling Christ?[2] In this sacrament of our "spiritual resurrection" (*Catechism of the Catholic Church*, n. 1468), we embrace truth, discover goodness, and receive new life or being.

Penance also reaches the transcendental one. Reconciliation brings about unity. Sin not only erodes the good of the individual, it also fragments the life that we live together. Penance aims to strengthen the human communion (or solidarity) that forms the ontological foundation for the Church. Sinful actions corrupt the *communio personarum,* which is the Pope's preferred way of expressing what constitutes the common unity that God ordains for every person to enjoy. In order for human persons to enter once again into a perfect *communio,* the sacrament of Reconciliation offers healing and re-establishment in ecclesial communion. Everyone needs this sacrament. St Augustine makes this clear when he writes that, "The beginning of good works is the confession of evil works."[3]

An adequate sacramental theology must explain that each sacrament comprises two moments: the first is that of image-perfection, and the second that of image-restoration. The expressions date back to Saint Augustine and help us ponder what God accomplishes in the sacramental system. We see this teaching verified in the way that the *Catechism* describes the grace of baptism: this grace comes to us for the forgiveness of sins (nn. 1263–1264). In other words, the work of image-restoration. Again, this grace accounts for the fact that the human person becomes through baptism "a new creature" (nn. 1265–1266). In other words, the work of image-perfection. To sum up, image-perfection implies the bestowal of a divine intimacy that only God can confer on the human creature, whereas image-restoration reminds us that this process of divinization occurs within the sinful circumstances of this present life, and so is unthinkable–in every case except one–apart from personal forgiveness. That Baptism introduces us into the communion of the Church, establishes a sacramental bond among all the baptized, and imparts an indelible spiritual mark (or character) (see nn. 1267–1274) follows upon the restoration and perfection of the godly image, originally bestowed on every human being at creation. A similar pattern of image restoration and image perfection can be discovered in the abiding sacrament (*res et sacramentum*) of the six other sacraments.

The sacramental system would be unintelligible apart from the call to ultimate communion with the Blessed Trinity that Christ reveals as the divinely willed destiny of every human person. This also explains why the Church teaches that only theology can provide a definitive analysis of human action and freedom. Pope John Paul II leaves no room for doubt: "Seen in any other terms, the mystery of personal existence remains an insoluble riddle."[4] This affirmation applies also to those persons suffering from addiction.

Recall that Aquinas began the second part of his *Summa theologiae* by appealing to the doctrine of the *"imago Dei."* He thought that nothing definitive could be said about Christian life without first making clear the pre-ethical conditions for human conduct. Appealing to the anterior tradition, Aquinas writes:

> Man is made to God's image, and since this implies, so Damascene tells us, that he is intelligent and free to judge and master of himself, so then, now that we have agreed that God is the exemplar cause of things and that they issue from his power through his will, we go on to look at this *imago*, that is to say, at man as the source of actions which are his own and fall under his responsibility and control.[5]

The Pastor of the Church is obliged always to consider human freedom as an instrument of God's wise providence for his creatures. On this point, Christian realism radically differs from the perspectives of Greek tragedy and philosophy, which often promote a pessimistic view about the durability of goodness in human life and about the capacity of man to embrace the good.[6]

For the sinner, especially one whose sin is grave, the restoration of the image of God always entails a turning away from some disordered attachment to a creature and a turning toward the mercy and the love of God. This is the case because, to borrow the lapidary phrase of Aquinas, sin constitutes both an *aversio a Deo* and a *conversio ad creaturam*. The "conversion" or clinging in a disordered way to some created good produces in the sinner certain effects immediately related with having embraced a good wrongly. We call this *vice*. Vices principally manifest themselves in the moral character of a person, impeding the sinner's full communion with God and with his brothers and sisters.[7] Further, vicious attachments sometimes leave physical traces. Think of the younger Hans Holbein's (d. 1543) characterizations of the drunkard, the lecher, and the miser in Tudor England. He exhibits the disordered attachments in the person's very physical appearance.

Or consider the descriptions of the punishments for the capital sins that Dante gives in the *Purgatorio*. Each one calculated to represent a suitable penalty for the nature of the fault: the slothful running furiously, shouting *"Faster! Faster! To be slow in love is to lose time . . . ."*[8] The poet's vision is that sin disforms, and that it possesses the power to accustom a person to the deformity. Dante's is a Christian vision.

From these considerations, it is possible to propose that the classical theological analysis of sin helps us understand present-day clinical and biological descriptions of addictions. Spiritual authors always have warned that vicious *habitus* can gain the upper hand in a person's life, and result in a vicious deformation of character. This state of the person explains the need for image-restoration, which must be accomplished either here on earth or, according to the truth of the Catholic faith, after death. Thus, the *Purgatorio*. Only those ready to love as God loves are ready to see God.

Satisfactory works, which are commonly referred to as penances, constitute the appointed means for this image-restoration. The Council of Trent (in 1551) provided explicit warrant for the Catholic teaching about sacramental satisfaction: "Absolution takes away sin, but it does not [*primo et per se*] remedy all the disorders sin has caused" (*CCC,* n. 1459, citing *DS* 1712). The complete remedy of course involves the practice of satisfaction, or making use of the gift of indulgence.[9] Unfortunately, many theologians have accepted the argument that St. Anselm exercised a negative influence on Western theology, and so much misunderstanding exists nowadays in Catholic theology about the place and role of satisfactory works.[10]

It is fair to say that theological misunderstandings of satisfaction arise from Reformation debates about justification. The sixteenth-century reformers argued that justification never really changes the sinner, who therefore abides *simul justus et peccator.*[11] By making the distinction between what absolution accomplishes and what satisfaction achieves, Trent challenged the claim that justification always remains "alien justification." On the contrary, the Council affirmed that the sacrament of Baptism (and Penance) changes the sinner into a justified soul, even though the lingering signs of sinful defect may still manifest themselves in the forgiven person's character. This affirmation provides a good example of the truth that the Church always judges on the basis of "what is" and not what appears to be.[12] Satisfactory works contribute toward healing this defect without involving the justified sinner in an endless rhythm of propitiation. The art of the Catholic baroque period provides a visual witness to this truth: the ornament, the spirals, the gold all exhibit a continuity between heaven and earth into which the Christian believer is inserted through the sacraments. The message was clear to anyone with eyes to see: grace transforms.

The theological issue at stake in the justification debate is profound. Because of her commitment to sacramental realism, the Church rejected and continues to reject an unmodified version of the *simul justus et peccator* account of justification.[13] Furthermore, the Church must insist that since the Incarnation nothing human remains alien to the work of divine grace. Once you believe that an individual human nature subsists in a divine person, there should be no difficulty believing that divine grace can heal the wounds of sin in any human nature. The Church also recognized that it would not be in keeping with the biblical revelation to announce a doctrine of reconciliation which sin seemed to hold the upper hand—trumping, as it were, both the work of creation and the work of redemption. Such considerations persuade us that debates about justification are not confined to theological subtleties. They affect the practices of salvation.

Consider the notion of penance. In the Catholic tradition, penance always expresses the joyful conversion that the grace of Christ accomplishes in the one who freely associates himself with the mysteries of Christ. Penance never amounts to a tribute paid to an angry god. The *Catechism* carefully selected a text from the Tridentine decrees that makes it plain that the efficacy of all penance derives from Christ, who Himself has first merited for us.[14] My own practice is to encourage young priests to use the prayer, "May the Passion of Our Lord Jesus Christ, the merits of the Blessed Virgin Mary, and of all the saints, and also whatever good you do and evil you endure be cause for the remission of sins, the increase of grace, and the reward of everlasting life." This prayer found in the Roman ritual sacramentalizes the whole of a sinner's life, placing the penitent, as it were, in a permanent state of making satisfaction. Because they have been associated in the sacrament to the atoning work of Christ's cross, our penances surpass whatever intrinsic worth for spiritual training they may possess. *Incarnationis mysterium*—the Bull of Indiction for the Great Jubilee—applies this same theological principle to the gift of the indulgence, which also purifies us.[15]

The spiritualization of penances should not lead us to forget that satisfactory works do possess their own psychological power: prayer, an offering, works of mercy, service of neighbor, voluntary self-denial all contain the ability to form our psychological powers (see *CCC*, n. 1460). More precisely, satisfactory works possess the power to shape our soul and its powers, both rational and emotional. Satisfaction is a work of both nature and grace; or, to be more precise, a work of uplifted nature in which the requirements of both human psychology and good theology are met. At the same time, penances are not magic, and should be administered based on a judgment about the spiritual maturity of the person.

A question about the utility of satisfactory works naturally arises in the case of persons who are described as suffering from an addiction. A standard 1997 dictionary used by physicians describes addiction as "the compulsive and overwhelming involvement with a specific activity which may lead to either psychologic or physical dependence or both."[16] The definition is broad, but serviceable for the present discussion. The question is simple: What spiritual benefits can people who are addicted to whatsoever kind of bad behaviors obtain from receiving the sacrament of Penance? To keep the discussion within a reasonable framework, I will not consider the capacity of the addicted person to conceive true contrition or to confess his or her sins. It is true that some psychologists would argue that both contrition and confession can be counterproductive activities for persons actually suffering from addiction, or who are in certain stages of recovery from addiction. The Church on the other hand offers another outlook.

We find evidence for this view in an apparently minor modification made in the *editio typica* of the *Catechism*. In the first modern language editions, the *Catechism* instructed confessors when dealing with the virtue of chastity to take into account "the affective immaturity, force of acquired habit, conditions of anxiety, or other psychological or social factors *that lessen or even extenuate* moral culpability" (emphasis mine, n. 2352). The authoritative text now reads: "... other psychological or social factors that can lessen, if not even reduce to a minimum, moral culpability" (see *CCC, editio typica*, n. 2352). I interpret this to mean that the Church does not encourage us to place vicious actions outside of all reference to the moral capacities of the person. We can conclude, then, that the Church does not envision a category of persons— other than those who are incapable of performing a human act—who by reason of some psychological description imposed on them stand outside the need for sacramental Reconciliation.

In order to discuss behavioral addiction and sacramental satisfaction, we need to consider more closely the reason why the Church made this small, but still significant, change in the *editio typica* of the *Catechism*.

What prompted making this precision in N. 2352? The answer lies, I submit, in the way that *Veritatis splendor* had explained moral imputability: "It is possible that the evil done as the result of invincible ignorance or a nonculpable error of judgment may not be imputable to the agent; but even in this case it does not cease to be an evil, a disorder in relation to the truth about the good" (n. 63).

To apply this principle to our discussion, when persons suffering from an addiction commit sins, even though their moral culpability may be reduced to a minimum, they nonetheless have made an "affective mistake" about the true goods of human perfection.[17] This mistake may be evident from the nature of the addiction, as is clear in the case of drunkenness or lechery, or not so evident, as with less demonstrative compulsions, like surfing the Internet or excessive shopping. In any event, a Pastor of souls is obliged to make a judgment about not only the origins of behavior but also about the harm that it causes in relation to the good ends of human flourishing.

Psychologists speak about addictions in terms of negative consequences and destructive patterns. The faith, however, enables us to make more definitive assertions. If addiction impairs human dignity, it is because it introduces a neglect of being, and causes a loss of touch with objective truth. Why is this affirmation from *Fides et ratio* important for everyone? *Veritatis splendor* offers a succinct answer: "Only the act in conformity with the good can be a path that leads to life" (72). Even granted diminished culpability, persons suffering from addictions to vicious actions do not stand on the path that leads to life. The faith teaches us that only satisfactory works accomplished in love can reestablish this conformity.

The Voluntariness of Christian Activity

In order to appreciate why satisfactory works can benefit even those who suffer from addictions, we need to recall those basic elements of Christian anthropology that explain the relationship of human nature and free activity. First, just as natural law inclinations arise from the specific nature that human beings possess, so also do the voluntary wellsprings of human behavior originate in both knowledge and rational appetite. Second, as a basic feature of every human action, voluntariness signifies the self-mastery that the human person can possess over his or her activity. From this we can conclude that not only does natural law reveal the imprint of the *imago Dei*, but also that the voluntary character of human activity manifests the human persons analogical participation in that divine nature wherein knowing the good and willing the truth are necessarily coincident. Third, the more the rational creature grows in holiness, the more he or she images God who is the cause of all voluntary movements. Anything that inhibits this kind of growth must be judged as harmful to the human person.

The Voluntary and the Free

From the foregoing, we see that Christian theology introduces a useful distinction between the voluntary and the free. Every free act is voluntary, but not every voluntary act attains the perfection of human freedom. When moral theologians discuss the voluntary, they explore the basic and indispensable conditions for human freedom, not the deliberate exercise of free choice itself. Some contemporary schools of Christian ethics prefer to adopt the dominant themes of the German *Aufklärung*, Enlightenment, with the result that we have become accustomed to read about human freedom as a transcendental category which, for all intents and purposes, obscures the status and purposes of human nature as they pertain to the moral life. Although the poetry of modern German Romanticism might lead us to conclude otherwise, transcendental freedom cannot explain those human actions which surpass the act of deliberate choice.[18] Yet, the Christian tradition numbers among such voluntary though technically nonfree activities realities as foundational to human life as the profound want of the human will for happiness and the ecstatic love of God which follows upon the beatific vision. So we are advised that impairment of the voluntary touches upon the most essential goods of human nature.

Some theologians have not understood how freedom fits into the anthropology of the *imago*, and so have concluded that impediments to deliberate choice (such as arguably are present in persons suffering from addictions) leave the person in a state of moral indifference, like an automobile running in neutral. Therapeutic treatments are conceived as a means to shift the gear into drive. But such a view of choice fails to take into account the intimate relationship between human nature and human freedom. With respect to choosing, there is no state of indifference, either we are moving toward God or away from him.[19] At the same time, anything that thwarts the voluntariness of human action, including addictions, impairs a human nature whose perfection depends on achieving conformity with the good.

Consider the difference between the human being and other beings whose actions depend on knowledge. Since only human knowledge can grasp the exact nature of purposeful activity, it is characteristic of human beings that they can properly deliberate about an end and the relationship that a means bears to it.[20] In this ability, human persons differ from brute animals, who perceive ends, but remain incapable of adapting themselves to creative ways of achieving them. Likewise, but for quite different reasons, angelic persons do not reflect about means, for their intuitive knowledge eliminates the need for deliberation about circumstantial means. As a result, in both angelic nature and angelic activity, the voluntary and the free coincide, although the angels remain capable of choice.[21] Because the capacity to engage in intelligent behavior forms the basis for imputing responsibility, moral theologians ascribe praise or blame only when it is a case of fully voluntary activity.[22]

Again, the Catholic tradition acknowledges a distinction in the human being between the free and the voluntary. The importance of this distinction for our present discussion should be obvious: whatever impedes the voluntary goes against the good of human nature, and so affects immediately the spiritual well-being of the human person. We can see this claim exemplified most clearly by recalling the ways that classical moral theology dealt with impairment to the voluntary: ignorance, violence, fear, and lust.[23] A review of these classical expositions would confirm, I submit, that addiction is best understood as a meta-category for whatever factors can impede voluntary action. Our concern is not only with bad choices or, for that matter, wrong or inappropriate choices, but with the dislocations of nature that impairment of the voluntary introduces.

Enemies of the Voluntary

What is a voluntary action? Again, to state it briefly: a voluntary action is one which finds its principle from within the agent and which proceeds with knowledge of the end.[24] When it comes to making a judgment about what affects the voluntary in a given circumstance, interiority and due knowledge serve as the criteria for evaluating a human action's voluntary character. Threats to voluntary action, such as those caused by addictions, arise from anything that can upset the psychological poise or balance in either of these areas.[25]

Established moral teaching identifies certain factors that affect voluntary activity. Violence, fear, ignorance, and lust constitute the *hostes voluntarii*, or the enemies of the voluntary.[26] These factors, when they affect a human person, either restrict the requisite knowledge for deliberate human activity or else intrude upon that interiority which distinguishes authentic human conduct, or "human acts," from what the tradition described as mere "acts of man." While this theory of how certain factors reduce the voluntariness of human action borrows from classical philosophy, its application belongs to the structure and the logic of *sacra doctrina*.

We are pursuing a properly theological discussion. The life sciences can aid our understanding of how such factors as collective ignorance, societal violence, personal fear, and heightened lust impair a person's ability to operate in a fully human way, but a proper analysis of these circumstances as they apply to a human person depends on theology. Only theology safeguards the relationship between being, acting, and the supernatural destiny of the human person.

Consider violence. It signifies some action imposed on a subject from the outside and against its natural bent; as such, it represents a form of coercion. Violence renders a given action involuntary, that is, an act which goes against willing, for the simple reason that an action so produced effectively results from the will of another person. Even when a person becomes an instrument of another's choice, this instrumentalization affects adversely his or her human dignity.

The second enemy, the emotion of fear, affects voluntariness in a different way.[27] Fear first arises through the contending or irascible emotions as a certain alarm of mind which shapes the way we react to some evil which is absent but likely to befall us. By contrast, those evils which already have befallen an individual generate the emotion of sorrow. The effect of fear on voluntary activity depends upon various and complex factors. The classical example of the rich merchant at sea illustrates a typical scenario. When the threatening storm arises without forewarning, the merchant on the high seas must immediately estimate the peril which presently endangers both his life and his merchandise. Once he determines that his life is actually jeopardized as long as he holds on to the merchandise in the boat, fear moves him to throw the goods overboard. While he does this freely, still throwing the goods overboard expresses voluntary action only after a fashion, for he certainly would act otherwise if not for the sure perception that his fragile bark might sink and his life would be lost. Acting under the aspect of simple voluntariness, the merchant would preserve both life and merchandise. Actions induced by fear, then, exemplify the voluntary only in a qualified sense of the term, for apart from the concrete circumstances that precipitate the fear, the individual would not have acted in such a way. One only has to consider apostasy born of fear to realize that sacramental satisfaction serves the healing of the person who acts as a result of undue fear.

In the context of human voluntariness, concupiscence or lust represents the basic human desire for pleasure, but does not necessarily imply a note of baseness. This emotion concerns the human response to things perceived as good, but not yet possessed in joy and delight. Lust ensures that human nature remains capable of moving towards the essential goods required for individual perfection and the perfection of the species. Precisely because of its drawing-from-within function, lust always increases the voluntary character of an action.[28]   In other words, lust draws the person toward a perceived good so that the interiority characteristic of the voluntary increases rather than decreases.

Since in conditions of lust the agent's interior movement follows its voluntary direction towards some object of desire, the lustful person is not said to act involuntarily. Instead, in cases where actions proceed from lust, the resultant action illustrates non-voluntary activity, that is, action proceeding from a strong interior drive while the agent lacks a keen comprehension of the object of his or her lust. Lust, it is true, can obscure the work of right reason, but even when it causes diminished culpability, there still remain the need for image-restoration. Think of the person caught in the practice of autosexual behavior and what is required to reintroduce such a-one into the full relational quality of sex that is required by the nuptial meaning of the body.

While such considerations obviously merit attention when it comes to evaluating a person's culpability for a particular action, emotional upset of the magnitude suggested by impaired volition clearly does not betoken a desirable state for human beings to foster. Consider the harm that living in a habitually disordered state brings to human happiness. For example, one who sins habitually against the virtue of temperance becomes, as it were voluntarily bound, to goods in a way that conform neither to integral human perfection and contentment nor to evangelical values and beatitudes. Some moral theologians argue that, since the lustful state of a person diminishes the voluntary character of human conduct, we should reclassify certain species of disordered activity, such as adolescent masturbation and daytime unchaste reveries. Such authors, it seems, grasp only half the truth about moral culpability, for while they aim to acknowledge the factors which depreciate the voluntary in certain persons, at the same time they risk exculpating whole classes of vicious behavior.

From these short remarks about the enemies of the voluntary, we learn that the juridical category of imputability and the psychological category of responsibility do not determine the moral status of the person whose volition is impaired. The standard teaching on the enemies of the voluntary persuades us that impairment of human nature at this level is neither a neutral matter nor a matter of no consequence for the moral life.[29] Human conduct that falls short of bringing a person to human perfection and Christian maturity requires forgiveness and restoration.

Sacramental Satisfaction and Addiction

Contemporary magisterial teaching provides a way to assess the effect of impaired human action on the agent. It goes without saying that we are in a better position to understand the interrelationship of physiological factors and human actions than were the theologians of yesteryear. Still, in order to maintain the radical spirituality of human freedom, it is necessary to consider any biological factor dispositive for rather than determinative of human action.

Otherwise, psychology produces determinism. This subject introduces another discussion that is not our purpose today.

We can conclude, however, that satisfactory works and the use of the gift of indulgences that is promised for the Great Jubilee Year can benefit spiritually every Christian, even those who are involved in treatment for behavior that is judged to flow from an addiction. The reason is simple: anyone who is impaired from pursuing the good ends that perfect the Christian life needs to embrace the work of image-restoration. The spiritual renewal complements psychological health. It does not impair it.

I recognize that associating sin with certain addictions, especially those for which the hypothesis of physical causation is largely accepted, challenges some suppositions of good counseling practices. If I were asked to begin a reply, I would begin with the Easter praeconium, the Exultet, where we read that it is better to have been redeemed by Christ than never to have sinned. It is a paradoxical exclamation, but warns us nonetheless not to find too much comfort in psychological strategies for easing guilt. For the Christian believer, the truth is that they are not necessary. What is more important, it would be an error only to correct bad behavior and not accomplish the complete renewal of the human person that Christian forgiveness promises.

It remains an exercise of pastoral charity to encourage those persons whose ability to choose the good in freedom is somehow impaired to seek the sacrament of reconciliation. The confessor, on the other hand, needs to be alert to the special conditions of the person. In a Christian context, both therapist and confessor aim to restore the person to freedom, so that he or she once again is able to embrace the Truth. The sacrament of Penance remains a privileged instrument of this renewal, one that enjoys the distinctive quality of being both sign and cause of that personal healing which consists "in restoring us to God's grace and joining us with him in an intimate friendship" (*CCC*, nn. 1468).

References

[1] Father Jaroslaw Kupczak will soon publish a study at CUA Press that reveals the Thomist background to John Paul II's action theory.

[2] For a development of this theme, see my recent article in the January 1999 issue of *Crisis*. And for a general account of the sacraments as placcs of encounter with Christ, see Colman O'Neill, *Meeting Christ in the Sacraments* (Staten Island: Alba House, 1988).

[3] *Commentary of the Gospel of John* 12, 13 (*PL* 35, 1491) cited in *CCC*, n. 1458.

[4] *Fides et ratio*, n 12.

[5] See the introduction before q. 1 of *Summa theologiae* Ia–IIae.

[6] For a detailed account of this view from both the perspectives of philosophy and literature, see Martha C. Nussbaum, *The Fragility of Goodness. Luck and Ethics in Greek Tragedy and Philosophy* (Cambridge, Cambridge University Press, 1986), 419. On Nussbaum's account, a tragedy such as Euripides' *Hecuba* "shows us a case of solid character and shows us that, under certain circumstances, even this cannot escape defilement. It also [shows] us that even the good character who has not suffered any actual damage or betrayal lives always with the risk of these events: for it is the nature of political structures to change, and in the nature of personal friendship that the confidence man should be indistinguishable from the trustworthy man . . . ."

[7] The teaching is expressed in *CCC*, n. 1472, which speaks about the "double consequence" of sin. Both the eternal punishment and the so-called "temporal punishment" (*poena*) due to sin is distinguished from the fault (*culpa*) of sin. It is called temporal, because the effects of sin are felt in this life.

[8] Dante Alighieri, *The Purgatorio*, trans. John Ciardi (The New American Library, 1961), canto 18, cornice 4, lines 103–104.

[9] For further background discussion for this topic, see my "Christian Satisfaction and Sacramental Reconciliation," *Communio* 16 (1989): 186–196.

[10] For further discussion of this topic, see my *The Godly Image: Christ and Salvation in Catholic Thought from Anselm to Aquinas*, Studies in Historical Theology VI (Petersham, MA: St Bede's Publications, 1990).

[11] For the latest developments in Roman Catholic approach to this question, see the "Joint Declaration on the Doctrine of Justification" and various official responses to it in the Pontifical Council for Promoting Christian Unity *Information Service* 98 (1998): 81–103.

[12] See *Fides et ratio*, no. 44: "Looking unreservedly to truth, the realism of Thomas could recognize the objectivity of truth and produce not merely a philosophy of 'what seems to be' but a philosophy of 'what is.'"

[13]The "Joint Declaration" (see note 11) confirms that this theological point is one that requires clarification to be made compatible with Catholic doctrine.

[14]*Incarnationis mysterium*, n. 10 makes the same point: "Revelation also teaches that the Christian is not alone on the path of conversion. In Christ and through Christ, his life is linked by a mysterious bond to the lives of all other Christians in the supernatural union of the Mystical Body."

[15]See *Incarnationis mysterium*, nn. 9–13 (The Bull of Indiction of the Great Jubilee), which explains the Catholic understanding of indulgences. For further explanation of the relationship of indulgences to satisfaction, see my "St. Thomas Aquinas on Satisfaction, Indulgences, and Crusades," *Medieval Philosophy & Theology* 2 (1992): 74–96.

[16]*The Merck Manual of Medical Information*, ed. R. Berkow Whitehouse Station, NJ: Merck Research Laboratory, 1997). Current usage extends the term addiction beyond its original psychophysiological meaning to include all harmful compulsive behavior. Some distinguish between substance addiction (stemming from drugs, alcohol, food, etc.) and a more general class of behavioral addictions. For a discussion, see H. Clinebell, *Understanding Persons with Alcohol, Drug and Behavioral Addictions* (Nashville: Abington, 1998). However, the psychological categories do not always serve the purposes of moral analysis.

[17]Addiction should not be confused with spiritual sloth. The same text from *Veritatis splendor* warns against "feeling easily justified in the name of our conscience" and cites Psalm 19: 12, "Who can discern his errors? Clear me from hidden faults." Pastors of the Church should excuse no one from the sacrament of Reconciliation.

[18]"Transcendental freedom" is taken to mean one's free basic stance toward being itself, as opposed to particular individual choices which may not fully reflect this basic stance. Yet, neither the embodied nature nor the teleological ordering of human freedom is sufficiently regarded by this teaching, which construes the whole providential ordering of creature to Creator as a supererogatory detail surpassed by naked, overarching, and disembodied will. The human will does in certain respects transcend facticity, but remains nonetheless a creaturely reality rationally specified by the whole natural hierarchy of ends, and further elevated and perfected in grace.

[19]"Freedom makes man a moral subject ... Human acts ... are either good or evil" (*CCC*, no.1749).

[20]See *Summa theologiae* Ia-IIae q.6, a. 2.

[21]See for example, the discussion in *Summa theologiae* Ia q. 60, a. 2, "Are the angels loving as choosing to love?," where Aquinas accounts for freedom of choice in the angels, even though the intuitive infallibility of their knowledge always shapes their prior and natural desire for only good ends.

[22]So when the lamb flees from the wolf, it receives neither praise nor blame; its reward consists only in its continued existence or, if it fails to flee successfully, its "punishment" amounts to death. On the other hand, we designate angels as either good or bad on the basis of their once-and-for-all choice whether to love God as the supremely desirable Good or not.

[23]*The Catechism of the Catholic Church* adjusts the list: "ignorance, inadvertence, duress, fear, habit, inordinate attachments, and other psychological or social factors" (see n. 1735).

[24]*Summa theologiae* Ia-IIae q. 6, a. 1.

[25]The pinball machine provides a helpful, albeit mechanical, metaphor for grasping the relationship of the voluntary to the free. Let the object of yesteryear's penny arcade game, namely, to score as many points as possible, represent the ultimate goal of a virtuous life. Now some intrusive factor, such as too much leaning on one's elbows, can interrupt the pinball game either immediately or at some point before the game's end. As a result of such external interference, the pinball machine tilts and the game abruptly ends. Let the intrusive factors which cause the machine to tilt represent the enemies of the voluntary. For to one degree or another, such intrusions tilt or upset the psychological balance or poise which is required for authentically free human behavior. Such factors affect the voluntariness of human activity so that the actions which result fall into the category of either involuntary or non-voluntary actions. When this occurs, we can designate the action as authentic moral behavior only in a depreciated sense of moral.

[26]For a concise account of this material, see Ralph McInerny, *Ethica Thomistica* (Washington, D.C.: The Catholic University of America Press, 1982), pp. 63–71. In *Aquinas on Human Action. A Theory of Practice* (Washington, D.C.: The Catholic University of America Press, 1992), the same author gives a lucid and readable account of Aquinas's complete theory of human action.

[27]See *Summa theologiae* Ia–IIae q. 6, a. 6.

[28]See *Summa theologiae* I-IIae q. 6, a. 7.

[29]Again, the sobering judgment found in *Veritatis splendor* is germane: "It is possible that the evil done as the result of invincible ignorance or an error of judgment may not be imputable to the agent; but even in this case it does not cease to be an evil, a disorder in relation to the truth about the good" (n. 63).

PRIESTLY IDENTITY AND THE REASONS FOR ADDICTIVE BEHAVIOR

ARCHBISHOP PAUL JOSEF CORDES, S.T.D.

In each of the past two years, some 700 priests submitted petitions for laicization which were granted by the Congregation for Divine Worship and the Discipline of the Sacraments. The figure amounts to less than two percent of the approximately 410,000 ordained priests in the world. The total number of those who applied for laicization and the number of the applications rejected are not published.

Anyone who studies the justifications cited by the ordinaries sponsoring these laicization requests and by the applicants themselves will recognize a clear dominance of psychological motivations. The keywords of psychoanalysis recur again and again as the grounds for requests: existential and family problems, father or mother domination, internalization of a conflictual parent-son relationship, emotional distress, sexual repression, anxiety in the face of intimate relationships. The symptoms of these problems are identified as: forms of depression and other psychosomatic illnesses, pathological shyness, obsession with pornographic magazines and films, alcoholism. In many cases celibacy is cited as the root cause of all these woes. The context of the faith, i.e. essentially religious motivations, remains excluded from all this. In the cases of five individuals seeking laicization with whom I was able to consult in detail on the matter—three of them from Germany— questions about priestly identity and the sacrament of ordination were in no way a component

141

of their reflection on their decision to leave the priesthood, and questions of spirituality and faith in general played only a marginal role. Also the minutes of the conversations between the bishops' representatives and the priests in difficulty at most touched tangentially on these issues. Theological points of orientation for the formation and guidance of priests were not taken into account.

A similar perspective is valid for a brochure I came across entitled: *A Reflection Guide on Human Sexuality and the Ordained Priesthood.* It was published by a committee of the National Conference of Catholic Bishops in 1982. The sixty pages of this publication contain only a few fleeting references to Holy Scripture and to theological issues. Affirmations on the sacrament of ordination are lacking. The analysis is for the most part concentrated on the findings and theories of modern psychotherapy. Sigmund Freud and his followers clearly inspired it a good deal more than did the faith.

Now, it has to be admitted that psychological factors generally seem easier to raise than those relating to spirituality. Thus, motivations for a laicization process can more readily be found in family background and complications in personal life than in questions of faith. Psychological data are, after all, more persuasive than spiritual ones, especially if a bishop wants to persuade an office of the Roman Curia to accept a laicization request.

Yet any such limitation of a human problem to a psychological perspective is mistaken. The psychological approach alone cannot remove the addictive behavior of the priest in question. In the short space at my disposal I would like to discuss the two fundamental errors involved in the prevailing psychological approach to addictive behavior.

Limitations of Psychological Analysis and Therapy

Psychological findings have proved useful in many respects for religious and moral life. That is quite obvious in those cases where psychiatry and psychotherapy help to rehabilitate a mentally ill or psychologically disturbed person and place him in a position to freely use his reason and his other powers of mind and spirit.

A theological anthropology must however go beyond the inherent limitations of empirical psychology. For it uses words like the love of God, grace, the light of faith, and many others to point to realities that appear, or are insensibly at work, in the consciousness or subconsciousness, without having their ultimate origin in human nature. The stream of spiritual life, as we can experience it, is nourished from two sources: from nature and from grace. Once they have merged, the two can no longer be separated.

No single empirical science as such is able to grasp this wholeness of being. Psychology, besides, is a hybrid science. It is not self-sufficient, and more than any other remains dependent on philosophy and theology. The science unavoidably enlists supplementary help from them, whether conscious of this or not.

The contrary opinion, however, is not infrequently voiced today, namely, that psychology is so self-sufficient that it can now perform unaided what previously was expected from philosophy and theology, that being the answer to the question, "What is man, how is he supposed to be, and how should he behave?" Psychology is unable to answer this question. But many psychologists believe that it is the job of psychology to provide just such an answer. When psychologists try to cut themselves off from faith and attempt to explain the world and man in isolation from it, their science then becomes an obstacle to God's saving grace.

A good deal is subsumed under the concept "psychology" that has little to do with science, the knowledge of man and reason. Under this term we find many human foibles, masquerading as psychology, ranging from ideological fads, unfounded opinions, and rash advice, to downright charlatanry. Not infrequently psychology is the opium of those who have lost their faith, a form of escape from fundamental truths under the guise of science. Not infrequently it denotes a narrow anthropocentrism and secularized doctrine of salvation. That is no cause for surprise, because it is now common practice for the faithless man to seek in psychology, and in the social sciences in general, ways of self-redemption that philosophy is no longer able to offer, and that theology has never aimed to offer.

A frank critique of the absolutist claims made by psychology is not aimed against well-founded, psychological, psychotherapeutic, or psychiatric findings. It is exclusively directed at ideological theories, with which these findings are sometimes confused. The Church cannot but oppose any attempt to interpret her factual and historical foundations, the life, teaching, death, and resurrection of Jesus Christ, and the content of her faith, as mere symbols of subconscious psychic phenomena. She must never forget that psychology alone can remit no sin, can work no redemption, can offer no ultimate goal or meaning to life.

The deepest tensions between faith and psychology arise where our faith shows man a goal that he can neither recognize nor attain by the forces of his own nature alone, and where it prescribes or recommends a form of conduct that seems to him unattainable, insupportable, or even downright injurious. For Revelation demands that we love our neighbor, and that we love our Father, as Jesus Christ did. It demands lifelong marital fidelity, abstinence from sexual relations outside marriage, love of our enemies.

Yet the contradiction between the claims of the Word of God and psychology's claims about man's natural inability to meet them is false. For it is faith itself that sometimes confirms the pessimistic findings of psychology. For instance, when the gospel declares about worldly riches —the same goes for marriage and celibacy— "For men this is impossible; for God everything is possible" (Matt 19: 26). All God's commandments and counsels can only be kept by those whose faith is founded in prayer and love of God.

Misinterpretations of scientific experience naturally follow popularization in the mass media. It is no doubt unavoidable that hypotheses that scientists perhaps are still trying to verify with scrupulous care are publicly used as reliable building blocks. This gives rise to confusion and untold harm. This popular psychology has played a disastrous role, especially in the field of basic human relations between the sexes and between generations, in the sphere of marriage, the family, and the bringing up of children. It turns meaningful scientific queries and hypotheses into foolish assertions with a high claim to truth.

Psychoanalysis, psychotherapy, and empirical psychology have undoubtedly helped to alleviate unimaginable suffering. They have helped to remove temptations to despair, to overcome dejection or apathy, and have made many burdens easier to bear. They are an irreplaceable help to man. But if they are absolutized, if they are no longer conceived as forms of assistance or therapy, they go astray and then have a destructive, not a therapeutic effect. Their overestimation in our society, together with the vehemence of their arguments, reinforces their harmful effects also for priests with existential and vocational problems.

Theology of Priestly Identity

If the confrontation with addictive behavior is limited to a psychological and psychotherapeutic approach, it deprives itself of powerful help. Anthropological-ascetic factors that guide the life of the priest are then seen as extraneous. They do not mesh with his religious identity as an ordained minister in the Church. Priestly identity and the claims of faith, on the one hand, and profession on the other hand, are located in separate compartments. Spirituality is raised into a "superstructure" (*Uberbau* in the Marxist sense) and thus retains purely theoretical or rhetorical character.

At this point I would like to have provided a detailed discussion of Vatican II's Decree on the Ministry and Life of Priests, with its presentation of the theological richness of the sacrament of ordination, illustrated by various key concepts from *Presbyterorum ordinis.* This would show how theology could not only help individual priests to be sure of their identity and their irreplaceable mission, but also show the reasons for priestly engagement and for a specific lifestyle that do not concern nonordained Christians: the importance of prayer, celibacy, the obligation to bear witness. Unfortunately the time for any exhaustive discussion of all these points is lacking. I will therefore confine myself to just one fundamental affirmation of the above-cited decree *Presbyterorum ordinis.*

The Decree recalls that Christ sent out the Apostles, just as he himself was sent out by the Father. Bishops and priests share in the same consecration and mission. By being anointed with the Holy Spirit they share in the priesthood of Christ; they are "signed with a special character and so are configured to Christ the priest in such a way that they are able to act in the person of Christ the head (n. 2)."

At the center of this affirmation is the reference to Christ the Lord. He is the real source of all authority in the Church, the salvific will of the Father who became a human being. Those who represent the ministry in the Church are— compared with Christ—no more than servants. Even if we must never lose sight of the fact that God does not want to renounce man's co-participation in the history of salvation, it yet remains true that Christ alone is effective in the action of those who hold office or exercise ministry in his name.

At the same time, however, it is Christ who raises the priest's action to a new rank, by virtue of which the priest receives a quality that differentiates him from the common priesthood of all Christians. To the priest is entrusted the office of announcing the gospel and acting in such a way that redemption is worked through Christ in word and sacrament. That is the precise content of the specific authority of the priest for the public ministry of the Church. Whoever understands the service of the priest and is ready to accept it, to him will happen in his time and place what the boldest imagination could scarcely conceive: the believer encounters the love of the Father in the salvific word and effective sign—the love that became person in Christ. It is this that determines the irreplaceability of the priest for all time. And one understands the emotion of the Holy Father in his *Letter to all Priests of the Church* on the occasion of Holy Thursday, 1979. There he states, think of the places where people anxiously await a priest, and where for many years, feeling the lack of such a priest, they do not cease to hope for his presence. And sometimes it happens that they meet in an abandoned shrine, and place on the altar a stole which they still keep, and recite all the prayers of the Eucharistic liturgy; and then, at the moment that corresponds to the transubstantiation a deep silence comes down upon them, a silence sometimes broken by a sob ... so ardently do they desire to hear the words that only the lips of a priest can efficaciously utter (n. 10).

The Holy Spirit

On the other hand, the priest's authority is not granted to him from the hands of those for whom he was appointed. Admittedly his service may at first sight be exclusively determined by pastoral needs or mainly determined by objectives of Church policy; perhaps he was even nominated by vote. Despite that, it is not delegation nor election that appoints him to his office, but the sacrament of ordination he receives. Neither an ecclesial group, nor the Church's superiors, can themselves establish the priest's mission. Since Christ himself must be present in the word and sign of the priest, Christ himself must also support his mission. He does so by imbuing candidates to the priesthood with his Spirit. For that Spirit is the power of the holy pneuma, in which the Lord himself went into action, so that the Apostle can declare: "This Lord is the Spirit" (2 Cor. 3: 17). It is this same Spirit of God that conceived the human life of Jesus in the womb of the Virgin Mary, the Bride of the Holy Spirit (cf. Luke 1: 35). Mary, in her exemplary submission to the will of God, is thus the model and guide through whom the Lord continues in time to make his presence felt in history. It is the Spirit of God in which we are able to experience the Son of God in all his power through his resurrection from the dead (cf. Rom. 1: 4).

From the very beginning the Church has understood appointment to the ministry as endowment with the grace of the Holy Spirit. The Pastoral Letters exhort us not to neglect the charism given to us by the laying on of hands, but to kindle it anew (cf. I Tim. 4: 14; 2 Tim. 1: 6). All the formularies of ordination speak in similar terms—beginning with the oldest surviving text that goes back to Hippolytus of Rome (died 235), through the early Christian sacramentaries right down to the pontificals of the medieval and modern periods. They all speak of the calling down of the Holy Spirit by the bishop and the praying community as the culminating moment of the ordination process. This interpretation is confirmed by a wealth of testimonies in the writings of the Greek Fathers and in the Orthodox ordination formularies.

It is this Spirit that creates the characteristic relation to Christ of the holder of ministerial office in the Church, a personal relation that is special to the ordained priesthood and not given with the basic Christian life.

Such a rooting of priestly life in theology ought to be the fundamental guideline of formation in seminaries and of continuing education after ordination. From faith itself it would then be recognized that the service of the priest, if devoid of any deep personal relationship to Christ, is doomed to fail. This means that from a positive perspective the spirituality of the priesthood has to follow organically from the sacrament of ordination. It does not need to be "superimposed" from outside, because there is a convincing and intrinsic connection with the priestly identity. Psychiatric counseling can still provide valuable assistance. But it has a purely secondary character and will never replace the spiritual principle that provides the foundation and mainspring of ministry.

Consecration and Mission

I would like to come back to at least one pair of biblical concepts of central importance for an understanding of the ordination process. The Second Vatican Council Decree on the Ministry and Life of Priests supports the above-cited central determination of the priest's identity and can help to explain the relevance of theology for the life of the ordained. *Presbyterorum ordinis* (December 7, 1965) speaks about the "consecration and mission" of Christ, the Apostles, and all holders of office in the Church. This expression—

in Greek AGIAZEIN KAI PEMPEIN—shows the richness that can be derived from biblical thinking for the spiritual motivation and reinforcement of priestly identity. According to John's Gospel, Jesus was "consecrated and sent" by the Father (John 10: 36).

In the context of religious history in general, and also in that of the Old Testament, "consecration" means, in the first place, being removed or separated from a "godless" environment; the Latin term *"sancire / sanctus*—to delimit, to be singled out" leads in the right direction. In the New Testament, too, the word retains its cultic background. Yet in the New Testament consecration or holiness by means of separation from pagans must not be understood in the direct empirical sense, as if separation from a pagan environment implied that holiness were achieved by distance from the world and history. It is not cultic-sacral singling out, but spiritual bond and inner relationship that is the means of sanctification. New Testament holiness thus grows in daily life, not in a glass structure of isolation.

This indication that holiness does not mean isolation in a place that only belongs to God, or separation from the surrounding world, is underlined by the concept of mission. Jesus' holiness is realized by being sent into the world. His mission is in the world. So " consecration" and "mission" reciprocally interpret each other. Indeed we can go further. "Consecration" and "mission" form an indivisible unity; they are not to be understood as a chronological sequence—as if mission only arose *after* consecration and as a result of it. The union between consecration and mission is dialectical. Holiness is both the result of, and the presupposition for, a successful mission.

Priesthood as Service

In the seventeenth chapter of John's gospel the verb "to consecrate" is used in the active sense: "for their sake I consecrate myself " (John 17: 19). At the beginning of the Passion it is revealed that Jesus fulfills his consecration voluntarily, i.e., consecrates himself by offering his own life. It is therefore by no means being singled out in isolated dignity. Indeed its only preeminence lies in the ignominy of a slave's death. In this respect consecration coincides with the New Testament teaching about service (*diakonia*), as this is emphasized by the words spoken by Jesus at the Last Supper in Luke's Gospel.

DIAKONIA originally meant service at table. It was precisely in this activity that the Jews felt the element of humiliation in service. That is why this term is closely related to the term DOVLOS, slave. The synoptic gospels show us in their choice of terms that they were quite conscious of the close connection between servant and slave (cf. Luke 17: 7–9).

The dispute between the disciples about which should be reckoned the greatest and Jesus' reference to himself as the servant, in Luke 22: 24–27, shows that any authority that flows from the sacrament of ordination is a form of service. This particular distinguishing qualification of ministry is, so to speak, the "reverse side of the coin" of being singled out. For it is participation in the particular authority of Jesus. It necessarily entails taking over the destiny of Jesus and hence the humble submission, the total abandonment of the person to his service. When the verses in question speak about "greatness," "those who lord it over" others, etc., it follows in the first place not only that the leaders chosen to exercise authority over the community do so according to Christ's will, but that even the "great" must recognize their having been chosen as an obligation to serve: "the leader [must behave] as if he were the one who serves" (Luke 22–26).

"Yet here am I among you as one who serves," the verse concludes. The model of Jesus implies both: leading and service. Jesus' own description of his role here is not an individual phenomenon confined to this particular passage: the service of the slave in the washing of the disciples' feet (John 13:1 ff) and the role that the Lord would play on the day of the completion of the Kingdom of God (Luke 12:37)— "he will put on an apron, sit them down at table, and wait on them"— clearly show that what is being described here is a salient feature of the specific way in which Jesus taught and lived his greatness. In the imitation of Jesus, therefore, those who represent the Church's ministry as a whole not only have the obligation to serve at table. They are expected to give proof of the diaconic life—the life of Christian service—that should characterize *all* their action. The whole extent of this service can be derived from Luke (10:45). Harking back to the words of Isaiah (53:10 ff), Jesus says that the last expression of his service would be, "to give his life as a ransom for many." Here lies the objective justification for the collocation of the two terms— *diakonia and dovlos*—in the way that Jesus describes service and the role of the servant at the Last Supper. They are intimately connected with the action that is heralded there, with the moment of the interpretation and symbolic anticipation of Christ's redemptive death on the cross.

Such biblical teaching removes any reproach of curtailment of freedom or ecclesial harassment from the specific spiritual claims of the life of the priest. Rather, it enables the priest—as love always does—to achieve a growing closeness to the Redeemer and a growing assimilation to him. It rests not least on the means of divine help and grace.

This theological foundation of the priestly identity admittedly does not have the power of magic formulas. It is not the immediate solution to all problems. However, it points in the right direction. It leads the priest suffering from psychological problems to look away from himself and confront himself with his alter ego. It points to Christ, who brought and who continues to bring salvation. He who takes a servant into his service, also wants to be the savior of that servant's body and soul. Peter says of Christ in the Acts of the Apostles (10:38), that "Jesus went about doing good and curing all who had fallen into the power of the devil." Should the ministerial servant of all people be excluded from Jesus' salvific will?

Bishop and Priest

I would like to conclude by addressing a personal word to you all. You have gathered together here as pastors, to tackle the problem of the addictive behavior of priests. You wish to discuss practical questions and seek practical solutions for priests. But you cannot delegate this task exclusively to experts or specialists. *Presbyterorum ordinis* reminds bishops that it is "on their shoulders particularly [that] falls the burden of sanctifying their priests" (n. 7). To one of these bishops, who is already in the presence of God in eternal life, I would like to entrust the concluding words of my talk. On the occasion of a meeting of the German Bishops' Conference on the life and faith of priests in their dioceses he said:

> The present conference must also have the significance for us of placing ourselves in question. What are we doing wrong? A certain estrangement between bishops and priests is unmistakable. Each of us always finds that painful. Where do the causes for this alienation lie? Priests can be heard saying: "... You [bishops] live high up in a pure world that is quite different from ours; we are down here below in the muck, and then you give us good advice about what needs to be done."

> Should we not set an example in many things simply by the way we live? Too little is radiated by the example we set, even at the spiritual level. Should we not admit this to each other? Spiritual life—the Spirit by which we are kindled—does not inflame us merely to give other people good advice. Rather, it should inspire us to act in such a way that the example we set is taken up and acted on by others. One basic evil is this: we are far, too far removed from priests, and priests often know next to nothing about our life. We must do something to counter this alienation.

On the other hand, a great yearning can be noted among priests, also among younger priests and right up to university professors, to see their bishop more often, to speak with him more often. Compared with the time when we were theology students, a great deal has quite definitely changed.

THE FAMILY AND DRUG ADDICTION

ALFONSO CARDINAL LÓPEZ TRUJILLO

I am deeply honored to participate in this meeting and to share some simple reflections not as an expert, but as a Shepherd interested in this pressing topic. Meetings such as this are a rich source of up-to-date information for groups of Bishops. This workshop is an example for other continents. The Roman Dicastery in which I work offers to the various Episcopal Conferences courses of reflection on the topic of Family and Bioethics; more than twelve hundred Bishops have taken part in our courses.

Some time ago the Pontifical Council for the Family organized a three-day international conference on the theme of the family and drug addiction. At the conclusion, we were received by the Holy Father, who, summarizing the road traveled by a drug victim, spoke of a shift "from despair to hope." Thanks to the contribution of institutions and individuals who have considerable experience in liberating people from this modern-day slavery, a final document of the conference was published, bearing the title *From Despair to Hope: Family and Drug Addiction.*

Some of the reflections that I will put forward involve elements taken from discussions that I have had on various occasions concerning the topic of the family and drug addiction. I am in close and permanent contact with institutions in Italy that have a rich experience on the complete and integral liberation of the person from drug addiction. Since that conference of the Pontifical Council for the family, I have been convinced of certain positions, rooted in a dynamic conception of man, that are indispensable.

A Profound Human Problem

The problem of drug addiction must be seen in an anthropological context, that is, in the context of the basic questions about the meaning of human
existence and the relationship of men and women to God in Christ. Drug
addiction reveals a whole set of symptoms that are evident signs of a distress-
ing problem which is related to the truth and dignity of man, and the very
meaning of existence. Drugs offer a kind of escape by which a human being
seeks to fill in gaps, to escape the emptiness of an existence that is not based
on fundamental values and thus remains rootless, unprotected, and exposed
to every storm. Such an emptiness deprives life of meaning. It is something
that touches the root of the identity of the individual, who, when caught up in
such emptiness, undergoes a terrible and painful experience of enslavement.
Because of the lack of orientation and the absence of a central point of reference, the weakened person gives in to despair. The gap may be filled, artificially (of course, thereby aggravating the despair) through turning to the drug.
Or the gap may be filled by a slow process of liberation: entering into oneself,
taking on the biblical attitude of the prodigal son (Luke 15:11–32), thus enabling the person to regain awareness of his human dignity. It is not merely an
individual problem, the core of the problem is anthropological and extends to
the relationships of life within the family and society.

The person experiencing drug-addiction is in a way both a victim and a
sad product of society, sick in many respects, incapable of giving meaning to
life and experience, who transmits only his own emptiness. Here we are dealing
with a confused society from which faith is uprooted, so that faith no longer
shapes either individual or collective existence. The value of life itself is overshadowed, producing a confusion that becomes a kind of gnawing at, or
nausea, of the soul.

A disconnected society produces the expected phenomenon. It transmits or transfers its disorder to families (without the deliberate intention of
parents, who are most often fine and well-intentioned persons with irreproach-
able behavior). These families suffer the impact of a society that suffocates
them, because of the void in their actual capacity to embody values that can
illuminate and orient existence. But, when we state that families are uprooted,
this is not to increase the dimension of their tragedy by making them feel guilty.
The intention is not to point out who is responsible, but to understand both
the causes and movement of pertinent phenomena.

I do believe that the so-called "Peter Pan syndrome" helps us to understand a number of phenomena by way of the general approach conveyed by
the book bearing that title. At one of our meetings some time ago, Professor
Tony Anatrella, a psychiatrist from France, who collaborates closely with us,
told us to watch out for "endless adolescence" (also a title of one of his
books), which is the state or situation of one who never matures. The Peter Pan
syndrome encompasses a whole set of behaviors according to which the

protagonist's choice to ever remain a child is linked in a disastrous conspiracy to the attitude of a family that hesitates to educate. Many families nowadays suffer a real crisis of parenthood because of the fear to educate their children, as if to educate were an abusive imposition. Such a family renounces its central mission. Today we are faced with parents who, though they are essentially generous, cannot be described as good parents, since they neglect the demands of their mission, appealing in fact to their children's right to be free. They do not educate because they fear encroaching on the freedom of their children. This is worse when the life of the parents themselves is not exemplary, either, and does not offer a process of self-realization in responsible love. I experience this during the recent wonderful celebration with the Holy Father in Mexico: a young driver told me that he had received many wounds in his parents' home because they quarreled much in front of him, wounds which deepened when they divorced. He felt his life to be without future and without meaning and he started to hear compulsively satanic voices. He ended a long dialog with a request for a priest to help him.

From our vantage point at the Pontifical Council for the Family, an observatory on the phenomena of family life, we can affirm that today many families are like a repeating recording of a wrong conception of man which produces children in its own likeness. The void in life becomes a caricature, a parody of an insufficient human project, or the lack of one.

What has been described so far contrasts with what the family ought to be, in line with authentic humanism: a place in which the person is rooted in the initial stage of developing his own personality. The family is a shaper, a builder of persons. This social and essential mediation of the family cannot be replaced. Many sociologists acknowledge that the social mediation of the family in the shaping of the personality cannot be replaced by the state or by any other instances. Allow me to use the expression of St. Thomas, which he attributes to early childhood, but whose significance can today be extended to adolescence and the process that fosters maturity. The expression of the holy doctor goes as follows: the family is the "spiritual womb" (*Summa Theologiae* II–II, 10.20). What significance does this concept have in terms of education, or integral formation? This notion removes us from the purely biological conception of birth. Giving birth to somebody is not to separate him from the process of education and formation in love and responsibility.

The Family as Community

The family is a life-long community, one of love in which education builds the children according to a model, the original project of God, i.e. what man really is. The family is an environment or an atmosphere of protection for the growth of the children as persons. One Polish professor recently told me that in Polish the word *rodjina*, "family," means originally to "make grow," or "give birth to." This is the reason why the two are inseparable: family and life.

A family that is not a dynamic source, cannot generate growth in the process of life and has no reason for existence! To seek to give life or make someone grow raises certain questions: What life, quality of life, and style of life? The resulting development of life is at the heart of an anthropological context in which the social being of man discovers its very self in the first community, the family, which is the primary cell of society.

Within the family there is contained the truth of man brought to life, not only in the perspective of human wisdom present in it in a precious synthesis, but also in the whole extraordinary illumination received from the Lord, in which the mystery of man is revealed and discovered. In the family the human person opens to his very reality, as an individual subject. Besides, in it the child's moral universe enlarges, according to the measure in which, through a dialogue of love, the child experiences his worth and dignity, by becoming an object of parents' love and the center of their life. This constitutes a prelude to the moment he will discover that, in the depth of his dignity as a person, he is loved as a person (one not treated as a thing or instrument) by the Creator himself.

Many of the great pioneers in the liberation of their brothers and sisters well knew how to accompany and guide them through this process in such a way that human beings manage to interiorize or enter into themselves, in order to begin the journey (which in most cases is one of conversion and return) that leads to the Father, to God. Man in his entirety needs to experience the reality of his worth by feeling that he is loved. This worth increases in unlimited measure when one becomes aware of the fact that he is an object of the love of God Himself.

May I here give two complementary examples, which for me were useful lessons of "anthropological experience." The first one was the reassuring example I received at the International Congress on the Meninos da Rua, "street children," which we organized in Rio de Janeiro. The fact that street children or abandoned young people have no fear of death had always attracted my attention. Often they are used to carry out criminal ventures, which they execute without even realizing what they are doing. They have no self-esteem. They believe they are expendable and have no place in society. A series of testimonies convinced me of one reality: when these children or young people start experiencing that they are loved, that they have a value and are persons, for them this is like a resurrection. For this reason, institutions that care for these children ought to transmit respect and love, which is like giving them what they missed in their families. I really saw many faces of children and young people being changed and brightening up, as if the light of the Word Incarnate, the image of God, was being reflected in them (and, indeed, it was). The other complementary example is what I experienced in a dialogue with drug addicts, during the first stage of their liberation, which is both difficult and painful. I asked them how they felt. Their answer was, "We are discovering what we are." All in all, every individual human being continuously discovers what he or she is or ought to be; however, for those who go through the drama of drug abuse, the road to liberation and hope is a special journey of discovery.

In many dialogues and visits to various institutions, above all in the diversity of positive Italian experiences, I gradually came to understand something which, I must confess, I did not understand entirely at the beginning: not only that "you cannot use drugs to fight drugs," but also that the problem of drug addiction, in which man is deeply entangled, is not a question without an answer or a tunnel without an exit. It is in the first place a question of values, one that calls for a return to the center of existence, where man is not an obscure entity, but a mystery (as expressed by Gabriel Marcel). Light is breaking on new roads out of the dark and restricted world in which those enslaved by the void are confined. Their journey leads to the Other, and to others, by way of incarnate values that are uncovered.

I have been deeply touched by some of the books of Victor Frankl and by what his own experience of Nazi concentration camps meant to him. Despite everything, some persons there managed to survive and overcome every torture and abuse. They loved life and still found meaning in it, for their ideals had not died. In contrast, those who lacked strong values were annihilated by suffering. Frankl has translated much of this experience into his theory of "logotherapy," a method used to revive ideals and transmit values when everything has been ruined and lost.

In view of these considerations, I very much agree with the idea of following ways of recovery based on profound anthropological insight into the processes of liberation. These have been used in some communities of therapy in Italy. Some of these communities pledge themselves in a liberating evangelization with the explicit proclamation of the Gospel. In fact, in societies that have deep Christian cultural traditions, presentation of values in general is not sufficient. Rather this process must take the form of a personalized evangelization. Let us return to the metaphor of the prodigal son (the parable is also that of the Merciful Father). The son's journey of self-discovery and return to the Father by interiorization becomes a passage into resurrection and hope, a meeting with the Lord, a meeting with God. A key word in the parable is the Greek term *anastasis*, meaning "resurrection," but also "standing up or rising to one's feet." It can be applied to a vital decision by one who is in an actual, if hidden, dialogue, and has managed to enter into and come to terms with himself. This liberation moves through a new network of human relations, whereby institutions or centers act as a family, a "community," in which one experiences new dimensions of a love that liberates, redeems, and transforms. In other words, the liberation process is a matter of personalization, which is not a medical process. At least it is a process in which medicine is an aid and not a principal factor. I know many young people, who have an almost monastic style of prayer life, meditation, and discipline, who have achieved a complete rehabilitation. This is possible with the help of a community that is like a family. The moment of understanding that their existence is very important and that they are the object of the love of God, is the moment of their Resurrection.

In a process of interiorization involving the identity of the human person, or the "irrepressible thirst for dignity," the life-giving blood, is the discovery that man is not an obscure entity, but that human existence and its profound reality is exalted in God. Christ is the Veritatis Splendor that illuminates the truth of man.

To one who has faith, and for cultures that have been profoundly penetrated by revelation, God does not reign in shadows. He is the sun from above that enlightens man's movement in the world, saving him from moving on hesitantly like a blind man. In a word, the way of interiorization entails the dialogue of man with God. Man alienated from himself, one who, according to the expression of Hegel, breaks away from his center towards X, becomes an obscure entity marked by "disenchantment." To fill life with values, better yet, to fill life with Christ means to overcome an existential emptiness not by an inconsistent or unreal dream but by personal dialogue: to meet Jesus is to meet freedom. Medicine can help in processes of detoxification, science can discover regions in our brain that we must know how to control, but all this must gravitate around what is central, the liberation of a person as a person. An Italian community of liberation of drug-addicts called The Cenacle gave me a beautiful icon painted using the best iconographic techniques. The artists explained to me that through the making of that icon of the Holy Family, which they could create only after a month of spiritual recollection, they had returned to the dialogue with God. Thus they felt redeemed.

On various occasions this incarnation of values has arisen when the recovery takes place in the presence of (at least implicit) faith and Christian values, or explicit evangelization, or where there is Christian culture (at least where it is not completely overshadowed or where it has not completely disappeared). In those cases a proclamation of human value is not enough, but we need to bring, to show, Christian values. This is the focus of the energy and the strength of the Church in this area. Liberation is a fruit of true evangelization, in which the good news of Christ operates in such a way that the lofty dignity of life is recuperated. In this case, if we are talking about physicians, Jesus is the physician. It is, however, obvious that in countries where the Gospel has not yet penetrated society or has not yet given rise to a Christian culture, the process cannot be identical. Nevertheless, even where the young have had some contact with a Christian education, the bulk of the liberating process is hard work permeated by reason illuminated by faith.

An Accompanying Family

Much thought can be given to the challenge of keeping people from the tentacles of the modern slavery of drug addiction. We may begin with the family. The complete solution is a profoundly evangelized family, rendered capable of fulfilling the sacred mission to which it is called by God Himself in which the duty of education is taken seriously. Forming families as domestic churches provides assurance of overcoming gaps and making family a mainstay. The duty of the family as a "shaper of persons," forming them in the true sense, where parents are the primary evangelizers, ought to be fulfilled step by step. Births lead to the formation of the family, which as a spiritual womb permits genuine growth analogous to that of the Son of God in the Family of Nazareth.

With regard to this mission, I would like to stress the importance of adequate sexual formation in love. Our Document on this subject is entitled *The Truth and Meaning of Human Sexuality*. In summary, we may briefly state that the truth of man embraces the unity of all that is truly human in terms of sexuality. This goes far beyond what is merely biological, to encompass altruism, responsibility, and respect for others. A love in matrimony becomes concrete and achieves its greatest depth and seriousness as total love and fidelity, both exclusive and fruitful, alone at the service of the family, which is in turn at the service of society.

I would now like to reflect on the issue of families hit by the crisis of having their own children caught up in drugs, families that are, however, not afraid of making an examination of conscience and deciding, in any case, to help their children overcome a struggle in which their own happiness is involved. It is not possible for families to ignore crises of their own children, as if they were something that did not concern them. In our experience, institutions of drug-rehabilitation do associate more and more with families at opportune moments during the process of liberation and reinforcement. Families need, above all, to be helped and formed, so that they may exercise a positive role and avoid being an obstacle on the way towards hope. One day I met a group of families that had gone to visit their children at a rehabilitation center. Someone said to me, "As usual, we are here this week 'to get a fill-up' (like filling up the fuel tank of a car): to be charged with all the necessary energy that enables them to be good collaborators in the complete recovery of their children.

One may not expect that those leaving recovery centers after having attained hope and in possession of new reasons for living can avoid falling back into the problem without the active involvement of their families. There is a great danger of relapse. The care of the families in this case must be permanent and continuous, with the strength of love and authority in tenderness. In this field we, Priests and Bishops, can give a very great service to society and to the family. We all need to fill their hearts with the fullness of the Gospel, that becomes a call to conversion (metanoia). "Because the goodness of God leads to conversion" (Rom. 2:4): *chreston tou Theou eis metanoian de agei.*

Certainly, there has been much progress in recent years, and new experiences have been accumulated in this field. Together with the Pontifical Council for Health Care Workers, we have for some time been thinking about and preparing a special meeting on this particular topic, with all the creativity that this challenge demands.

The Role of Society

Here we are taking the concept of society in its broader dimension, above all in reference to the wide scope of culture. Cultural changes today have a lot to do with the political community and the role of legislators and governments because many laws that concern the common good involve implicit anthropological concepts or forms of behavior.

When we speak of serious gaps within the social order, one might think that we are exaggerating. However, there are many thinkers, many highly qualified, who today complain of a situation of pronounced pessimism and desperation, in a society that is intoxicated, if you will, with its successes and the myth of a sustained and constant progress. I would like to place myself in the perspective of what, after various clarifying discussions, the Apostolic Exhortation *Reconciliatio et poenitentia* (RP) called "social sin." Today there are many widespread accepted lifestyles reinforced by laws and institutions that have all the qualifications to be labeled social sin. In a society bombarded day after day by numerous messages and experiencing a series of disturbances in its spirit, to the point of undergoing serious forms of spiritual illness, we cannot but be preoccupied about the human beings, especially the frail ones, who thirst for truth and meaning in life in order to emerge from their tragedy.

Here we have to take into consideration two complementary conceptions concerning the significance of original sin which are treated in the Apostolic Exhortation. The first one refers to the human solidarity of original sin, which is very mysterious and imperceptible, yet very real and concrete. One could speak of a "communion in sin" because "a soul degraded by sin degrades the Church, too, and to some extent the entire world. In other words, no sin exclusively concerns the one who commits it, even that which is innermost and secret or most strictly individual" (*RP* no. 16). We could speak of an expansive force, like an explosion of sin, that pulverizes human relationships and ruins both human society and the individuals themselves. The second aspect is *social*, inasmuch as sin tends towards direct aggression of one's neighbor. This implies sins committed against justice, sins against the community: aggression against the rights of the human person, beginning with the right to life and including that of the unborn; sins against the common good; the sin of commission or omission by leading politicians and economists, etc. (*RP* no. 16).

Social sin is more or less bound up with and permeated by considerations of an anthropological nature. This does not just concern the severe conditioning which the individual suffers in a society where moral oxygen is rarefied, but, what is worse, it is connected with a certain conception of man that debases him. It is a conception that generates a particular type of person. This is the crisis of this age, in which, amid moral erosion and conceptual confusion, hypotheses that destroy man are being spread. It is not only a question of a wrong attitude, but also a defense and dissemination of error as if it were the truth. The Apostle of Gentiles shouts with pain that "The wrath of God reveals itself against all impiety and injustice of men who keep truth imprisoned in injustice" (Rom. 1:18), and he denounces: "some have changed the truth of God into a lie" (Rom. 1:25). This amounts to defending a situation where disorder and deterioration pass for the achievement of freedom. With things like this, we find ourselves in a sick society, which not only does not educate, but also disintegrates, and does not allow the family to fulfill its essential function. Just as Cyprian back in his time complained of crimes which, when committed by the State, passed for virtue (*De unitate Ecclesiae*), so *Evangelium vitae* denounces the acceptance of crimes as rights because of unjust laws.

In this case the social illness is more dangerous and disastrous, for both the individual and society at large, because it is equivalent to a systematic burying of values which are necessary for the formation of a person within the dimension of true humanism and also for the building of society. In such cases the "culture of love" becomes a mere abstract ideal, for time bombs have been put in place to demolish the human person. Is this not a disastrous situation, one which like a wave uproots, disturbs, and confuses man? I do think that all this is characteristic of what we call an empty society.

All that concerns the relationship between the family and the state ought to be given special attention so that the family may not only be respected, but also helped in its duty of formation. When, with the conspiracy of mass media, attempts are made to harm human ecology, the result is that the foundations are laid for a dangerous increase in the number of persons who take refuge in drugs. These are especially people who not only have experienced a void, but have also been disturbed by the disorganization of life offered by a crumbling culture, commonly known as the "culture of death."

Let us return to the parable of the prodigal son. Regarding this heavy human concern of the family and drug addiction, it is evidently necessary to the son to recover certain truths which allow him to look honestly into himself, rise to his feet, and embark on the return journey, a journey of freedom, which in the Gospel parable is described as a "resurrection." He who was dead has come back to life. This resurrection is possible because man recovers his dignity at the very moment when he meets God and in Him comes to terms with himself. Therefore, this resurrection becomes a passage from despair to hope. The Church must occupy a prominent position in this undertaking, and that is why we are gathered here.

In these simple reflections, then, rather than insisting on the obligations of organized society or of the state in relation to the crime of drug trafficking or instead of reminding them of the assistance they ought to give to institutions

159

that are dedicated to the liberation of the young from drugs, I would like to make an appeal in favor of societal conversion to the dignity of man. We must advise caution so that the comfortable but destructive permissiveness of governments may not be used as an instrument for further aggravating the existing problem. This social conversion goes hand in hand with the conversion of the family to that which constructs the plan of God. At the International Meeting of the families with the Holy Father at Rio de Janeiro, His Holiness John Paul II, in a beautiful improvisation, referred to both the divine and human architecture of Rio de Janeiro. All this concerns the family, which is, above all, the architecture of both God and man. It is the harmony of its construction that will permit the harmonious development of children in such a way that they both grow in humanity and do not become tragic victims of drugs.

Scientific Analysis

THE NATURE OF DRUG ADDICTION

ROBERT MORSE, M.D.

I was asked to talk to you about the nature of drug addiction. I told a friend last night that if I had been asked to talk to you about alcoholism, I would say much the same thing. I hope that is one of the messages you take away from this meeting, that alcoholism is addiction to the legal drug alcohol, and the addictive disorder that we associate with that drug is virtually the same as other drug addiction.

What I would like to do with you this morning is review some of the symptoms of addiction, talk about the difference between abuse of drugs and addiction to drugs, and discuss a theory that was first introduced in 1972 (addiction as an artificially induced drive) which has probably come into its own with our new neurobiology.

The brain is an extremely complex organ. (This data is from a recent article by Dr. Hyman, head of the National Institutes of Health.) What we are talking about today are theories only, and they are theories about an organ that has over a hundred billion nerve cells, with thousands of types of cells. Morphology, chemistry, and physiology of these cells differ. Each cell may have thousands of synapses, or connections between cells. There are over ten trillion synapses in the brain, more than 100 chemical neurotransmitters in the synapses, and the total system changes dynamically. So to say that we know what's going on is not exactly true!

We have some excellent researchers and have come a long way in understanding addiction and mental health, but we have far to go. Please keep this in mind while I try to present current theories for you today.

163

As we have mentioned, alcohol is a drug, and what I am going to say about drug addiction we can say about alcohol and vice versa. Is drug addiction a disease? I will leave that up to you, but by the end of my "stimulating" talk, maybe you will be able to answer that. Often, addiction is called a disease, but treatment of it often ends up in the prison hospital or jail. It is still thought of as a moral weakness by many of us who are otherwise well educated.

Why have men and women over the years, even without scientific knowledge of what alcoholism or addiction is, empathized with its power? Abraham Lincoln, in 1842, speaking to the Washington Temperance Society said. "In my judgment, such of us who have never fallen victims have been spared more by the absence of appetite than from any mental or moral superiority over those who have." Isn't that another way of saying that nonalcoholics are not necessarily stronger or in better mental health; they just do not have the appetite for this substance that victims of the addiction do.

What Is Addiction?

Lincoln's suggestion is not far from the way scientists might define addiction today: having an abnormal appetite that makes the compulsive use of a drug or alcohol necessary.

Some of you may know of DSM-IV (Diagnostic and Statistical Manual of Mental Disease, fourth edition, put out by the American Psychiatric Association). This manual contains the official way to make diagnoses in psychiatry. The following is the definition of addiction, which is called substance dependence. Keep in mind we will use the term drug dependence and addiction interchangeably.

Three or more of these seven criteria qualify for diagnosis of dependence or addiction:

1. A tolerance to the drug (a need for higher doses)
2. Evidence of withdrawal symptoms
3. Using the substance in larger amounts than intended
   (that is the loss of control)
4. Unsuccessful efforts to cut down or stop
5. Increased time devoted to obtaining the substance
6. Compulsive use
7. Continued use despite knowledge of problems caused by the drug.

If you had to boil down a definition of substance dependence to its very essentials, it probably would be "continued use of the substance (drugs, alcohol) despite the adverse consequences suffered from its use" (continued use despite adverse consequences).

Over the years there has been much data generated from addiction research. We continue however to lack a unified theory of what addiction is, despite the knowledge from biology, psychiatry, psychology, sociology, criminology. We clinicians, and I consider myself first of all a clinician, have learned what this disorder is and what it does to people.

No matter what you call it: disease, bad habit, clinical syndrome, these five characteristics of addiction seem to be well accepted:

1) People don't set out to become addicted. **It's a disorder nobody wants.**

2) **It may no longer be pleasurable**, as opposed to drug abuse or alcohol abuse, which may feel good. The addict is often trying to cut down or trying to abstain.

3) It is **insightless** before it's diagnosed. In other words, seldom do people who have addiction know that they have it. The type of early intervention which we often preach suggests that people should know when they are becoming addicted. It just will not work, almost by definition. Alcoholics do not know when they are becoming dependent; alcoholics do not know when they have gone across the line. If we are going to help these people, we have to help them by being responsible others who observe their behavior and reflect this back to them.

4) It becomes a **primary disorder**; then you can no longer call it a symptom. It leaves you with a recurrent desire to use the substance you've become addicted to—predictably, intermittently, perhaps forever. For example, when addiction or dependence occurs in a person who initially began to use alcohol to relieve stress or anxiety, there is a temptation to believe that drinking might return to "normal" if the stress or anxiety were treated or disappeared. However, the loss of control over alcohol (or other drug of addiction) will remain even after improvement in the stress, etc. In other words, what began the alcohol use (stress) is no longer the reason for drinking. It now occurs because of the addictive disorder which has evolved and become a primary and independent condition. We have recovered alcoholic counselors who work in our program, some of them abstinent for fifteen or twenty years, and they tell me that they, occasionally, think about drinking, dream about drinking, want to drink. They do not drink; but they have had to learn to deal with that **artificially induced drive.**

5) **It is irreversible**. This does not mean it is not treatable! But once you reach the stage of being addicted to a drug, there is no going back; no going back, that is, to the point that you can take the drug, use a little bit, predict what's going to happen, stop it when you wish, and start it again at your will. You lose control over the time, circumstances, and quantity used. One can recover from addiction, then, only by abstinence.

Addiction as an Artificially Induced Drive

Dr. Neil Bejerot, a Swedish psychiatrist, published a small monograph in 1972 that contains one of the most influential theories that I have come across in my thirty years of trying to understand addictions. It was called simply, "Addiction is an Artificially Induced Drive." He notes, "hardly any psychiatric condition is more difficult to treat than a well established addiction. This is partly because the addict does not suffer from his disease, he enjoys it. The drug effects take on the strength of libidinal desires and outweigh all mental, physical, social, and economic complications arising from the abuse. He also said, "I look upon euphoric or pleasurable drug effects as a kind of short circuiting of the pain-pleasure principle. The final result is an artificially induced drive. No disturbed personality and no underlying social problems are required."

According to Bejerot, addiction is really akin to an artificially induced drive. There are two stages: drug abuse, which is under one's control, and drug addiction, which becomes a condition of its own, a disease or primary disorder, which has its own dynamics and characteristics. My profession of psychiatry, perhaps your profession, and many of the mental health professions, unfortunately often continue to see addiction as being a symptom of an underlying disorder. In other words, as "abuse" rather than "dependence" or addiction.

Symptoms vs. Disorder

Let me give you a couple of examples of how the symptom becomes a disease, or how the abuse of a drug may become an addiction.

Let us take tobacco, the most mundane of our addictions. Virtually all scientists agree that the tobacco user who uses it compulsively after a few months is certainly addicted. Many young people begin to use tobacco in part because their peers use it and to look grown up. Ten years later, does it make any sense to say that the reason that this person is addicted to tobacco is because he wants to look grown up, which was the initial cause of his abuse? Something has changed over this period of time.

Let us say I am an alcoholic; at the age of 18 I began to drink in part because I am a neurotic, anxious, insecure young man who can not ask girls to dance. I get flustered easily, and I learn that alcohol is a great tranquilizer and sedative. So I begin to drink, because quite obviously, it helps me with these symptoms. Twenty years later, I am a "card-carrying alcoholic." do not know it, but I have all the characteristics of alcoholism. Then you take me to the Mayo Clinic or some other famous place, where you find a good psychiatrist who helps me with my insecurity, my neuroticism, my anxiety, and lo and behold, my mental health is improved tremendously. Now I should be able to go out and drink normally, right? No, you all know the answer to that, I cannot drink normally. The cause of my drinking, the beginning of the abuse of alcohol, now has nothing to do with why I continue to drink. The addiction has taken on a life of its own. You could be as mentally healthy as anyone in the country (have no diagnosable psychiatric disorders), and you still are addicted.

Pain Disorders. One of the things that we struggle with a lot in our work is chronic pain and addiction. Let us say I have chronic back pain and my doctor is giving me one of the popular opiates to use for pain relief, and I become addicted to it. You then take me to a clinic where good doctors find out that I do have something wrong with my back which requires surgery. They operate on it, correct the defect. Then, I should be able to use the opiate normally, right? No. Because the pain, the origin of my abuse at this time, has nothing to do with the addiction itself. Once I have used this over a period of time, the addiction becomes primary. As long as the drug is around me and I use it, I will use it addictively.

Anxiety Disorders. One of the common drugs to treat anxiety disorders is Xanax, alprazolam. Many of you have heard of it as modern Valium. It's very effective in reducing anxiety, and as a first-line drug, it is preferred by many psychiatrists. If you use it more than a few months, you become physiologically dependent, and many people become addicted to it.

Let us say I am using Xanax to quell my anxiety and I get into a psychiatric treatment program that allows me to treat the anxiety disorder with behavioral therapy and other medications that are not addicting. After relieving the anxiety, I should be able to use Xanax normally, without trouble, right? No, because the addiction to that drug remains. The anxiety symptoms now have nothing to do with the ongoing addiction.

So I hope you can see that there is a gross difference between use/abuse and addiction. We should never speak of addiction as a symptom. We can speak of drug use/abuse and alcohol use/abuse as symptoms; addiction is never a symptom. Addiction becomes a disorder of its own.

Neurobiology of Addiction

Let me talk a little bit about the biology of this condition. In the 1950s, a Canadian scientist named Olds and a colleague Milliner demonstrated that after putting electrodes into a certain area in rats' brains (which we later identified as the pleasure center) the animals could be electrically stimulated by pressing a bar in their cages. They would keep active at the bar until they were exhausted, even unto death. They would do this in preference to food, water, or sex. Stimulation of this center in the brain, the reward center, the addictive center, if you want to call it that, was so powerful that these animals would prefer to satisfy it rather than other instinctual drives.

This anatomical area has been increasingly studied to the point where scientists now believe that we now know the area that is the addiction center.

These terms may not mean much to you, but they include the ventral tegmental area, the basal forebrain with several components, the nucleus accumbens, and olfactory tubercle. There are several neurotransmitters or chemicals that activate this system: dopamine, serotonin, endorphin GABA (gamma amino butyric acid). These influence what is called the limbic system of the brain, the area which is associated with emotions and mood states.

Increasingly, it has been thought that dopamine itself (the neurotransmitter chemical dopamine), is the primary neurotransmitter for virtually all the drugs of addiction. So whether you're using opiates, alcohol, cocaine, nicotine, or marijuana, the activation of the dopamine system in this particular anatomical area may occur, perhaps indicating a common bond for all the addicting substances.

Dr. Alan Leshner, director of the National Institutes of Drug Abuse, has said this relatively recently and eloquently, "Addiction is a brain disease." There is a single pathway for all the drugs of abuse (the pathway that I've mentioned to you). Activation of this pathway seems to be the common element in compulsive or addictive use. All addictive drugs affect this circuit. The addicted brain differs from the nonaddicted brain in several ways: metabolic activity, receptor availability, gene expression, and responsiveness to environment cues. Conditioned responses also have a lot to do with developing addiction. The "anticipation," in animals, by being in an environment where they have been rewarded by cocaine, will actually release dopamine in this neuroanatomical area, even without the presence of cocaine. So a lot of very interesting and elegant study is being done to help us specify the anatomy and physiology of addiction.

Let us look at the difference in brain reaction to short-term alcohol use (social use) versus long-term or addictive use.

In short-term use, the inhibiting neurotransmitters, the transmitters that slow down the action of the brain, GABA and glycine, are enhanced, so there is a sedative effect throughout the nervous system. The activating transmitters, glutamate and aspartate, are inhibited. So the entire nervous system responds to the short-term use of alcohol by sedation or inhibition.

Over the long term, it is just the reverse. If you are drinking addictively, the inhibiting side of the nervous system (GABA, glycine, etc.) is reduced, and the activating neurotransmitters are enhanced, so that you have an activation which makes this individual feel uncomfortable, nervous, and anxious. One of the currently interesting theories is that this has something to do with why alcoholics cannot stop drinking. Once they get into the activation phase, then they feel anxious much of the time, have trouble sleeping, have trouble relaxing, have anxiety symptoms. Of course, the alcoholic says to himself or herself, "It is because of these systems that I need to drink," when in fact, it is the drinking that has caused the symptoms. The alcohol itself then has induced a hyperactive state which may propel the addictive disorder.

Leshner then says, "A metaphorical switch in the brain seems to be thrown as the result of prolonged drug use. Initially, drug use is voluntary behavior, but when the switch is thrown, the individual moves to a state of addiction, characterized by drug seeking and use, and compulsive drug seeking." In other words, drug use/abuse becomes a brain disease which is addiction. It is induced, that is what our friend Bejerot said twenty-five or more years ago! Without his having the biological explanation, his clinical experience and foresightedness helped us to think of this as being an artificially induced type of drive.

Conclusion

Even as we understand more of the biology and technology of addiction, the clinical side has not changed. There is a lot we *do* know about the signs, symptoms and cause of this disease! If you can keep this in mind, it will help you understand your colleague or parishioners who may have addiction. It's a disorder no one wants! Drinking or using drugs initially is pleasurable; but when you become addicted and you have lost control, and you are preoccupied with it all the time, you are trying to cut down or control it or stop using, and you continue to use despite your best efforts to stop, it's not fun anymore.

I think of this in the current climate of our elderly people. Too many of us in medicine, and our culture in general, say things like, "Well, good old Bob. He worked a long time at a tough job. He deserves to have a little fun and pleasure in his retirement. So he drinks a little too much, so what? Let's let him enjoy his last years."

Folks, if Bob is drinking in an alcoholic manner, that is not fun! No matter what he tells you, if he is drinking in the way that I just described to you, that's not fun. We should never assume that addictive drug use is fun for anyone, in our elderly or middle-aged or young people.

It is insightless. You have all heard the overused term "denial," but it is very real. Before they are diagnosed or someone explains it to them, virtually no addict understands what is going on. If we stand back and wait for this insight to occur, we may wait a long, long time. Usually insight does occur spontaneously only after an accumulation of adverse consequences or problems. Sometimes those problems result in death (of the individual or others) before the insight is gained, so intervening to bring it to their attention is very worthwhile and almost necessary.

Again, the addiction becomes a primary disorder, and this concept is perhaps the key to understanding it. This is Bejerot's idea: abuse can be controlled, but once you develop the addictive disorder, you have lost control. It has assumed a different quality and has become a primary disease. It leaves the victim with a recurrent desire. Addicts will have the urge to use in predictable situations, for example, an area where they've procured drugs or around a

169

hospital where they got a prescription. However, they may also have a spon-taneously urge to use for no obvious reason. It may be generated somehow internally.

Addiction is irreversible. We don't know how to help an addict become a nonaddict and continue to use their drugs of choice in a normal, controlled manner. We do know how to help people recover with abstinence.

References

American Psychiatric Association. 1994. *Diagnostic and Statistical Manual of Mental Disorders*, 4th ed. (DSM IV). Washington, D.C.

Bejerot, N. 1972. *Addiction: An Artificially Induced Drive*. Springfield, Ill.

Leshner, A.I. 1997. Addiction is a Brain Disease, and It Matters. *Science*. 278: 345–347.

Olds, J. and P. Milner. 1954. Positive reinforcement produced by electrical stimulation of septal area and other regions of rat brain. *J. Comp. Physiol. Psychol.* 47: 419–427.

THE NATURE OF ALCOHOL ADDICTION

MICHAEL M. MILLER, M.D., F.A.S.A.M.

I practice addiction medicine, being one of 3,000 physicians who is a member of the American Society of Addiction Medicine (ASAM). The terminology of addiction is a problem; even within ASAM, we struggle with it. Usually, when people hear the word "addict," they immediately think "drug addict," and that conjures up certain concepts, certain ideas. This starts a process of myth making (O'Brien, C.P., and A.T. McLellan).

Myths about Addiction

The first myth is that the problem is drugs. Certainly in America the cocaine epidemic was very shocking to us, but the rise of this epidemic served to reinforce the myth that drugs are the problem. *Figure 1* on cost-of-illness studies for alcohol and drug abuse, adjusted for inflation and population growth (alcohol is on the left, drugs are on the right) shows that alcohol is far more costly to our society than all illicit drugs combined. *Figure 2* shows that premature deaths from alcohol are roughly 100,000 a year in America; from all illicit drugs, one-fourth of that; but from tobacco, four times that. In the medical specialty of addiction medicine, I know what the big drug problem is in America, and it is nicotine. I know that tobacco rarely causes problems in your parishes with regard to the daily functioning of your priests; it simply kills them. The Number One cause of death in alcoholics is tobacco.

A contributor to this volume, Dr. Pat Owen, is from the internationally respected addiction rehabilitation center directed by the Hazelden Foundation in Minnesota. Another myth is that all this addiction treatment, going to

Figure 1

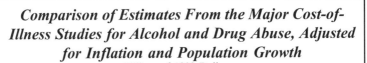

Comparison of Estimates From the Major Cost-of-Illness Studies for Alcohol and Drug Abuse, Adjusted for Inflation and Population Growth

Billions of 1992 Dollars

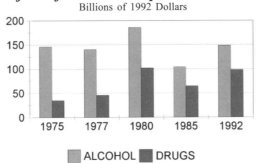

ALCOHOL ■ DRUGS

Sources: 1975 alcohol: Berry et al. (1977); 1975 drugs: Rufener et al. (1977); 1977 drugs and alcohol: Cruze et al. (1981); 1980 drugs and alcohol: Harwood et al. (1984); 1985 drugs and alcohol: Rice et al. (1990); 1992 drugs and alcohol: Analysis by The Lewin Group; price and population data: *Statistical Abstract of the United States 1993*, U.S. Department of Commerce 1993.

Figure 2

Premature Deaths Attributed to Addiction to Various Substances (U.S.A.)

Nicotine Dependence	approx. 400,000 deaths/year
Alcohol Dependence	approx. 100,000 deaths/year
Cocaine, heroin, and all other illicit drug dependence	approx. 25,000 deaths/year

Figure 3

Where the Burden of Alcohol and Drug Problems Falls, 1992 (Billions of dollars)

	Alcohol	Drugs
Abusers and Households	$67	$43
Government	$57	$45
Private Insurance	$15	$3
Victim losses	$9	$7
TOTAL	**$148**	**$98**

Hazelden and similar treatment centers, is breaking the bank, that it costs insurance companies too much, that it costs government too much. But *Figure 3* describes who actually pays for the drug problem in America.

The next myth is that addiction disproportionately affects blacks. For alcohol addiction, the data is very clear, as *Figure 4a* shows. The onset of drinking is much later in black youth than in white youth. Examining the percentage of people addicted to alcohol, whites are far higher than blacks (see *Figure 4b* which shows the percentage of whites and blacks in the population as a whole). So alcoholism is not a disease of African Americans. It is a disease of white Americans (and, of course, proportionately, it is a disease of Native Americans).

Myth Number Four is that alcoholism is not very relevant for women. Alcoholism is admittedly a male-dominated disease, with a 4:1 ratio of males : females for some kinds of alcoholism, and a 9:1 ratio for other kinds of alcoholism. But while it is a very male disease, women get affected, and they develop physical damage from alcohol quicker than do men. They die from cirrhosis at lower levels of alcohol consumption than do men. Women are more sensitive to being killed by this drug.

Then we have another myth: that addiction is only a problem of working-class people or people who are "losers" or are on the fringe of society; and that the best and the brightest are protected. There are some very interesting data that challenge that myth. Let me just share with you some information that's close to me, and that's the data about impaired physicians. I've done a lot of work with sick doctors, sick from alcoholism and other drug dependencies and psychiatric disturbances. One-third of all chemically dependent physicians graduated in the top 5% of their medical school class. If you think that alcoholism in the clergy is only amongst the marginal members, I'm sorry. It does happen to the best and the brightest.

Regarding a final myth, here's where I'll take a risk. I am going to take a risk and state to this audience that it is a myth to contend that alcoholism is best understood as a sin. I will tell you I do not think that is a useful model. I am not going to say I believe that morality has nothing to do with it; but if you want to consider alcoholism a sin, you'd better get in line and consider cardiovascular disease a sin, epilepsy a sin, obesity a sin, diabetes a sin, and schizophrenia a sin. If you choose to go the route of calling addiction a sin, that's your right. But addiction is a brain disease (Leschner, A.I.) (O'Brien, C.P.) like manic depressive illness, epilepsy, Parkinson's disease, and cerebrovascular disease. Putting it in a special category which considers it first and foremost a sin is not supported by the evidence.

Why Learn about Alcohol Addiction?

In preparing today's talk, I thought of you as "customers" of my presentation, and I considered, "What do my customers need regarding alcohol ad-

Figure 4a

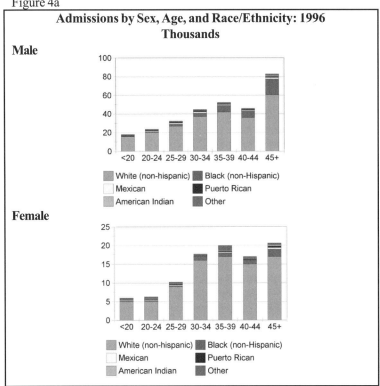

Figure 4b

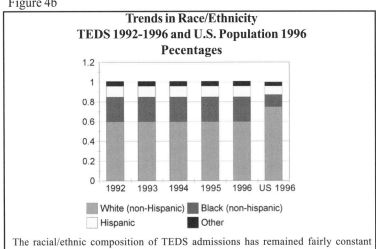

The racial/ethnic composition of TEDS admissions has remained fairly constant since 1992, at about 60 percent non-Hispanic whites, 25 percent non-Hispanic black, 11 percent Hispanic, and 4 percent other groups.

diction?" I determined that you likely have four different kinds of needs. First, I think you would agree you need to know about this because of your faith: you need to know about alcoholism for the people you minister to. Alcohol and other drug addiction affects roughly 10% of the public, roughly 20% of people that go to doctors' offices, and roughly 30% of people who are in hospitals. So alcoholism is extremely prevalent. It is very prevalent in all congregations, among many types of parishioners. There are variances in prevalence, of course. Alcoholism is more prominent in Native Americans, less prominent in Asian-Americans (Crum, R.M.). There is a lot of different variability, ethnic and otherwise; for instance, alcohol addiction is much more prominent in men than in women. But it is everywhere.

Another reason you, as bishops, as "customers" of today's talk, need to know about alcoholism is—obviously—for your clergy. You are going to hear from Fr. David Carey later this afternoon from Guest House, describing addiction as an affliction that affects clergy. Thirdly, the topic of alcoholism is important for yourselves. General statistics are that 10% of priests have alcoholism, which is roughly the same as the general population. Alcoholism is simply a very prevalent condition in the laity and in the clergy.

Finally, I believe you have the need to know about the nature of alcoholism because it is prevalent in your families. I do know that physicians, nurses, clergy, and religious often come from families where there is a strong dysfunction, quite often alcoholism. For people who help other people, there is often a spiritual calling, but there is also a psychological set of variables that helped influence your choice. The spiritual calling was more important, but I know that many of you come from families where alcoholism has been significant. So this is a topic where I don't think I'm going to have any trouble holding your attention. So let's proceed.

Major Points

What are some of the highlights of my presentation—the big points I hope you will take away? My three main points are these: (1) the etiology of alcoholism is multi-factorial (2) the manifestations of alcoholism are multiple, and (3) the course of alcoholism over time is varied. So alcohol addiction waxes and wanes, it comes and goes, it looks different in different people, and it is caused by a lot of different things. If you say it is all caused by chemistry, that's wrong. If you say it is all caused by genetics, that's wrong. If you say it is all caused by neighborhoods, that's wrong. If you say it is all caused by families and spouses, that's wrong. If you say it is all caused by moral weakness, that's wrong. Alcoholism results from multiple factors that influence its onset and its progression (Morse, R.M., and D.K. Flavin).

Definitions and Terminology of Alcohol Addiction

I mentioned that terminology can be problematic, even among professionals. Let me try to walk you through a little bit of the jargon. The Diagnostic and Statistical Manual of the American Psychiatric Association, the D.S.M., (American Psychiatric Association) is the standard of nomenclature. The current edition is the fourth, the D.S.M.-IV. Addictive disorders are included in this manual, and that causes some controversy, because calling addiction a psychiatric problem is, and is not, a valid formulation. Under the general category of "substance related disorders," the D.S.M. describes substance use disorders, which are substance dependence *(see Figure 5)* and substance abuse *(see Figure 6),* as well as other conditions. Those other

Figure 5

Criteria for Substance Dependence

A maladaptive pattern of substance use, leading to clinically significant impairment or distress, as manifested by three (or more) of the following, occuring at any time in the same 12-month period:

(1) tolerance, as defined by either of the following:
  (a) a need for markedly increased amounts of the substance to achieve intoxication or desired effect
  (b) markedly diminished effect with continued use of the same amount of the substance
(2) withdrawal, as manifested by either of the following:
  (a) the characteristic withdrawal syndrome for the substance (refer to Criteria A and B of the criteria sets for Withdrawal from the specific substances)
  (b) the same (or a closely related) substance is taken to relieve or avoid withdrawal symptoms
(3) the substance is often taken in larger amounts or over a longer period then was intended
(4) there is a persistent desire or unsuccessful efforts to cut down or control substance use
(5) a great deal of time is spent in activities necessary to obtain the substance (e.g., chain-smoking), or recover from its effects
(6) important social, occupational, or recreational activites are given up or reduced because of substance use
(7) the substance use is continued despite knowledge of having a persistent or recurrent physical or psychological problem that is likely to have been caused or exacerbated by the substance (e.g., current cocaine use despite recognition of cocaine-induced depression, or continued drinking despite recognition that an ulcer was made worse by alcohol consumption)

Specify if:
With Physiological Dependence: evidence of tolerance or withdrawal (i.e., either Item 1 or Item 2 is present)
Without Physiological Dependence: no evidence or tolerance or withdrawal (i.e., neither Item 1 or Item 2 present)

---

substance-related disorders *(see Figure 7)* are intoxication, withdrawal, substance-induced psychiatric illness, and substance-induced physical illness. So alcohol can cause psychiatric problems, it can cause biomedical problems, it can cause intoxication, it can cause withdrawal—and none of those things is the syndrome of alcohol dependence, which is synonymous with the term alcohol addiction for our purposes today.

You will be graced tomorrow by hearing the coauthor of a paper from *JAMA* which provides a definition of alcoholism. Dr. Robert Morse from the Mayo Clinic was the cochair of a committee that worked in 1990 on developing a consensus among experts as to what is alcoholism.

Alcoholism is a disease. It is characterized by things that can occur either continuously or periodically. The features of alcoholism usually occur periodically; not often do the manifestations of alcoholism occur continuously. So what are these things that can occur every now and then, or much of the time, or even all the time? First, there is impaired control over drinking. Next, there is preoccupation with the drug alcohol. Next, there is the persis

Figure 6

Criteria for Substance Abuse

A. A maladaptive pattern of substance use leading to clinically significant impairment or distress, as manifested by one (or more) of the following, occurring within a 12-month period:

(1) recurrent substance use resulting in a failure to fulfill major role obligations at work, school, or home (e.g., repeated absences or poor work performance related to substance use; substance-related absences suspensions, or expulsion from school; neglect of children or household)

(2) recurrent substance use in situations in which it is physically hazardous (e.g., driving an automobile or operating a machine when impaired by substance use)

(3) recurrent substance-related legal problems (e.g., arrests for substance-related disorderly conduct)

(4) continued substance use despite having persistent or recurrent social or interpersonal problems caused or exacerbated by the effects of the subset (e.g., argument with spouse about consequences of intoxication, physical fights)

B. The symptoms have never met the criteria for Substance Dependence for this class of substance.

Figure 7

Substance Related Disorders

Substance Intoxication
Substance Withdrawal
Substance Induced Disorders
- Mental/Emotional
- Physical/Biomedical

tence of use despite adverse consequences. Next, there are distortions of thinking, most notably denial. I'm going to spend a little bit of time on each of these features, because of their importance.

So what is addiction? I think that the underlying process involves some sort of problem with satiation. The organism doesn't say, "I've had enough." The usual meters that would say "I've had enough" don't turn on. There's something wrong with satiety, something involved in the reward pathways we heard about this morning. But at its core, what separates the alcohol or drug addict from the nonaddict, is **impairment in control**. This is a concept that is very hard for people to understand if they have not experienced it themselves. The vast majority of the public—and, I would dare say, 96% of the people in this room— have no personal experience with loss of control over substance use. "Loss of control" doesn't make sense to you; it is not part of your experience. It is easier to think that it is fictional, because you haven't experientially been there. What an addict will tell you is, "I planned to have four, but I had twelve. I have no clue what happened." Usually they really don't have a clue as to what happened; it is not a 'cop-out' when they say this. Impairment of control does not specifically refer to whether they have the drink or not; it has to do with what happens when they drink and the ability to predict how much will be consumed and what the consequences will be. Loss of control occurs continuously or periodically. Early in the course of alcoholism it occurs in 10% of the use episodes: you drink ten times in a month, and one of those times you lose control, nine times you don't. Later, let's say in the middle stages of the disease, loss of control is experienced with about 40% of the use episodes. In advanced stages of alcohol addiction, loss of control occurs maybe seven out of ten times that the person drinks alcohol. Only rarely is loss of control experienced essentially every time the person samples alcohol.

Use despite adverse consequences can be described as "not heeding stop signs." A nonaddict, when experiencing problems from substance use, will change their use; if they have lots of problems, they will stop their use. "Duh!" as the youngsters say—it's not a very tough concept. It is the way normal organisms work: they learn from adverse consequences. We don't put our hand on the hot stove ten times; once is enough. But addicts tend to not heed the signs to stop behaviors that are detrimental to themselves and to their loved ones. It is puzzling and baffling to everyone around them, and it is puzzling and baffling to themselves—especially when their IQ is 150 and they know it is 150 and they say to themselves, "What am I doing acting like this?" I don't know the actor Robert Downey, Jr., whose case has been in the media recently. I have no idea what his moral structure is, but I bet that guy is just baffled. I mean, what has he thrown away through his substance use? And how many times does it take to learn and adapt one's behaviors based on previous negative consequences?

Denial is another central aspect of alcohol and other drug addictions, but it is also normal human experience. It is a psychological defense mechanism. Freud did a great job describing defense mechanisms. Human organisms don't like emotional pain. So if there is something that would tend to cause you to hurt, your mind takes steps so that you won't. You will deny it—tell yourself "It is not there." Or you will project it—tell yourself "It is them, it is not me." Or you will minimize it—tell yourself "It is not that bad." Or you will sublimate it, or rationalize it. Calling psychological defense processes "denial" is shorthand for a lot of mechanisms.

Let us consider a scenario that demonstrates how these aspects of alcoholism become intertwined. Say that you have been a priest for eight years. You've been successful in your parish, and your drinking is about to get you fired by your bishop. How does that make you feel? Awful. If you tell yourself it is not happening, you don't have pain. It is very simple. So the process that occurs is that the individual has problems due to drinking, continues to drink despite that, and—because of genetic vulnerabilities—he experiences loss of control periodically, and then tells himself that he doesn't have loss of control. Then what he does is to re-evaluate reality. The good things about drinking are overvalued. The bad things are minimized and denied. The fact that loss of control is periodic confirms for alcoholics that they're not alcoholic because they have control in 70% of their drinking episodes! "I can't be an alcoholic. I have control with 70% of my drinking episodes. What kind of numbers do you want?" he'll say.

Here is another puzzle. You will often experience, when you interact with an alcoholic, that they are lying to you. I encourage each of you to not take anything personally in such situations. Alcoholics are lying to themselves, because they do not want to hurt. So they tell themselves, "My wife isn't really going to leave. It is a bluff." Or, "I'll be able to scramble together the money for my taxes this year." Or, "My liver is really not all that bad." The First Step of AA says, "We admit that we are powerless and our life has become unmanageable." The life of the alcoholic is indeed unmanageable, and they may acknowledge it is unmanageable, but they will attribute it to something else. It takes a long time for the alcohol addict to say, "Yes, my life is unmanageable. And it is because of my drinking," which is the truth.

Next is a slide I put together a number of years ago on "the core features of alcoholism." It helped me understand things. I use it for teaching, and I'll use it for you today *(Figure 8)*. The first core feature I list is "loss of control"; the best term is "inconsistent control" or "loss of consistent control over use." The next core feature is "loss of ability to abstain." You stay away from it for three to six months and suddenly find yourself doing it again. Preoccupation with obtaining the substance, or with using the substance, comprises the next core feature. This includes a cognitive and a behavioral manifestation: you think about it a lot or you pursue it a lot. Next we have "substitution of use activities for other activities"; I call this "atrophy of other interests," whereas

Figure 8

Core Features of Alcoholism

1. Loss of consistent control over use.
2. Loss of ability to abstain.
3. Preoccupation with return to use.
4. Substitution of use activities for other activities (atrophy of other interests).
5. Restriction of social network to a using network (atrophy of a healthy peer group).
6. Atrophy of personal values - including honest and personal responsibility.
7. Atrophy of executive functions - including judgment, planning, priortization, and completion of tasks.
8. Biological markers (blackouts).
9. Inability to tolerate experiencing of feelings, with defensive reactions including denial and projection.
10. Defocusing from the need to work on addiction as the primary source of unmanageability.
11. Caretaking of others as a method of defocusing (not always present).
12. Genetic penetrance (positive family history).

some authors refer to this as "salience of alcohol-related behaviors." Thus, amongst the things you could do, your behavioral repertoire narrows down, and the thing that takes salience, takes prominence, is substance use activities. Next is "restriction of the social network" to a network dominated by substance users, which I call "atrophy of a healthy peer group." This involves salience of relationships with drinking buddies over all other people. Later in the list we find "atrophy of personal values," including honesty and personal responsibility, and "atrophy of executive functions," including judgment, planning, and the prioritizing and completion of tasks.

I list as another core feature of alcohol a biological marker of alcoholism: the alcohol "blackout." This phenomenon involves the individual being unable to remember things the next day after a drinking episode. It has to do with the brain's not being able to put down memory traces. The memory proteins are not made in the brain, and the memory is not stored. So the next day the alcoholic may not remember who called on the phone. There is 30 minutes gone, or 10 minutes, or 90 minutes, so you don't know how you got home, don't know where the car is, don't know where the car keys are, don't remember the date you had, don't remember the person you kissed, don't remember anything of that particular point in time. There is a gap in one's subjective experience. You can do a lot of things during this period of time that will not be recalled later. You are awake; you may or may not appear drunk to people around you. If someone asks, "Did you or did you not?" your honest answer is "I don't know." The important thing about blackouts is they are a biological marker: they are a physiological abnormality that can identify and foretell cases of alcoholism. Nonalcoholic sons of alcoholics may have blackouts.

When they have developed blackouts, their risk of developing alcoholism is increased. In your family, if you have a nephew or a great nephew who has an alcoholic dad, and this youngster at age 16 or 21 experiences blackouts after drinking, even if he is not alcoholic yet, he should be advised to become an abstainer.

Another core feature is positive family history, in which an enhanced genetic risk has come through. An important recent finding about the genetics of alcoholism has to do with another phenomenon: the ability to "handle one's alcohol." Male offspring of male alcoholics—even if they have not developed alcoholism yet themselves—tend to be able to drink without experiencing as many intoxicating effects as do their drinking buddies who do not have a positive family history. Those males who do manifest this ability to "handle" their drinks better are at increased risk of developing alcoholism later in life (Schuckit, M.A., and T.L. Smith). Again, advice is in order for such young men, for, as a group, we can say that the future for these men—who share with others both (a) this characteristic and (b) this type of family tree—is more likely to involve impairment of control over alcohol use, an inability to abstain, persistence of use despite adverse consequences, etc.

Other core features of alcoholism include the inability to tolerate the experiencing of feelings, resulting in defensive reactions which may include denial and projection, as well as defocusing from the need to work on addiction as a primary source of one's unmanageability.

Control and Will

If I might digress a bit, I'd like to reflect on some comments from this morning's speakers. People frequently confuse problems due to substance use and problems due to substance addiction. One gets blamed for the other. As one author so succinctly put it, "In the public eye drug dependence equals illegal drug use ..." (Terenius, L.). This morning, Dr. Haas welcomed us and presented us with an overview of the program and then described the benefits of temperance. "You should establish well-ordered use," he said, "not nonuse." I am not trying to pick on Dr. Haas for his views on this matter, but relevant to all this is that there are two syndromes which are quite different. One is called substance dependence, and the other is called substance abuse (and the terminology has changed in the last twenty years, which makes it all the more confusing at times) (Kosten, T.A.). Addiction is what's now called substance dependence, and that's what involves loss of control. Substance abuse is use despite problems, and that is the totality of that condition. Someone experiencing drunk driving incidents, or someone who strikes somebody while under the influence, or somebody who keeps on using despite having problems from use, but who does not necessarily have loss of control, is said to have the syndrome of substance-abuse. The issues of culpability are really different, in my opinion, between substance dependence, which is a biological illness, and substance abuse, where the biological substrate is less clear. To suggest well-established, well-ordered use, one needs to be clear as to whether one is recommending this for individuals with substance abuse or for individuals with substance dependence. There has been an argument in the alcoholism treatment field for decades about whether one can or should teach controlled use to people. My experience is that teaching controlled use to a nonaddict with substance abuse is not an unreasonable process. They have the ability to control use, and you can teach them coping skills and behavior methods. But trying to teach controlled use to an addict is almost an oxymoron, because they have a physiologic defect in control which cannot be reconditioned through psychological or behavioral means. We can speak about "hoarding, grasping, self-indulgence," and how destructive these are. I would concur. But these features can be isolated problems, recurrent problems, or manifestations of addiction.

Use and choice: free will has a lot to do with use. But once addiction develops, the situation becomes different. Choice and free will may not be the sole explanation for persistent use in the addict. As Dr. Lukas said in his presentation this morning, there are different factors involved in initiating use and in continuing use, and I will go into some detail about this in the last sections of my presentation. But later this morning, Father Giertych presented a fascinating paper in which he spoke about will, and this brings to mind the whole issue of "willful misconduct" in alcoholics. You may remember the story in the news several years ago when either Congress or somebody in the executive branch described alcoholism as "willful misconduct," and disability benefits were summarily denied for alcoholics. The matter went to the U.S. Supreme Court. The justices did not rule that alcoholism was not a disease. The Court said that the civil servants who wrote the regulations had the right to draft regulations with any kind of language they wanted: if they wanted to say alcoholism was willful misconduct, it was not unconstitutional for them to use such phrases when they were trying to express the intent of the Congress, whether it be scientifically accurate or not. But still, today, alcoholics are discriminated against in more ways than I could ever mention. For example, they can not get Social Security disability benefits. You can get disability benefits for defective hearts, lungs, diabetes, or other bodily dysfunction. But if it is alcoholism, forget it!

Addicts want it all! Don't we all? Even if you have a very wonderful spiritual life and understand the difference between ultimate good and earthly good, you're still human, and as a human being, you want it all. That's just the way we're made—just as the Adam and Eve story depicts it. What happens with addicts is that they end up misdirected because of their beliefs and judgments, manifesting the thinking problems mentioned in the ASAM-NCA definition (Morse, R.M., and D.K. Flavin). Number One, they believe they can have it all. Number Two, they pursue having it all. Number Three, even if they don't have anything, they may think they have it all. Alcoholics simply want what nonaddicts have: they want to be controlled drinkers so they can enjoy all the positive aspects of alcohol (like most of us enjoyed last night) with none of the negative aftereffects. Addicts want all the goodies and none of the baddies. It takes them a long time, lots of pain, and lots of trouble in their lives for them to finally accept they can not have it their way. Many who achieve acceptance lose sight of it and revert to former patterns of thinking and behaving anyway. But do they manifest willful misconduct? No, they don't will to be addicts. A kid picking up a cigarette doesn't will to be on a ventilator. A drinker doesn't want cirrhosis or dementia. A heroin addict doesn't will to get hepatitis. A heroin addict wants to get high. They don't want to be an addict. They are convinced they won't become an addict. So addiction is not aspired to by anyone.

Father Giertych writes in this volume about substance abuse being repeated use, and states that repeated use is a neurotic pursuit of an altered emotional state. Substance use is a pursuit of an altered state. It can be neurotic to see that state as a reasonable good that should be pursued, but it doesn't necessarily constitute addiction.

A lot of our problems with street crime and the like are attributable to substance abusers. Some of them are addicts and some of them aren't. I'm not going to suggest that this is easy to clarify, or that it is easy to develop social policy, medical policy, or medical morality. It is not. But as we try, it is important to maintain clear thinking about the distinctions between "substance abuse" and addiction.

Summary of the Definition of Alcoholism

Now back to my original outline. The ASAM-NCADD definition of alcoholism (Morse, R.M., and D.K. Flavin) as crafted by Morse et al. attests that addiction is a primary illness. It is not secondary to something else. Somebody may use substances because of sadness, loneliness, or anxiety; substance use may be secondary to such states. But to say that addiction is secondary to psychopathology is generally not accurate. Alcohol addiction is a primary disease; other things are secondary. One distinction is that in women, depression is usually primary and alcoholism is secondary, whereas in men, it is generally the rule that alcoholism is primary and depression is secondary. Depression comes later, when alcoholics begin losing things in their lives, which saddens them.

Alcohol addiction is a chronic illness, usually progressive. It is a behavior disorder. The behaviors to seek, pursue, and consume persist despite problems. It is appropriate to understand alcoholism as a behavior disorder: you cannot have active alcoholism unless you engage in the behavior of drinking! (Parenthetically, I do believe you can have alcoholism and never have been a drinker. I say this because alcoholism involves having a biological defect in your brain reward pathways. If you never challenge those pathways

183

with molecules of ethanol, you'll never know what would occur with your behavior were you to expose your brain to ethanol.) For the condition to be expressed and active, you have got to drink! When alcoholics drink, they will periodically lose control, and problems will happen in their lives. It is a bio-psycho-social-spiritual condition: it involves physiology, thinking, feeling, acting, relationships, and your connectedness to the transcendent. All of the above are involved in the consequences of loss of control, inability to maintain abstinence over time, preoccupation, and use-despite-consequences. I think you now know the definition of addiction.

More on the Features of Alcohol Addiction

Now on to other features. We have discussed the cognitive changes, wherein the addict rethinks things, or makes erroneous evaluations of his or her life or false attributions regarding the source of life difficulties. As mentioned, "the goodies" of use will be overemphasized (the euphoric effects of the substance, the social aspects of using) and "the baddies" will be deemphasized.

Tolerance and withdrawal used to be thought necessary for a diagnosis of alcoholism or alcohol dependence. If a person didn't have tolerance or withdrawal, they were given the diagnosis of "abuse," not "dependence" (Kosten, T.A.). We now know that's really not the proper way to look at it. The current view says you can have dependence with or without the physiologic signs of tolerance and withdrawal *(see Figure 5)*.

In general, half of alcoholics have physical symptoms of tolerance and withdrawal. Half of alcoholics (the people with loss of control, the people with the problem of not maintaining abstinence consistently) don't have physiologic tolerance and physiologic withdrawal.

So we have done the DSM-IV criteria *(see Figure 5)* and the definition written conjointly by ASAM and the National Council on Alcoholism. I know that you may not care whether the condition is abuse or dependence, an academic distinction to some extent. I know that nonaddicts who use despite problems go on to cause more problems in their families and in your congregations. Whether it is abuse or dependence, it is still a challenge to you in your multiple roles. Alcohol dependence remains an intriguing illness; it affects about 6% of the adult population of America; addiction to alcohol plus other drugs affects about 10%. But even though alcoholism is a very prevalent condition, there are other problems that are not just alcohol addiction. It is a continuum.

We do know that it generally takes a long time for alcoholism to develop. You heard that this morning. It can take thirty years. It can take ten years. In women it takes less time, overall. With early onset alcoholics, the boys who start drinking at twelve and fourteen, the addiction to alcohol develops much

Figure 9

Functional Continuum
- abstinence
- use
- regular use
- problem use
- regular misuse ("SUBSTANCE ABUSE")
- habituation
- compulsion
- physical dependence
- ADDICTION
- chronic physical complications
- chronic psychological complications
- permanent disability
- incompetence

quicker: it can develop in five years. So age of onset of use is extremely important.

Figure 9 summarizes that continuum. We can go from abstinence, to use, to regular use, to problem use, to regular misuse, to habituation and compulsive use, to physical dependence, to addiction, to chronic complications, and all the way to disability and complete mental incompetence requiring legal guardianship. Those who are permanently disabled comprise about 3% of alcoholics; 97% of alcoholics never become totally disabled by the disease. There are various factors which appear to provide protection against progression to disability. College education is one. The socioeconomic status of college graduates gives them some protection from really hitting bottom, as may happen to a working-class person. The age of onset of addiction is later in life for college-educated alcoholics vs. working-class alcoholics. (This comes from the studies of the natural history of alcoholism, by Dr. George Vaillant from Harvard (Vaillant, 1983), which I'll go over in more detail later this afternoon.) One of the more fascinating observations of Vaillant's work (Vaillant, 1998) is that problems still wax and wane in alcoholics who have college degrees, maybe because of some level of "protection" imbued by social status. You, as bishops, probably have an average of three college degrees each. You folks are the equivalent of CEOs, correct? You're high in the socioeconomic scale. You don't have all the materialistic stuff that people in business do, but your status, success, and talents make you high-level executives. So you enjoy the same level of sociological "protection" from addiction as do other executives. Once you develop addiction, however ... well, more on the Grim Reaper later.

The general statistics are that two-thirds of American adults consume, and one-third are total abstainers from alcohol. You hear a lot about habituation: "Can you change that habit?" You can change habits, but in addicts there's something else going on chemically. The biochemical processes happening in addicts down at the level of the nucleus accumbens and the dopamine that you heard about this morning are not subject to conditioning or re-learning. Part of all this has to do with something that's beyond the level of this talk; it is called unconscious craving. We're beginning to learn about unconscious craving. Conscious craving says, "I'm hungry for a drink," and I'm aware of that drug hunger. In unconscious craving, your deep brain structures chemically want to have a molecule fit into their receptors, but up at the level of your cerebral cortex, you don't think about it. This silent craving, that you have no conscious thoughts about, is a very scary phenomenon. Addicts have unconscious craving. The only thing you can make them aware of is what alcoholism is, and why total abstinence is important.

Types of Alcoholics

What are the different types of alcoholism? Jellinek wrote a very famous book in 1960, (Jellinek, E.M.) describing five types of alcoholics, though we won't go over all that today. When you came here you probably had an idea of what an addict was in general. You had an idea of what a crack addict was— you had a mental image, and I would guess your mental model of a crack addict did not include "white" and "employed." Similarly, you probably had an idea of what an alcoholic was, and maybe your model was of someone sloppy or rude or irresponsible. Most likely you thought of intoxication, and you thought of somebody that you had seen repeatedly intoxicated. Well, about fifteen years ago, Dr. Robert Cloninger from Washington University in St. Louis described Type I and Type II alcoholics (Cloninger, 1996). The validity of his typology is still debated. Cloninger's model describes a subset of alcoholics—roughly half of alcoholics—who are very hard-working and over-responsible; Jellinek had described this variant as well. Cloninger called these folks Type I alcoholics; individuals in this group can be male or female. Type I alcoholics tend to be filled with guilt and shame. Numerous workaholics are in this group. They're very responsible, and they often end up with a deep-seated fear of failure, fear of disaffecting people, and with a profound self-loathing. Type I alcoholics are plagued with guilt and shame, they feel awful, and they feel like you're going to yell at them like so many others have.

One of the things I do in my professional life is take care of patients. When I take care of alcoholic patients, there are a lot of things that I'm supposed to be doing in my medical role, but I know that one of the most important things for me to do is to love them. It is most important for me to do nothing that will amplify their self-loathing, because they've got an overabundance of self-loathing already.

Type I alcoholics *(see Figure 10)* are said to have high "reward dependence," high "harm avoidance," and low "risk taking." Dr. Cloninger defined those variables (Cloninger, 1996) and contrasted their appearance in his Type

Figure 10

Type I Alcoholism
- male and female
- hard-working/over-responsible
- filled with guilt and shame
- fearful and self-loathing
- high "reward dependence"
- high "harm avoidance"
- low "risk-taking"
- onset at any age
- relapsing and remitting
- good treatment response

Figure 11

Type II Alcoholism
- 25% of all alcoholics
- almost all male
- strong father-son genetics
- early onset
- rule-breaking (criminal)
- rapid progression
- low "harm avoidance"
- low "reward dependence"
- high novelty-seeking
- little guilt, fear, or remorse
- antisocial/irresponsible
- high rate of physical dependence
- poorer work record
- poorer treatment response

I and Type II subtypes of alcoholics. "Reward dependence" refers to the extent to which one feels an emotional boost from a positive event: good things make people with high "reward dependence" feel better, and they may shift focus in their lives to seek out positive emotional rewards from others. Good things can "fill up" emotional deficits or needs within, and alcoholics often have big emotional holes inside. They can also be people-pleasers who try to make themselves feel better by making others feel better. Booze can be seen by them as emotionally rewarding and will be pursued to "fill up" their sense of emotional emptiness. Next, Type I alcoholics are said to have high "harm avoidance." They're scared! They tend not to be risk taking. The Type I alcoholism described by Cloninger can have its onset at any age; it tends to come and go (remit and relapse) through the life span; and it tends to respond to treatment well. Hazelden and similar treatment centers were made for these people; traditional treatment (M.M. Miller) has helped thousands and thousands of Type I alcoholics. Guest House also works ideally for Type I's. Type

I's comprise 75% of alcoholics. About 80% of Type I alcoholics are males and about 20% are females.

Type II alcoholism *(see Figure 11)* has a much earlier onset in the life cycle, usually appearing in the early to mid-teens. The Type II subtype described by Cloninger is almost exclusively male. There are very strong father-to-son genetics. These people have lots of sociopathic tendencies: they break rules at a very early age. The disease progresses rapidly, and is more continuously manifest through the life cycle. Type II individuals have low "harm avoidance": they are afraid of hardly anything. They have low "reward dependence": nice things won't fill them up emotionally. Warm fuzzies don't do a lot for them; they'll make gestures with their fingers at warm fuzzies! These individuals can almost at times look a little psychopathic. They tend to be very novelty seeking, with little guilt, fear, or remorse. They tend to be antisocial, irresponsible, with poor work records, and a poor treatment response. Cloninger also notes that they have high rates of physical dependence, which means that Type II alcoholics manifest tolerance and withdrawal more commonly than do Type I alcoholics.

Type II alcoholics can cause lots of social problems, and not just absenteeism at work. They break laws. They beat their spouses. They're bad actors overall in general. Now we get to the issue of people's attitudes about alcoholics, the "unlikeability" of many alcoholics. It is because of the unpleasantness and intransigence of Type II alcoholics that most people don't like alcoholics: they think of all alcoholics as the antisocial, irresponsible Type II. But seventy-five percent of alcoholics aren't this type. Type I alcoholics are ashamed and try to hide their alcoholism; but Type II's don't bother to hide it. They screw up and they don't care what you think about them! So Type II's are very transparent in their dysfunction, whereas Type I's tend to try to be very hidden and secretive—the "closet alcoholic," for example the alcoholic housewife who hides her problems, or the alcoholic clergy person. Type I alcoholics certainly can experience problems and can create problems—impaired work performance, infidelity, or domestic violence. But they're very remorseful once they sober up and look at what they've done, and their remorse is sincere.

Occurrence of Alcoholism

Next we will try to examine "Who has alcoholism?" and "How much alcoholism is out there?" There are two types of frequency statistics: prevalence and incidence.

Prevalence is the measure of the rate of occurrence of a condition in a population. How much of it is out there? The answer depends on the time window in which one examines the population. The prevalence in one month is the number of persons who, when examined in this month, meet criteria for alcohol addiction, current or past. If one-year prevalence is measured, more people will meet diagnostic criteria. If one measures across the entire life span of the individual—lifetime prevalence—one measures the occurrence in that person at any age, i.e., whether he/she meets the diagnostic criteria in youth, or middle years, or only during senior years.

Incidence is the measure of the rate of development of new cases in a population: the rate of appearance of the illness. Alcoholism appears in the population and it disappears in the population. During the teenage years six per thousand will develop alcoholism. During the next decade of life three per thousand will develop it. By age 30 there will not be as many new cases developing. There can be new cases developing in the 30s, 40s, 60s, and 70s. (Onset in the senior age groups is a very different kind of syndrome than early-onset or midlife-onset alcohol addiction.) Much alcoholism, and virtually all of Type II alcoholism, begins in the early adult years or younger.

What's the rate of disappearance of alcoholism? Two percent of active cases vanish every year. They can vanish by the person dying or by the person getting well. Statistics on the rate of disappearance of cases include those disappearing due to treatment, those occurring spontaneously without treatment, and those occurring due to mortality. So alcohol addiction appears and it disappears.

Figure 12 shows prevalence of use. Is it problem use, or is it abuse, or is it addiction? Now use itself can be a problem; I expect this will be in Dr. Morse's talk tomorrow. Use of a dirty needle a single time can cause HIV transmission. Use of an inhalant by a teenager a single time can cause a cardiac arrhythmia and death. Use can be a really bad thing even in the absence of addiction. With alcohol, for instance, a single instance of use can lead to a car being driven into a tree—you're dead, okay? So use can be bad. The preceding example is a public health issue, but it is not necessarily addiction.

Figure 12

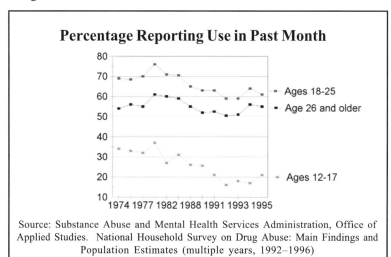

Percentage Reporting Use in Past Month

Source: Substance Abuse and Mental Health Services Administration, Office of Applied Studies. National Household Survey on Drug Abuse: Main Findings and Population Estimates (multiple years, 1992–1996)

Figure 13

Prevalence of Alcoholism

(estimates from various studies)

Lifetime Prevalence - will manifest active disease (meet diagnostic criteria) at some point during one's lifetime

Annual Prevalence - will manifest active disease within the one-year time-frame under study

6-month Prevalence - will manifest active disease within a given 6-month time-frame

1-month Prevalence - will manifest active disease within a given 30-day time-frame

	Males	Females	Combined
Study 1			
Lifetime Prevalence	24.0 %	5.0 %	14.0 %
6-month Prevalence	12.0 %	2.0 %	5.0 %
1-month Prevalence			3.0 %
Study 2			
Lifetime Prevalence—Dependence	20.0 %	8.0 %	
Lifetime Prevalence—Abuse	13.0 %	6.0 %	
1-Year Prevalence—Dependence	11.0 %	4.0 %	
1-Year Prevalence—Abuse	4.0 %	2.0 %	
Study 3			
1-Year Prevalence—Dependence	6.0 %	2.0%	
1-Year Prevalence—Abuse	5.0 %	2.0 %	
Study 4			
Lifetime Prevalence if in stable marriage		9.0 %	
Lifetime Prevalence if cohabitating outside of marriage		29.0 %	

Other Studies
Males with alcoholic father: 3X lifetime prevalence compared with nonalcoholic biological father

But getting back to prevalence statistics for alcoholism in American adults, let me attempt to summarize the data in *Figure 13* and just say that in general, about 12% of males and about 3% of females will develop active alcoholism in their lifetime, averaging out to 6% of the public. The prevalence amongst male offspring of Type II alcoholics is closer to 60%, however. So the genetic issues with regard to Type II alcoholism are profound.

A Brief Look at Cultural Influences

In genetics, scientists distinguish between genotypes and phenotypes. The genotype is the internal genetic makeup; the phenotype is manifested externally in organisms as they develop in their environment. An individual will not manifest alcoholism externally unless he or she drinks! If you have a nonalcoholic genotype and you drink, you'll simply be a drinker (the statistics will show that there is a case of alcohol use). If you have an alcoholic genotype and you drink, you may experience loss of control and you may develop alcoholism, because of the way your constitution is set (and the statistics would then show that there is a case of alcohol addiction). The prevalence of addiction in the population is a function of consumption, which is a behavior under a variety of environmental/cultural influences. The more the population consumes, the higher the addiction rates will be in that population. If a society raises taxes on alcohol, you'll see a reduction in consumption, and addiction rates go down. These patterns have been studied by sociologists and economists worldwide for years, for different substances, and at different points in history, such as during World War II, during Prohibition in the U.S., etc.

So to illustrate in the case of another kind of addiction, what are the implications for the debate about legalizing marijuana? If you legalize it, there will be more addiction—because the base rate of addiction genotypes in the population is set, and if there is increased availability and if there are decreased social proscriptions against use, use will increase (among both addict and nonaddict genotypes), and the number of phenotypically-expressed addicts will increase. Does that mean you shouldn't do it, or you should do it, or whatever? There are other reasons for evaluating the complex question of drug policy and whether marijuana should be decriminalized; but we need to keep in mind the truism that the base rate of addiction in the population is a function of how much consumption of a substance there is.

Another relevant cultural topic is the role of advertising and the capitalist drive on the rate of substance addiction in a population. You saw the slides this morning regarding advertising for alcoholic beverages. I've attended two-hour presentations on the effects of advertising on alcohol consumption. Advertising is needed to generate customers for alcohol beverage makers. Remember that two-thirds of Americans drink, but 90% of Americans don't have alcoholism. But half of all the beverage alcohol in America is consumed by alcohol addicts. Anheuser Busch, Miller Brewing, Seagram's Distillery and the like would not be able to generate revenues and maintain their corporate existence if they were not supplying addicts. Of course, direct advertising to influence alcohol addicts to purchase alcohol is part of this business. You can ponder the morality of that these issues if you choose. I am just sharing with you the facts. Half of all the alcohol sold in America is sold to addicts, to alcoholics! Alcohol marketing must therefore target and appeal to the alcohol addicts in our culture to be commercially efficacious.

Initiation and Continuation of Use and Addiction

One of the things we heard this morning is that initiation of use, continuation, cessation, and resumption of use after a period of abstinence all depend on certain factors *(see Figure 14)*. There is overlap in these factors, but some sort out into different categories. Whether or not somebody develops addiction depends on factors, some of which can be in the person, some in the substance used, or some in the sociocultural environment in which the person uses substances *(see Figure 15)*. So the host (the person consuming the substance) and agent (the substance consumed) and their environment (the

Figure 14

Initiation of Use -	Cessation of Use -
►Availability	► Negative Effects of Agent
►Cost	► Use-Incompatible Behaviors
►Cultural Attitudes	► Behavioral Contingencies
►Approval/Proscription/Taboos	► Supervision/Monitoring
►Personality Traits/Styles	
►Low Harm Avoidance	**Onset of Addiction -**
►High Novelty Seeking	► Personal Vulnerabilities
►Comorbid Drug Use Disorder	► Continuation of Use
	► Genetic Risk
	► Cultural Instability
Continuation of Use -	
► Reward/Reinforcement	**Progression of Addiction -**
► Peer Influences	► Genetic Risk
► Occupation	► Social/Cultural Approval
► Personality Traits/Styles	
► High Reward Dependence	

Figure 15

	Remission of Addiction -
	► Productive Daily Activity
Onset of Addiction -	► Supportive Living Environment
► Personal Vulnerabilities	► New Culture/Social Network
► Continuation of Use	► Prolonged Cessation of Use
► Genetic Risk	
► Cultural Instability	**Relapse of Addiction -**
	► Genetic Risk
	► Conscious Craving
Progression of Addiction -	► Unconscious Craving
► Genetic Risk	► Triggers
► Social/Cultural Approval	► Conditional Cues
	► Negative Affective States

context) all affect whether or not addiction will develop (see the Morse and Flavin article in JAMA (Morse, R.M., and D.K. Flavin) once again).

Looking at the "agent factors" *(see Figure 16),* there are certain things in the molecule of the substance, whether it is cocaine, nicotine, or ethanol, that affect addiction potential. Also, there are certain things about the route of administration that affect whether or not the user develops addiction to the substance. You heard this morning that the smoking and "snorting" intranasally delivers a drug to the brain in seven seconds; intravenous administration gets the agent to the brain in ten seconds; taking the agent orally gets it to the brain in 30 minutes or so. So the schedule of reinforcement, the route of administration, and the frequency of dosing of the reinforcer all make a difference. Environmental factors include all sorts of cultural issues, such as whether or not the culture says it is okay to use. The base rate of alcoholism in Saudi Arabia is very low, largely because the culture says alcohol use is absolutely not okay. Host factors are largely genetically determined. They include gender, personality style, and psychiatric co-morbidities. It is thought that maybe one of the reasons that women have more trouble with alcohol is that they don't have a particular kind of metabolic enzyme called alcohol dehydrogenase (ADH) in the lining of their stomachs. So men have this big "filter," such that when they drink alcohol, it enters the stomach, and gastric alcohol dehydrogenase in the men will break it down and the ethanol will never get absorbed. In women, who lack the filtering effects of gastric alcohol dehydrogenase, the molecules of ethanol reach the small intestine directly and get absorbed. The result is that serum alcohol levels rise in women after drinking to a greater magnitude than occurs in men of comparable body size who drink the same amounts. Therefore, the woman gets more alcohol to her brain than a man of similar body weight. Also, there can be more organ toxicity from 200 drinks per month in a woman than in a man, because of these genetically driven gender differences in alcohol metabolism.

A "host factor" *(see Figure 17)* which has been determined to be significant in the question of the presences of addiction is whether the patient has a psychiatric problem. The coexistence of a psychiatric disorder and an addictive disorder is referred to as a psychiatric co-morbidity with the addiction (or an addiction co-morbidity with a psychiatric disorder). The coexistence of these two types of conditions is also referred to as "dual diagnosis." In Type II alcoholism the antecedent psychiatric co-morbidity is most likely antisocial personality disorder, a condition which in itself does predispose the individual to addiction. In Type I alcoholism, psychopathology is a generally a consequence of addiction, not an antecedent. So this is a major issue. Alcoholics tend to be anxious. In general, alcoholics can't cope well, alcoholics are sad, alcoholics don't have good executive functions. But these aren't predisposing factors. Alcoholics can have bad marriages, but this isn't a predisposing factor. One of the great quotes I have read says that alcoholism causes bad marriages a lot more than bad marriages cause alcoholism. This really is true, in my clinical experience—but of course the alcoholic blames the spouse because that's the thinking pattern of alcoholics that protects the addict from emotional pain.

Depression, in female alcoholics, is generally a primary condition (that is, it precedes alcoholism), and it is associated with an improved prognosis!

Do not ask me why, but it is fascinating, and it is true: a woman going into alcoholism treatment with major depression has a better prognosis, in general, than a woman without major depression. Depression, in male alcoholics, is generally a secondary condition (that is, it follows alcoholism). In fact, male alcoholics, in general, tend to develop secondary depression. They're morose, possibly they've lost their money, they've lost their physical health,

Figure 16

Agent Factors
Availability
Intrinsic Addiction Potential
Route of Administration
Absorption

Figure 17

Host Factors
Genetic risk
Gender
Metabolism
Gastric ADH
Hepatic ADH
Personality style
Harm avoidance
Novelty seeking
Reward dependence
Psychiatric co-morbidities

Figure 18

Environmental Factors
Cultural Variables
Use with food/eating rituals
Use within religious rituals
Peer Influence
Socioeconomics
Recovery Environments
(availability; stress; domestic violence)

they've lost their life partner, they've lost their job—and they may kill themselves. Secondary depression in a middle-aged male alcoholic priest, especially one with physical problems as well—that can be dangerous!

Here's another host factor we should mention—the co-morbidity of addiction. This is kind of one of those "Duh" items, so obvious, but still often ignored: being a drug addict makes it more likely you'll drink and being an alcoholic makes it more likely you'll use drugs. Those are factors influencing alcohol use and progression of alcoholism—and being a nicotine addict makes it more likely that you'll be an alcohol addict or addicted to another drug. The prevalence of alcohol dependence is 7% in the general population, but among drug addicts it is 47%. The prevalence of drug dependence is 6% in the general population, but among alcohol addicts the prevalence of drug addiction is 21% (Crum, R.M.).

Here's an interesting irony: the factors influencing stopping alcoholism may be the same factors influencing progression of alcoholism. This differs from the pattern with other diseases: if you have lots of factors for heart disease, it increases your chance of mortality due to heart disease. But if you have lots of factors leading to drinking, this may lessen your chance of mortality due to drinking! You may get well because, maybe, finally, the "stop signs" just overwhelm you. The usual pattern is that the stop signs do not overwhelm the alcoholic, but they overwhelm the people in the alcoholic's social network. The social network goes, "Knock, knock, knock, there's a problem here! Lots of problems, okay?" It is the nonaddicts who complain; the addict is the last one to know there's something greatly amiss—as you heard this morning.

People start using alcohol because their peers do, because it is available, because it is cheap *(see Figure 18)*. But why do they stop using? One of the reasons people stop using is because of what are referred to as "use-incompatible behaviors." Being a college student is not incompatible with being a drug or alcohol user and with being frequently intoxicated; but through normal development people acquire life chores that are incompatible with drinking—a first full-time job, then a spouse, then a mortgage. So as we go through normal human development, we acquire more use-incompatible behaviors, and drinking levels tend to drop. Going to a seminary is not terribly compatible with substance use or frequent intoxication: it does happen that people drink bigtime in seminaries, but it is not a good fit. That fact that it is not a good fit makes it easier to stop drinking or using drugs. It is very hard to stop drinking on the University of Wisconsin-Madison campus—the Number One binge-drinking campus in America.

Other factors affecting cessation of use, other than use-incompatible behaviors, include supervision and monitoring, and behavioral contingencies. You're getting a whole talk later in this symposium on behavioral contingencies and coercion—that's a really important topic. Linking together "carrots" and "sticks" is extremely important in changing this behavior.

Natural History and Mortality of Alcoholism

The Natural History of Alcoholism by Dr. George Vaillant from Harvard, is a wonderful, not-too-technical, book (Vaillant, G.E., 1983), understandable by all. Vaillant compared Harvard undergraduates with age-matched working-class Boston males, and followed them from the onset of his study in the 1940s to the 1980s. College-educated males, like yourselves here, have onset of alcoholism later in life than do blue-collar males who develop alcoholism *(see Figure 19)*; but college-educated male alcoholics are less likely to fully remit and become total abstainers than a comparable cohort of inner-city males. This may be because college-educated males are insulated from negative social consequences. The Harvard educated alcoholics didn't end up in detox centers, didn't end up losing their jobs. They sure as heck were alcoholics, and they sure as heck died from their addictive disease. They just died ten years later than the working-class cohort.

So to wrap up: What kills alcoholics? Most of you would say cirrhosis or something else like that. But our final slide shows that forty-five percent of alcoholics die from accidents, homicide, and suicide, and only ten percent die from cirrhosis. Forty-five percent of alcoholics die from heart disease, but probably 40% of that 45% is tobacco-related heart disease. My guess is that only around 5% of the 45% is alcohol cardiomyopathy or an alcohol arrhythmia. Nicotine is the Number One killer of alcoholics. I'll repeat that: the

Figure 19

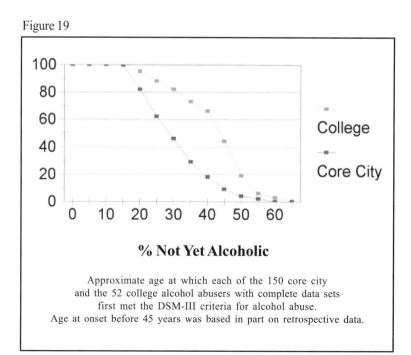

% Not Yet Alcoholic

Approximate age at which each of the 150 core city
and the 52 college alcohol abusers with complete data sets
first met the DSM-III criteria for alcohol abuse.
Age at onset before 45 years was based in part on retrospective data.

Number One cause of premature deaths in alcoholics isn't alcohol, it is nicotine.

Roughly 15% of all alcoholics die via suicide, and roughly 15% of all suicides occur in alcoholics. Alcohol addiction is a lethal disease, even in the absence of co-morbid major depressive disorder. We have been acculturated to laugh about drunks on TV shows and in stage plays. But alcohol addiction is a very, very lethal disease.

References

American Psychiatric Association 1994. *Diagnostic and Statistical Manual of Mental Disorders, 4th ed. (DSM-IV)*. Washington, DC: American Psychiatric Press.

Cloninger, C.R. 1981. Inheritance of alcohol abuse. *Archives of General Psychiatry* 38: 861–68.

_____. (1996). Type I and Type II alcoholism: an update. *Alcohol Health and Research World* 20: 30–35.

_____. (1987). Neurogenic adaptive mechanisms in alcoholism. *Science* 236: 410–16.

Crum, R.M. 1998. The epidemiology of addictive disorders. In *Principles of Addiction Medicine.* 2nd ed. A.W. Graham and T.D. Schultz, eds. Chevy Chase, MD: American Society of Addiction Medicine.

Jellinek, E.M. 1960. *The Disease Concept of Alcoholism.* New Haven, CT: Hillhouse Press.

Kosten, T.A., and S.A. Ball 1998. Diagnostic classification systems. In *Principles of Addiction Medicine.* 2nd ed. A.W. Graham and T.D. Schultz, eds. Chevy Chase, MD: American Society of Addiction Medicine.

Leschner, A.I. 1998. What we know: Addiction is a brain disease. In *Principles of Addiction Medicine.* 2nd ed. A.W. Graham and T.D. Schultz, eds. Chevy Chase, MD: American Society of Addiction Medicine.

Miller, M.M. 1998. Traditional approaches to the treatment of addiction. In *Principles of Addiction Medicine.* 2nd ed. A.W. Graham and T.D. Schultz, eds. Chevy Chase, MD: American Society of Addiction Medicine.

Morse R.M., and D.K. Flavin 1992. The definition of alcoholism. *JAMA* 268: 1012–14.

O'Brien, C.P. 1997. Progress in the science of addiction. *American Journal of Psychiatry* 154: 1195–97.

O'Brien C.P., and A.T. McLellan 1966. Myths about the treatment of addiction. *Lancet* 347: 237–40.

Schuckit, M.A., and T.L. Smith 1996. Eight-year follow-up of 450 sons of alcoholic and control subjects. *Archives of General Psychiatry* 53: 202–10.

Terenius, L. 1998. Rational treatment of addiction. *Current Opinion in Chemical Biology* 2: 541–47.

Vaillant, G.E. 1983. *The Natural History of Alcoholism.* Cambridge, MA: Harvard University Press.

_____. 1996. A long-term follow-up of male alcohol abuse. *Archives of General Psychiatry* 53: 243–49.

_____. 1998. Natural history of addiction and pathways to recovery. In *Principles of Addiction Medicine.* 2nd. ed. A.W. Graham and T.D. Schultz, eds. Chevy Chase, MD: American Society of Addiction Medicine.

THE BIOLOGICAL BASES OF CHEMICAL DEPENDENCIES

SCOTT E. LUKAS, PH.D.

Definitions, Terms, Concepts

Terms like "addiction" and "addict" have long outlived their usefulness. They are often used to judge an individual's character, implying that the subject is "weak willed" or has a character flaw. *Abuse liability* and *dependence potential* are more accurate terms as they convey the more fundamental notion that individuals can engage in certain types of behaviors that are reinforcing, resulting in their continued use. Further, chronic use can lead to biochemical and physiological changes in the brain and body that cause a withdrawal syndrome when the drug is stopped.

It is important to realize that drug abuse is fundamentally a brain disease. Continued use of drugs changes the brain in basic and long-lasting ways. These biological changes occur at the neuron, cellular, and molecular level, and collectively they cause compulsive behaviors that recur multiple times. Drugs are taken repetitively because there are reward circuits in the brain that affect a number of emotions. Drug use induces mood states like euphoria, feeling "high," and craving. All of these mood states are pleasing, and so the drug-taking behavior is repeated. The fact that common mechanisms in the brain are triggered by every major chemical that is abused suggests that there is a common pathway in the brain that is responsible for modulating these positive mood states. However, whether or not chemical dependency develops is controlled by many other factors such as the environment, history/ experience, physiology, and genetics.

From an etiologic point of view, the "cycle" of drug abuse can be illustrated by the graph depicted in Figure 1. The "drug-taking" event is central to the concept of chemical dependence, as it serves as the focal point that has a clear set of antecedent behaviors and physiological and behavioral consequences that can be independently studied in the laboratory. The concept of "reinforcement" is fundamental to understanding the biological basis of chemical dependence as it is the driving force behind the behavior. Thus, chemical-seeking behavior can be measured using techniques such as self-administration while the effects of chronic high doses of a chemical on biochemical and physiological processes serve as a measure of physical dependence. The appeal of this model is that the two basic processes involved in chemical abuse can be separated and the impact of one can be studied while the other is held constant.

A *reinforcer* is anything that, upon its delivery, can increase the probability that the response that preceded the event will occur with a higher frequency. A close inspection of *Figure 1* reveals that the concepts depicted do not apply solely to chemicals, but can be applied to a number of items such as eating food or sweets, craving salt, buying lottery tickets, watching television, using a computer, jogging, engaging in sexual activity, etc. What is now clear is that in a more universal theory of chemical abuse/dependence, it is a form of "stimulus abuse." The identity of the particular stimulus may not be as important as the willingness to engage in the behavior that causes the stimulus. In addition, the acute effects of the chemical need not be dramatic as long as the net result is to increase the likelihood of future use.

Perhaps the most significant development to understanding chemical abuse is recognizing the role that operant conditioning plays not only in the initiation of the behavior, but in its maintenance as well. Initiation and maintenance are very distinct and have different profiles as well as different conditions that facilitate them. For example, an individual may initiate chemical use, gambling, or some other behavior solely out of curiosity, as a result of peer pressure, or simply just to "see what it's like." However, the maintenance of the behavior occurs only after a series of instances of taking the chemical or performing the act have been rewarded or reinforced in some manner. In the case of chemical abuse, however, neurochemical, metabolic, and physiological changes can occur as a consequence of long-term exposure to these agents. Some of these changes actually result in the need to increase the amount of the chemical in order to achieve the original effect. This phenomenon is called tolerance and results in exposure to higher doses over time.

Physical dependence is a state that develops after chronic exposure to a chemical such that an individual experiences unpleasant behavioral and physi-

Figure 1

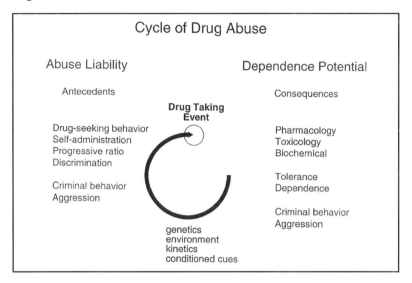

A theoretical cycle of drug abuse depicting the factors that precede the drug-taking event and the consequences of acute or chronic drug administration.

ological effects when the use of the chemical is abruptly stopped. Typically, the profile of this "abstinence syndrome" is specific to the drug class involved and often includes signs and symptoms that are opposite to those produced by acute administration of the chemical. Further, it is possible that nonchemical reinforcers can induce similar changes such that a withdrawal syndrome results upon abrupt termination of the behavior.

An alternative scenario is that individuals having a psychiatric or other medical disorder discover (often quite by accident) that certain illicit drugs alleviate some of the symptoms. When mental anguish or physical pain is reduced by taking a drug or another chemical, the association between the two is made rapidly, and so the drug-taking behavior can increase proportionally. This "self-medicating" theory is very compelling, as it explains many fundamental observations by health care professionals.

That is, many persons who are diagnosed with a chemical dependency often have a second psychiatric diagnosis. This so-called "dual diagnosis" is a common finding, now that health care professionals are trained to identify chemical dependent persons. In addition, the drug abuse problem often abates when the primary psychiatric problem is treated.

Neurobiological Bases of Reinforcement

As a wide variety of biologically important stimuli can serve as reinforcers, maintaining stimulus-seeking behavior, it is tempting to hypothesize that such stimuli act through a common brain mechanism. This is likely to be the case because these brain mechanisms involve chemicals normally found there called neurotransmitters that are either blocked or mimicked by a variety of psychoactive substances, that is, substances affecting the mind or behavior. Interestingly, most of these psychoactive chemicals are derivatives of plants.

Although there are over two dozen chemical messengers in the brain, most of the evidence points to dopamine as being the major mediator of reinforcement. Dopamine was the first neurotransmitter to be seen as communicating the reinforcing effects of brain electrical stimulation of the medial forebrain bundle (Liebman and Butcher, 1973; Fouriezos and Wise, 1976). Soon thereafter, it was also implicated in the effects of amphetamine (Yokel and Wise, 1975) and cocaine (de Wit and Wise, 1977). While these drugs also elevate brain norepinephrine and serotonin levels, the reinforcing effects of these drugs are reduced by drugs that are selective for dopamine receptors, and not for norepinephrine or serotonin receptors (Yokel and Wise, 1975; de Wit and Wise, 1977; Lyness and Moore, 1983). It is now believed that every major chemical that is abused, including cocaine, heroin, nicotine, alcohol, and marijuana alter dopamine levels in the same general area of the brain.

Dopamine is found in only two major brain circuits: the mesolimbic and the mesocortical systems. These circuits project from an area deep in the brain called the ventral tegmental area to the nucleus accumbens and frontal cortex. It is believed that the elements of the brain-reward circuitry are located in these two circuits (Wise, 1998). Not all drugs of abuse increase dopamine directly, however, those that affect mainly another transmitter, GABA, (e.g., benzodiazepines and barbiturates) may ultimately alter dopamine activity. Thus, drugs that belong to distinct classes appear to be linked in some way to a central common brain reward circuit.

Instruments to Measure Behavior

There are a number of useful tools that have been used to measure changes in mood state, particularly those that occur after consuming a drug. Historically, these have involved "paper and pencil" tests that are administered a number of times during a session. Typically, these questions are open ended or "true-false" questions. A variant of these assessments is the visual analog scale, or VAS. This type of question offers the subject the opportunity to respond by placing a mark along a horizontal line to describe the magnitude of their mood state. For example, to the question "How much do you crave cocaine right now?" the subject can indicate along a continuum from "not at all" to "most ever." As these questionnaires are rather easy to administer, frequent assessments of mood states can be collected and correlated with

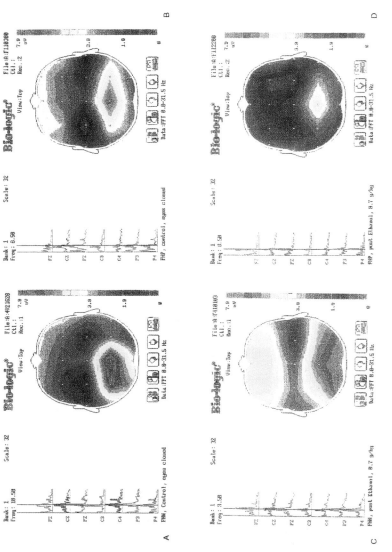

Figure 7. A-D. Topographic brain maps of EEG alpha activity of two individuals having either a negative (**A,C**) or a positive (**B,D**) family history of alcoholism after both placebo (**A,B**) and 0.7 g/kg ethanol (**C,D**). The colors are scaled to represent a range of voltages in microvolts. Increased alpha activity is defined as an increase in the voltage (μV).

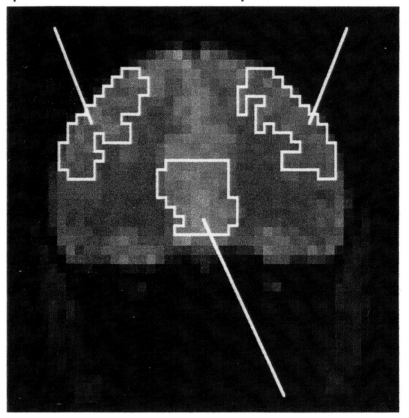

right dorsolateral
prefrontal cortex

left dorsolateral
prefrontal cortex

anterior cingulate gyrus

*Figure 9. Outline of anterior cingulate and left and right dorsolateral
prefrontal cortex for functional MRI assessments during cocaine cue-
induced craving.*

other measures.

Attempts to simulate the drug-like experiences resulted in the formation of the Addiction Research Center Inventory, or ARCI (Hill et al., 1963). This series of 550 "true/false" questions provided an insight into a broad range of physical, emotional and subjective effects of drugs. Because many experiments thrive on tracking the onset, peak, and offset of drug effects, the original ARCI has been edited to a series of 49 questions that, upon scoring, provide a measure of euphoria (morphine, benzedrine group or MBG scale); sedation (pentobarbital chlorpromazine, alcohol group or PCAG) and psychotomimetic (LSD group) effects (Martin, 1967; Jasinski et al., 1971).

Principles of Brain Imaging Techniques

Spontaneous fluctuations in human brain electrical activity, as measured from the scalp, are typically quantified using two basic parameters: amplitude and frequency. The frequency of a biological signal from the brain has been divided into four main bands, but additional smaller divisions have been added for special considerations. In 1929, Hans Berger (1931) discovered the first waveform in scalp recordings: the *alpha* band. Waves in this band oscillate between 8 and 13 cycles per second, or Hertz (Hz). Typically, alpha activity is most prominent over the occipital and parietal areas of the human scalp and is highest in individuals who are awake but resting quietly. Alpha waves are immediately suppressed during any type of activity, such as physical exercise or when concentrating. Frequencies below 4 Hz are defined as *delta* activity; these waves are of usually large amplitude. Delta activity is considered pathological if the subject is awake but such slow wave activity is quite normal during various stages of deep sleep. The theta rhythm contains activity between 4 and 8 Hz and is typically not localized over any specific area of the scalp. Beta activity is defined as that above 13 Hz and does not have any specific topography. Beta activity has been further divided into beta$_1$ and beta$_2$ to reflect a more restricted frequency range.

Amplitude, measured in microvolts (μV), provides a quantitative measure of the size of a specific waveform. The amplitude measures on the scalp EEG depend on the number of neurons firing synchronously, on the distance between these neurons, and the recording electrode, and, to some extent, on the source of the activity being measured.

Magnetic resonance imaging, or MRI, exploits the built in magnetic properties of the hydrogen atoms found in water. In a strong magnetic field, these elements will align with or against the north and south poles of the magnet. Then, radio frequency (RF) waves are played to rotate these atoms. When the RF pulse is stopped, the atoms will return to their original positions and will give off RF signals of their own, which are detected using an antenna. Images, which are essentially maps of the location from which these RF signals arise, are constructed by plotting these signals (Kucharczyk et al., 1994).

203

Functional Magnetic Resonance Imaging, or fMRI, studies are used to map specific functions of the brain. The development of high-speed, echo planar imaging (EPI) devices has greatly increased the speed with which these images can be collected (Stehling et al., 1991). With EPI, single image planes may be acquired in 50–100 msec and multiple image planes may be acquired each second. The development of EPI has greatly hastened the development of a family of techniques which are generally referred to as functional magnetic resonance imaging, or fMRI. These methods are generally designed so that changes in cerebral blood flow or blood volume lead to changes in image signal intensity.

There are two separate classes of fMRI studies: *noncontrast* techniques, which make use of body functions to detect changes in cerebral activation (Ogawa et al., 1990; Kwong et al., 1992), and *contrast* techniques, which require the intravenous injection of a chemical that helps "light up" areas of interest (Belliveau et al., 1990; 1991). Noncontrast techniques detect changes in blood flow or, more commonly, changes in the local concentration of deoxyhemoglobin, the protein that carries oxygen. The latter method has been referred to as *B*lood-*O*xygen-*L*evel-*D*ependent, or BOLD, imaging. BOLD experiments take advantage of the fact that regional brain activation is associated with changes in both blood flow and blood volume (Ogawa et al., 1993).

The promise that fMRI holds for studies of individuals with mental illness and chemical dependencies has been reviewed previously (Levin et al., 1995; Kaufman et al., 1996a). Levin et al. (1995; 1996) have pointed out that this technique may offer a more robust means to evaluate the acute effects of drugs on brain hemodynamics. Kaufman et al. (1996b) have recently used this technique to evaluate the vasoconstrictive effects of an acute i.v. injection of cocaine. They reported that 0.4 mg/kg cocaine is associated with an 18% decrease in global cerebral blood volume as well as a significantly shorter mean time for the contrast to pass through the central nervous system.

There also have been relatively few reports of using fMRI in individuals with chemical dependencies, despite the fact that radionuclide imaging studies have consistently demonstrated changes in brain blood flow and metabolism in substance abusers (Mathew & Wilson, 1991). However, there are likely to be several important areas for fMRI research. One example includes the use of BOLD fMRI to record brain changes to drug-related cues (Childress et al., 1993). Another area of research might include the use of fMRI to check the efficacy of interventions designed to block the effects of cocaine on blood vessels (Nolte et al., 1996). Thus, it is likely that fMRI will ultimately play a very important role in understanding clinical chemical dependence.

Merging Brain Imaging with Behavior

One of the biggest problems plaguing electrophysiologists who search for correlations between EEG activity and behavior has been the lack of a method to accurately identify specific mood changes using techniques that do not, in and of themselves, alter the measured brain electrical activity. The use of questionnaires or verbal responding techniques would introduce movement artifact into the EEG recording, and thus make it difficult to measure the brain activity that is associated with a specific change in mood state. To some extent, research comparing the correlation between brain electrical activity and various traits has not had similar problems, since traits tend to be more stable over time while mood states frequently change during an experimental session. With respect to procedures for monitoring brain electrical activity changes during drug-induced behavioral states, one advantage is that the drug taking event can be used as the focal point for initiating the recording procedure. Again, depending on the route of administration and the rate of onset of pharmacological effects of the drug, the procedures can be optimized to accurately detect changes in brain electrical activity during the drug-induced behavioral states.

In order to accurately measure changes in brain wave activity during a specific mood state, the subject must be provided with a method of communicating to the researcher when such specific subjective changes have occurred. Some form of an instrumental joystick or switch closure device has been most frequently used by researchers in this field (Koukkou and Lehmann, 1976; Lukas et al., 1995; Lukas and Mendelson, 1988; Lukas *et al.*, 1986; Lukas et al., 1990; McEachern et al., 1988; Volavka et al., 1973). The premise behind using an instrumental device is that the subject is not required to verbalize the response which significantly reduces the potential for artifact in the EEG recordings. In addition, the instructional set can be kept very basic and simple such that only selected behaviors of interest are measured. One possible interrelationship between the joystick device, spontaneous brain electrical activity, and its mapping are shown in *Figure 2.* Movement of the joystick device (lower right panel of figure) causes a corresponding deflection directly on the polygraph tracing. Thus, an immediate temporal relationship between changes in subjective mood state can be tracked along with corresponding changes in brain electrical activity. By keeping the response requirements as simple and as unobtrusive as possible, the amount of artifact on the resulting electroencephalogram is greatly reduced or eliminated.

It is important to segregate any evaluation of brain function measures and behavior into "trait" and "state" categories. With respect to the former, many investigators have documented specific brainwave changes in individuals with chronic schizophrenia (Goldstein et al., 1963; Goldstein et al., 1965; Sugerman et al., 1964), depression (D'Elia and Perris, 1973; Goldstein, 1979; Von Knorring and Goldstein, 1982), neuroticism (Hoffman and Goldstein, 1981), hyperemotionality (Wiet, 1981) and anxiety (Koella, 1981). To some extent, these changes have been used diagnostically, but their utility in this regard (especially for a specific patient) is questionable. There also is the problem of identifying an organic source of the observed changes.

Figure 2

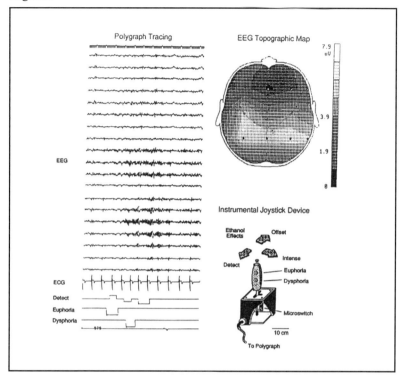

Key elements of an electrophysiologic study in which subjective effects of a drug are correlated with specific brain wave patterns. The left side displays raw tracing from conventional EEG polygraphs. The right side shows a representative topographic brain map for a specific epic of EEG activity. An instrumental joystick device is depicted in the bottom panel, the output of which is directly recorded on the polygraph paper left side thus facilitating location of specific events. The position of the joystick conveys information relating to detection of ethanol effects and whether the effects have become intense. (From London, 1993, with permission.)

Changes in state have been studied using the EEG for quite some time, but recently other brain imaging techniques such as positron emission tomography (PET) and magnetic resonance imaging (MRI) have been used. One of the features of human behavior is that it changes so quickly and so is unpredictable. This makes it difficult to measure the various mood states and then draw conclusions. Mental fatigue, premenstrual tension, pain, sexual arousal, meditation, and chemical-induced intoxication have all been quantified using

206

brain electrical waves.

Of particular importance are changes immediately *after* a reinforcing chemical has been taken, since it is presumed that the resultant mood state might reflect reinforcement and thus may dictate, to some extent, whether the individual will take that particular chemical again. In this regard, it is perhaps useful to think of pleasurable chemical-induced behaviors such as feeling extremely good, high, or even "euphoric" to be on a continuum with other chemical- or nonchemical-related behaviors. The fact that individuals can have "cravings" for various foods (e.g., chocolate, candy, sweets) and a variety of activities (e.g., jogging, gambling, sex) argues that the neurobiological basis of "craving" may be similar regardless of the target item.

Regardless of the source of the change in state, measures of brain electrical activity are well suited for the task. For example, the EEG is available for

Figure 3

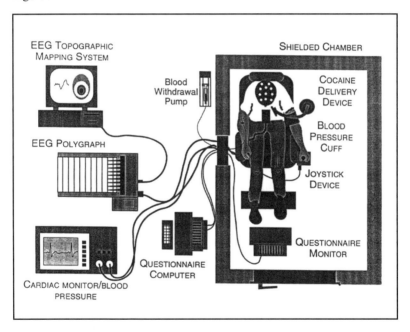

Schematic diagram of an electrophysiological laboratory in which measures of brain electrical activity are collected simultaneously with drug-induced behavioral changes. The subject is seated inside a shielded chamber and reports changes in mood state (via a joystick device) which are recorded on a computer located outside of the chamber. Responses on the joystick device are time locked with the EEG recordings so that changes in brain electrical activity can be directly correlated with changes in mood state.

measurement on a continual basis, i.e., the subject is not required to "do" anything. Thus, the measurements obtained are free of problems that are often associated with techniques that require more attention by the subject. With the advent of high-speed computer technology, the methods for recording, quantifying, and displaying brain electrical activity have changed dramatically in the last decade.

Studies designed to measure changes in brain electrical activity and subjective mood states after acute drug administration are typically done along with the collection of other data (Lukas, 1997). In addition, the lab must be protected from interference from radio and TV stations. Subjects also are typically required to sit relatively motionless in a comfortable chair while re-cordings are collected (*Figure 3*). This procedure minimizes the amount of artifact that would typically occur while collecting physiologic and behavioral data during the study. Thus, while these experiments do not simulate a natural-istic setting in which subjects are free to move about and engage in conversa-tion with other subjects, they do provide a very well-controlled environment such that the effects of the drug can be directly measured without interference from other variables present in the environment.

Once the subject has had the opportunity to adapt to the environment, baseline data is collected. Typically, heart rate, blood pressure, and skin tem-perature are measured during the course of drug-related studies. When enough baseline data have been collected, the drug is given, and EEG and other physi-ologic and subjective data can be collected.

Brain waves are recorded just like the heart's activity during an EKG test. Gold or silver electrodes are glued to the scalp and the wires are attached to a high powered amplifier. The placement of the scalp electrodes has been stan-dardized using the international 10-20 system reported by Jasper (1958). This method ensures that electrodes are placed not on the basis of an absolute measurement, but on a percentage of the distance from key external landmarks on the skull. Using this technique, electrodes are placed over similar brain structures regardless of the subject's head size. The first step in measuring brain electrical activity is to convert it to a digital signal by a high-speed computer. The next step is to apply some mathematical equations to the data in order to measure the amount of activity or μV in a particular frequency. This process is depicted in *Figure 4*. As the amplitude is relatively small in beta waves, the amount of activity is correspondingly small in the average power spectrum.

Traditional methods of measuring the electrophysiological effects of drugs have relied on visual inspection of up to 21 channels of brain electrical activity. While the human eye is very good at detecting subtle aberrations or asymmetries, the observed changes are impossible to quantify. Such tracings often provide too much information to be synthesized in a relatively short period. Nuwer (1988) commented on the utility of quantitative electroencephalography as a metric of central nervous system excitability.

Figure 4

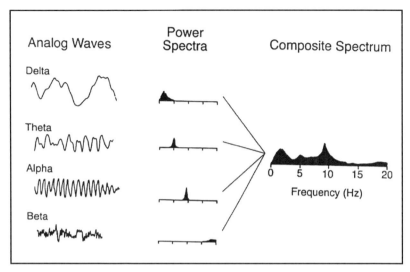

Diagrammatic representation of the generation of power spectra from analog EEG waveforms.

Topographic brain mapping is one such method that has been developed to provide a more complete view of the distribution of brain electrical activity over the scalp.

Topographic brain mapping is essentially an extension of the data analysis procedure described in the previous section except that the amount of activity located *between* electrode sites is actually estimated using mathematical interpolation procedures. Essentially, a power spectrum is generated for the electrical activity that has been recorded at each of the individual electrode sites. The value of each data point located between electrode sites is a compilation of the amount of actually measured values from the electrode to which it is most closely located plus a percentage of the activity from surrounding electrodes. Once these intermediate values are calculated, topograms can be drawn by connecting the data points that have similar values. Values of similar amplitude or power can be color-coded to aid in the identification of patterns over the scalp.

Brain Imaging of Ethanol-Induced Intoxication

Only recently have measures of EEG activity been exploited to their full potential with respect to assessing changes in mood states after a psychoactive drug administration (Lukas et al., 1989; Lukas 1993). The acute behavioral effects of ethanol are well known (Begleiter and Platz, 1972; Davis et al., 1941;

Figure 5

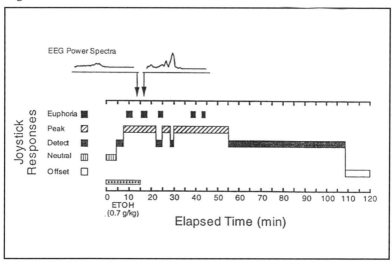

Behavioral profile of a subject after receiving 0.7 g/kg of ethanol.
Power spectra were generated for the EEG data that occurred just
before and during one episode of euphoria or intense well-being.

Doctor et al., 1966; Engel and Rosenbaum, 1945) and the acute effects on the EEG have been well described in the literature (Alha, 1951; Bjerver and Goldberg, 1950; Ekman et al., 1964; King, 1943). With the use of a continuous joystick device such as that described above, another behavioral profile emerged that was not expected. As is seen in *Figures 5 and 6*, 0.7 g/kg of ethanol is detected very quickly and paroxysmal bursts of intense well-being or "euphoria" result. Lower doses of ethanol and even placebo solutions are detected but fail to produce intense well-being or euphoria. It was found that large increases in EEG alpha activity occurred during the periods of ethanol-induced euphoria (Lukas et al., 1986; Lukas et al., 1989).

The implications of these findings are substantial, as they help provide a "window" into which we can see how brain/behavior relationships are wired. For example, increases in EEG alpha activity are often associated with pleasurable, free-floating, and extremely relaxed states (Brown, 1970; Lindsley, 1952; Matejcek, 1982; Wallace, 1970). In addition, similar levels of increased alpha activity are seen in individuals who practice transcendental meditation (Wallace, 1970). The direct relationship between increased EEG alpha activity during reports of euphoria after ethanol (Lukas et al., 1988), cocaine (Lukas et al., 1991), and marijuana (Lukas et al., 1995) suggests that this neurophysiologic response may be associated with the reinforcing effects of these drugs. Given the generality of alpha activity and its association with pleasurable mood states, it is plausible that increased EEG alpha activity may be associated with drug-induced reinforcement in general and may not be selective for a single drug class. This interpretation is consistent with the notion that drug-seeking behavior is a form of stimulus self-administration that produces a change (regardless of the direction) in subjective state. These relationships can be exploited to study other aspects of chemical dependencies.

Brain Imaging to Identify Genetic Markers of Vulnerability

One of the most interesting areas of research in the field of drug abuse has been the finding that alcoholism may be inherited. The children of alcoholics are 4–5 times more likely to develop alcohol-related problems than the general population (Cotton, 1979; Goodwin et al., 1974). Well-controlled studies of adopted children have verified that genetic factors do play a role in the development of alcoholism (Goodwin et al., 1973, 1974; Schuckit, 1986).

The use of topographic brain mapping techniques permits not only an evaluation of the acute effects of ethanol on human EEG, but also has revealed

Figure 6

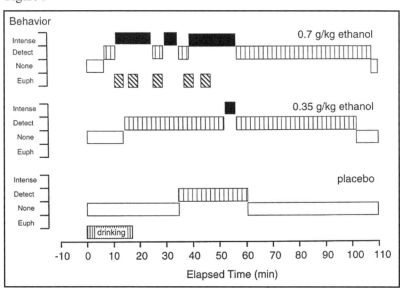

Behavioral profile of 3 different doses of ethanol: 0.7 g/kg (high), 0.35 g/kg (low), and placebo. Behaviors were reported via a joystick device and included: Intense—very strong effects; Detect—subject is aware of ethanol's effects; None—no effects; Euph - euphoria or intense good feelings.

distinct differences in individuals with and without a family history of alcoholism (FHP and FHN respectively) (Lukas et al., 1989). It also documents differences in recovering alcoholics (Pollock et al., 1992). As can be seen in *Figure 7* (see color plate), EEG alpha activity is high over the back of the scalp as indicated by the large amounts of brown and red colors (depicting larger amplitudes in μV) in the upper left hand panel of the figure. This is a typical topographic map of EEG alpha activity in an individual who does not have a family history of alcoholism. The effects of 0.7 gm/kg of ethanol (about 3 shots of vodka) in this individual are shown in the lower left panel. The increase in EEG alpha activity over the entire back of the scalp is clearly visible, as are increases in frontal alpha activity. These abrupt changes in EEG alpha activity corresponded to the subjective reports of intoxication and euphoria.

Baseline EEG alpha activity in a representative FHP individual is shown in the upper right-hand panel of this figure. It is also evident that there is more alpha activity during the baseline recording period in this individual. Similar differences have been observed for both EEG activity (Propping et al., 1981; Gabrielli et al., 1982; Bauer and Hesselbrock, 1992; Ehlers and Schuckit, 1991; Lukas et al., 1989) and event-related potentials (Begleiter et al., 1984; O'Connor et al., 1987; Polich et al., 1994). The effects of ethanol in this individual are shown in the lower right panel and clearly show that there is even a slight reduction in the amount of spontaneous alpha activity after the same dose of ethanol. However, what is also different is that individuals with a positive family history of alcoholism do not report feeling intoxicated and certainly did not experience euphoria after this dose of ethanol (Lukas et al., 1989). These topographic maps were taken during the same time as the FHN subjects' data when plasma ethanol levels were approximately 70 mg/dl. Thus, while the timecourse in the plasma ethanol levels were exactly the same in these individuals, their EEG and subjective response to ethanol was very different. The group data (*Figure 8*) demonstrates that FHN individuals have a much larger increase in alpha activity than those who have a positive family history of alcoholism (and feel more intoxicated after the same dose). As all subjects had the same drinking history, these differences in alpha activity may reflect an "innate" tolerance which may be tied to the genetic predisposition to alcoholism.

Thus, FHP individuals have an attenuated response to an acute dose of ethanol. It is believed that the reason that these individuals are more likely to develop alcohol-related problems is because of this lowered sensitivity to ethanol's effects. As a result, in a social drinking setting the FHP individual will not become as intoxicated as his/her FHN friends. They will likely stop after a few beers, but the FHP individual has yet to feel the desired effects of the alcohol. Thus, he or she will order 2–3 more drinks than everyone else. Over time (this can take years) the FHP individual is exposed to greater amounts of alcohol and so can develop a real tolerance to its effects. This, in turn, causes them to drink even more alcohol until finally they are drinking a substantial amount on a daily basis.

Brain Imaging Cue-Induced Craving Using fMRI

Echo planar functional magnetic resonance imaging (fMRI) is based on BOLD techniques and has been quite useful in measuring brain activation in response to specific stimuli. This imaging capitalizes on two of the most important aspects of brain imaging and behavior—high spatial resolution and fast temporal resolution (Kwong, 1995; Rauch and Renshaw, 1995). This technique was recently used to measure areas of the brain reacting to the cocaine-related cues (Maas et al., 1998).

This technique has been used to measure changes in brain blood flow during a specific mood state. One state that is of great importance in relapse to drug use is craving. The premise of drug-induced craving is not unlike that proposed by the Russian physiologist Ivan Pavlov. The phenomenon Pavlovian conditioning bears his name. In essence, a response is said to be "conditioned" when it is paired with a specific stimulus. Pavlov rang a bell as he presented a dog with its daily meal. After a few pairings of the bell with food, the dog began to salivate upon hearing the bell; this response persisted even

Figure 8

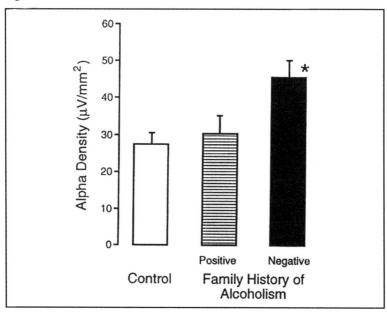

Group data from males subjects with and without a positive family history of alcoholism who received an acute dose of ethanol (0.7 g/kg). The density of alpha activity was obtained by summing the amount of activity from the central/occipital scalp leads.
(From London, 1993, with permission).

213

in the absence of the food. Drug-related cues can do the same thing and it is believed that these stimuli (which can be visual, sounds, smells, situations, a person, or virtually anything that has been associated with the drug-taking behavior) are responsible for relapse to drug use, especially after a few weeks or months of being "clean."

These cues are often specific to the drug and are certainly specific to the individual drug user. However, they are powerful "reminders" of the drug-taking experience and their importance in any drug abuse treatment program cannot be underestimated. Humans often respond to these cues with an over-whelming desire to use the drug (i.e., craving) along with a variety of other changes such as heart rate, skin temperature, and blood pressure. This cue-induced hyperaroused state can mimic the effects of taking the drug and so the individual may lose control over his or her ability to resist using. Once the drug is used, the cycle can return to the pretreatment level very quickly.

In the study by Maas et al. (1998), six male subjects with a history of using crack cocaine at least once every two weeks during the previous six months participated. Subjects who had never used cocaine served as controls. Using segments of a crack cocaine videotape (Childress et al., 1996) as the cocaine-cue stimuli, and clips from a public broadcasting tape on butterflies as neutral cues, a single ten minute videotape was constructed consisting of four 150-second segments that alternated between the two in the following order: neutral/cocaine/neutral/cocaine. The tape was played to the individuals while they were in an fMRI scanning session. Subjective reports of strength and frequency of desire for cocaine (i.e., craving) were collected before and after scanning, using a standardized visual analog scale (Weiss et al., 1995). Regions of interest were identified from high resolution MR images and mapped to the functional image set by two raters (*Figure 9*, see color plate). Significant elevations in activation magnitude between the cocaine and comparison groups were detected in the anterior cingulate and left dorsolateral prefrontal cortex (*Figure 10*). These areas of the brain are known to control emotional states and memory. Subjects also craved cocaine more after the session (Maas et al., 1998).

There are multiple significant implications of these findings. First, these results are consistent with both metabolic (Grant et al., 1996) and blood flow (Childress et al., 1996) changes found with PET. Second, this technique proved to be sensitive enough to measure subtle and rapidly changing levels of a subjective mood state. Third, and perhaps more importantly, is the fact that craving appears to be a very dynamic process that can wax and wane depending on the immediate surroundings. This alone provides a very important insight into the neurobiological bases of craving and altered mood states that relate to clinical dependencies. Finally, because changes in brain activation paralleled the changes in mood state so quickly, these techniques may be useful in studying new agents to modify or reduce craving.

214

Figure 10

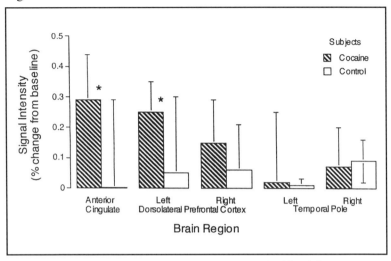

Group effects of cocaine-related cues on the blood flow in certain brain regions.
* indicates statistically significant at the p < 0.05 level.

Relationship to Other Compulsive Behaviors

It is now clear that a variety of compulsive behaviors such as gambling, overeating and hypersexuality share many attributes with drug abuse. Indeed these behaviors are more similar than different because these excessive behaviors share many behavioral, social, economic, and physiological constructs. One other compulsive behavior, gambling, shares many of these attributes with drugs of abuse (at least when individuals are winning). This concept was suggested 13 years ago by Hickey et al. (1986), who used the ARCI to measure changes in mood state in gamblers as they "simulated winning at gambling." The resultant euphoria was indistinguishable from that produced by psychoactive stimulants. More recently, Koepp et al. (1998) demonstrated that brain dopamine levels were increased while subjects played a video game for money. As nearly all abused drugs have an impact on the dopamine system, it is enticing to speculate that gambling (and perhaps the other compulsive habits) somehow influences the same basic reward circuits of the brain.

Implications for Counseling and Treatment

The use of new brain imaging techniques has revealed a number of key elements about chemical dependence. Scientists can now see a person's "brain on drugs" and thus begin to piece together the many pieces to the puzzle of why people take and abuse chemicals. Because of the complexities of drug abuse and the fact that it is a recurring problem that has clear brain chemistry correlates, a successful treatment program must incorporate a relapse prevention component. Further, the changes in brain function that occur over time is another piece of evidence that the most critical phase of a treatment program begins right after detoxification. Because a chronic drug abuser's brain has undergone a number of changes that may not be reversible for quite some time, it is important to remember that a successful treatment does not occur overnight. In addition, the first attempt at treatment is not always successful. Knowing this, one realizes that a relapse to drug use is not necessarily a failure as long as the individual is willing to try again. Often the reason for failure is that the individual is exposed to a conditioned cue that "reminds" him or her of the drug. The resultant increase in craving can overpower the individual, who succumbs to the urges and uses the drug again. As a result, cue-desensitization behavioral techniques as well as drugs that alter craving may have a place in the future for dealing with chemical dependencies.

References

Alha, A. R. 1951. Blood alcohol and clinical inebriation in Finnish men. *Ann. Acad. Sci. Fenn.* 26: 1–92.

Bauer, L. O., and V. M. Hesselbrock. 1993. EEG, autonomic and subjective correlates of the risk for alcoholism. *J. Stud. Alcohol.* 54: 577–589.

Begleiter, H. and A. Platz. 1972. The effects of alcohol on the central nervous system in humans. In *The Biology of Alcoholism Vol. 2*, ed. B. Kissin and H. Begleiter, 293–343. New York: Plenum Press.

Begleiter, H., B. Porjesz, B. Bihari, and B. Kissen. 1984. Event-related brain potentials in boys at risk for alcoholism. *Science* 225: 1493–1496.

Belliveau, J. W., B.R. Rosen, H.L. Kanto, R.R. Rzedian, K.N. Kennedy, R. C. McKinstry, J.M. Vevea, M.S. Cohen, I.L. Pykett, and T.J. Brady. 1990. Functional cerebral imaging by susceptibility contrast imaging. *Magn. Reson. Med.* 14: 538–546.

Belliveau, J. W., D.N. Kennedy, R.C. McKinstry, B.R. Buchbinder, R.M. Wiesskoff, M.S. Cohen, J.M. Vevea, T.J. Brady, and B.R. Rosen. 1991.

Functional mapping of the human visual cortex by magnetic resonance imaging. *Science* 254: 716–719.

Berger, H. 1931. Uber das Elektrenkephalogramm des Menschen. [On the electroencephalogram of man: third report]. *Arch. Psychiatr.* 94:16–60. Translated in Hans Berger ,1969, *On the Electroencephalogram of Man. Electroenceph. Clin. Neurophysiol. Suppl.*, ed. P. Gloor, 95–132. Amsterdam: Elsevier Publishing.

Bjerver, K., and L. Goldberg. 1950. Effects of alcohol ingestion on driving ability. *Q. J. Stud. Alcohol* 11: 1–30.

Bradley, W. G., W.T.C. Yuh, and G.M. Bydder. 1993. Use of MR imaging contrast agents in the brain. *J. Magn. Reson. Imaging* 3: 199–218.

Brown, B. B. 1970. Recognition of aspects of consciousness through association with EEG alpha activity represented by a light signal. *Psychophysiology* 6: 442–452.

Childress, A. R., A.V. Hole, R.N. Ehrman, S.J. Robbins, A.T. McLellan, and C.P. O'Brien. 1993. Cue reactivity and cue reactivity interventions in drug dependence. *NIDA Res. Monogr.* 137: 73–95.

Childress, A., W. McElgin, D. Mozley, M. Reivich, and C. O'Brien. 1996. Brain correlates of cue-induced cocaine and opiate craving. *Abstracts—Society for Neuroscience* 22 (part 2): 933.

Cotton, N. S. 1979. The familial incidence of alcoholism: A review. *J. Stud. Alcohol* 40: 89–116.

Davis, P. A., F.A. Gibbs, H. Davis, W.W. Jetter, and L.S. Trowbridge. 1941. The effects of alcohol upon the electroencephalogram (brain waves). *Q. J. Stud. Alcohol* 1: 626–637.

D'Elia, G., and C. Perris. 1973. Cerebral functional dominance and depression. *Acta Psychiatr. Scand.* 49: 191–197.

Doctor, R. F., P. Naitoh, and J.C. Smith. 1966. Electroencephalographic changes and vigilance behavior during experimentally induced intoxication with alcoholic subjects. *Psychosom. Med.* 28: 605–615.

Ehlers, C. L., and M.A. Schuckit. 1991. Evaluation of EEG alpha activity in sons of alcoholics. *Neuropsychopharmacology* 4: 199–205.

Ekman, G., M. Frankenhaeuser, L. Goldberg, R. Hagdahl, and A.-L.Myrsten. 1964. Subjective and objective effects of alcohol as functions of dosage and time. *Psychopharmacologia* 6: 399–409.

Engel, G. L., and M. Rosenbaum. 1945. Delerium III. Electroencephalographic changes associated with acute alcohol intoxication. *Arch. Neurol. Psychiatry* 53: 44–50.

Gabrielli, W. F., S.A. Mednick, J. Volavka, V.E. Pollock, F. Schulsinger, and T.M. Itil. 1982. Electroencephalograms in children of alcoholic fathers. *Psychophysiology* 19: 404–407.

Goldstein, L. 1979. Some relationships between quantitated hemispheric EEG and behavioral states in man. In *Hemispheric Asymmetries of Function and Psychopathology*, ed. J. Gruzelier and P. Flor-Henry, 237–254. New York: Elsevier Publishers.

Goldstein, L., H.B. Murphree, A.A. Sugerman, C.C. Pfeiffer, and E.H. Jenney. 1963. Quantitative electroencephalographic analysis of naturally occurring (schizophrenic) and drug-induced psychotic states in human males. *Clin. Pharmacol. Ther.* 4: 10–21.

Goldstein, L., A.A. Sugerman, H. Stolberg, H.B. Murphree, and C.C. Pfeiffer. 1965. Electrocerebral activity in schizophrenic and non-psychotic subjects: Quantitative EEG amplitude analysis. *Electroenceph. Clin. Neurophysiol.* 19: 350–361.

Goodwin, D. W., F. Schulsinger, L. Hermansen, S.B. Guze, and G. Winokur. 1973. Alcohol problems in adoptees raised apart from alcoholic biological parents. *Arch. Gen. Psychiatry* 28: 238–243.

Goodwin, D. W., F. Schulsinger, N. Moller, L. Hermansen, G. Winokur, and S.B. Guze. 1974. Drinking problems in adopted and nonadopted sons of alcoholics. *Arch. Gen. Psychiatry* 31: 164–169.

Graham, G. D., J. Zhong, O.A. Petroff, R.T. Constable, J.W. Prichard, and J.C. Gore. 1994. BOLD MRI monitoring of changes in cerebral perfusion induced by acetazolamide and hypercarbia in the rat. *Magn. Reson. Med.* 31: 557–560.

Grant, S., E.D. London, D.B. Newlin, V.I. Villemagne, X. Liu, C. Contoreggi, R.L. Phillips, A.S. Kimes, and A. Margolin, A. 1996. Activation of memory circuits during cue-elicited cocaine craving. *Proc. Natl. Acad. Sci. U.S.A.* 93: 12040–12045.

Hickey, J. E., and C.A. Haertzen. 1986. Simulation of gambling responses on the Addiction Research Center Inventory. *Addict. Behav.* 11: 345–349.

Hill, H. E., C.A. Haertzen, A.B. Wolbach, and E.J. Miner. 1963. The Addiction Research Center Inventory: Standardization of scales which evaluate subjective effects of morphine, amphetamine, pentobarbital, alcohol, LSD-25, pyrahexyl and chlorpromazine. *Psychopharmacologia* 4: 167–183.

Hoffman, E., and L. Goldstein. 1981. Hemispheric quantitative EEG changes following emotional reactions in neurotic patients. *Acta Psychiatr. Scand.* 63: 153–164.

Jasinski, D. R., C.A. Haertzen, and H. Isbell. Review of the effects in man of marijuana of tetrahydrocannabinols on subjective state and physiologic functioning. *Ann. N.Y. Acad. Sci.* 191: 196–205.

Jasper, H. H. 1958. The 10-20 electrode system of the International Federation. *Electroenceph. Clin. Neurophysiol.* 10: 371–375.

Kaufman, M. J., J.M. Levin, J.D. Christensen, and P.F. Renshaw. 1996a. Magnetic resonance studies of substance abuse. *Semin. Clin. Neuropsychiatry* 1: 61–75.

Kaufman, M. J., J.M. Levin, J.D. Christensen, S.E. Lukas, J.H. Mendelson, L.C. Maas, S.L. Rose, B.M. Cohen, and P.F. Renshaw. 1996b. Dynamic susceptibility contrast MR measurement of cerebral blood volume reduction following intravenous cocaine administration to human subjects. *Proc. Int. Soc. Magn. Reson. Med.* (April): 448.

King, A. R. 1943. Tunnel vision. *Q. J. Stud. Alcohol* 4: 362–367.

Koella, W. P. 1981. Electroencephalographic signs of anxiety. *Progress in Neuro-Psychopharmacology* 5: 187–192.

Koepp, M. J., R.N. Gunn, A.D. Lawrence, V.J. Cunningham, A. Dagher, T. Jones, D.J.Brooks, C.J. Bench, and P.M.Grasby. 1998. Evidence for striatal dopamine release during a video game. *Nature* 393: 266–268.

Koukkou, M. ,and D. Lehmann. 1976. Human EEG spectra before and during cannabis hallucinations. *Biol. Psychiatry* 11: 663–677.

Kucharcyzk, J., M. Moseley, and A.J. Barkovich, eds. 1994. *Magnetic Resonance Neuroimaging*. Boca Raton: CRC Press.

Kwong, K. 1995. Functional magnetic resonance imaging with echo planar imaging. *Magn. Reson. Q.* 11: 1–20.

Kwong, K. K., J. W. Belliveau, D.A. Chesler, I.E. Goldberg, R.M. Weisskoff, B.P. Poncelet, D. N. Kennedy, B.E. Happel, M.S. Cohen, A. Turner, et al. 1992. Dynamic magnetic resonance imaging of human brain activity during primary sensory stimulation. *Proc. Natl. Acad. Sci. U.S.A.* 89: 5675–5679.

Levin, J. M., M.H. Ross, and P.F. Renshaw. 1995. Clinical applications of functional MRI in neuropsychiatry. *J. Neuropsych. Clin. Neurosci.* 7: 511–522.

Levin, J. M., L.L. Wald, M.H. Ross, M.J. Kaufman, B.M. Cohen, and P.F. Renshaw. 1996. Investigation of T1 effects as basis for residual contrast agent effects seen in sequential dynamic susceptibility contrast experiments. *Proc. Int. Soc. Magn. Reson. Med.* (April): 441.

Lindsley, D. B. 1952. Psychological phenomena and the electroencephalogram. *Electroenceph. Clin. Neurophysiol.* 4: 443–456.

Lukas, S. E. 1993. Advanced electrophysiological imaging techniques for studying drug effects. In *Imaging Drug Action in the Brain,* ed. E.D. London, 389–404. Boca Raton: CRC Press.

Lukas, S. E., and J.H. Mendelson. 1988. Electroencephalographic activity and plasma ACTH during ethanol-induced euphoria. *Biol. Psychiatry* 23: 141–148.

Lukas, S. E., J.H. Mendelson, R.A.Benedikt, and B. Jones. 1986. EEG alpha activity increases during transient episodes of ethanol-induced euphoria. *Pharmacol. Biochem. Behav.* 25: 889–895.

Lukas, S. E., J.H. Mendelson, B.T. Woods, N.K. Mello, and S.K. Teoh. 1989. Topographic distribution of EEG alpha activity during ethanol-induced intoxication in women. *J. Stud. Alcohol* 50: 176–185.

Lukas, S. E., J.H. Mendelson, E. Kouri, M. Bolduc, and L. Amass. 1990. Ethanol-induced alterations in EEG alpha activity and apparent source of the auditory P300 evoked response potential. *Alcohol* 7: 471–477.

Lukas, S. E., R. Benedikt, and J.H. Mendelson, 1995. Electroencephalographic correlates of marihuana-induced euphoria. *Drug Alcohol Depend.* 37: 131–140.

Maas, L. C., S.E. Lukas, M.J. Kaufman, R.D. Weiss, S.L. Daniels, V.W. Rogers, T.J. Kukes, and P.F. Renshaw. 1998. Functional magnetic resonance imaging of human brain activation during cue-induced cocaine craving. *Am. J. Psychiatry* 155: 124–126.

Martin, W. R. 1967. Clinical evaluation for narcotic dependence. In *New concepts in pain and its clinical management*, ed. E.L. Way, 121–132. Philadelphia: F.A. Davis Co.

Matejcek, M. 1982. Vigilance and the EEG: Psychological, physiological and pharmacological aspects. In *EEG in drug research,* ed. W. M. Herrmannd, 405–508. Stuttgart: Gustav Fischer.

Mathew, R. J.,and W.H.Wilson. 1991. Substance abuse and cerebral blood flow. *Amer. J. Psychiatry* 148: 292–305.

McEachern, J., L. Friedman, M. Bird, S.E. Lukas, M.H.Orzack, D.L. Katz, E.C. Dessain, B. Beake, and J. O. Cole. 1988. Self-report versus an instrumental measure in the assessment of the subjective effects of d-amphetamine. *Psychopharmacol. Bull.* 24: 463–465.

Nolte, K. B., L.M. Brass, and C.F. Fletterick. 1996. Intracranial hemorrhage associated with cocaine abuse: A prospective autopsy study. *Neurology* 46: 1291–1296.

Nuwer, M. R. 1988. Quantitative EEG: II. Frequency analysis and topographic mapping in clinical settings. *J. Clin. Neurophysiol.* 5: 45–85.

O'Connor, S., V.M. Hesselbrock, A. Tasman, and N. DePalma. 1987. P3 amplitudes in two distinct tasks are decreased in young men with a history of paternal alcoholism. *Alcohol* 4: 323–330.

Ogawa, S., T.M. Lee, A.R. Kay, and D.W. Tank. 1990. Brain magnetic resonance imaging with contrast dependent on blood oxygenation. *Proc. Natl. Acad. Sci. U.S.A.* 87: 9868–9872.

Ogawa, S., R.S. Menon, D.W. Tank, S.G. Kim, H. Merkle, J.M. Ellerman, and K. Ugurbil. 1993. Functional brain mapping by blood oxygenation level dependent contrast magnetic resonance imaging. *Biophys. J.* 6: 803–812.

Polich, J., V.E. Pollock, and F.E. Bloom F. E. 1994. Meta-analysis of P300 amplitude from males at risk for alcoholism. *Psychol. Bull.* 115: 55–73.

Pollock, V. E., L.S. Schneider, M.F. Zemansky, R.P. Gleason, and S. Pawluczyk. 1992. Topographic quantitative EEG amplitude in recovered alcoholics. *Psychiatry Res.* 45: 25–32.

Propping, P., J. Kruger, and N. Mark. 1981. Genetic disposition to alcoholism: An EEG study in alcoholics and their relatives. *Hum. Genet.* 59: 51–59.

Rauch, S. L., and P.F. Renshaw. 1995. Clinical neuroimaging in psychiatry. *Harvard Rev. Psychiatry* 2: 297–312.

Schuckit, M. A. 1986. Genetic and biological markers in alcoholism and drug abuse. In *Genetic and Biological Markers in Drug Abuse and Alcoholism, NIDA Research Monograph No. 66,* ed. M.C. Braude and H.M. Chao, 97–108. U.S. Government Printing Office, Washington, D.C.

Stehling, M. K., R. Turner, and P. Mansfield. 1991. Echo-planar imaging: magnetic resonance imaging in a fraction of a second. *Science* 254: 43–49.

Sugerman, A. A., L. Goldstein, H.G. Murphree, C.C. Pfeiffer, and E.H. Jenney. 1964. EEG and behavioral changes in schizophrenia: A quantitative study. *Arch. Gen. Psychiatry* 10: 340–344.

Volavka, J., P. Crown, R. Dornbush, S. Feldstein, and M. Fink. 1973. EEG, heart rate and mood changes ("high") after cannabis. *Psychopharmacologia* 32: 11–25.

Von Knorring, L., and L. Goldstein. 1982. Quantitative hemispheric EEG differences between healthy volunteers and depressed patients. *Res. Comm. Psychol. Psychiat. Behav.* 7: 57–67.

Vorstrup, S., L. Henriksen, and O.B. Pauson. 1984. Effect of acetazolamide on cerebral blood flow and cerebral metabolic rate for oxygen. *J. Clin. Invest.* 74: 1634–1639.

Wallace, R. K. 1970. Physiological effects of transcendental meditation. *Science* 167: 1751–1754.

Weiss, R., M. Griffin, and C. Hufford. 1995. Craving in hospitalized cocaine abusers as a predictor of outcome. *Am. J. Drug Alcohol Abuse* 21:289–301.

Wiet, S. G. 1981. Some quantitative hemispheric EEG measures reflecting the affective profile of students differing in university academic success. *Biol. Psychiatry* 12: 25–42.

Wise, R.A. 1998. Drug-activation of brain reward pathways. *Drug Alcohol Depend* 51:13–22.

HOMOSEXUALITY AND COMPULSION

CHARLES W. SOCARIDES, M.D., F.A.C.PSA.

Development of Homosexual Attraction

In the debate over homosexuality one frequently hears some variation of the following: *Sexual attraction is genetically determined—one is born heterosexual or homosexual and nothing can be done to change this inherited characteristic. Homosexual attraction and behavior are simply normal human variations and should be accepted as such.*

While the idea of a "gay gene" has received media coverage, there are no replicated scientific studies proving that homosexual attraction is genetically determined. The confusion springs in part from the mistaken belief that sexual object choice is predetermined by chromosomal tagging. Human beings are born with a natural capacity for heterosexual desire, but that capacity must be developed through a series of learning experiences. Heterosexual object choice is outlined from birth by anatomy and then reinforced by cultural and environmental indoctrination. It is supported by universal human concepts of mating, the tradition of the family unit, and the complementary nature of the two sexes. Heterosexual attraction can be viewed as the outcome of healthy psychosexual development.

One of the most influential studies of homosexuality was done by Bieber, et al. (1962). Based on extensive clinical experience the authors described the environment in which healthy male heterosexuality develops:

A mother who is pleased by her son's masculinity and is comfortably related to his sexual curiosity and heterosexual responsiveness to her and other females, encourages and reinforces a masculine identification. A father who is warmly related to his son, who supports assertiveness and effectiveness, and who is not sexually competitive, provides the reality testing necessary for the resolution of the son's irrational sexual competitiveness. This type of parental behavior fosters heterosexual development which in adult life is characterized by the ability to sustain a gratifying love relationship (313).

Homosexual attraction, on the other hand, occurs in situations where massive childhood fears have damaged and disrupted the development of the standard male-female pattern. Such homosexual attractions can be considered as obligatory or compulsive, in that the person does not freely choose homosexuality but is pushed by unconscious fear away from heterosexuality. Such early unconscious fears are responsible not only for the later development of homosexuality, but also for all other modified sexual patterns of the obligatory type, e.g. fetishism, transvestitism, voyeurism, exhibitionism, pedophilia, etc. Individuals suffering from these conditions have in common the inability to perform in the standard male-female design and attempt to achieve orgastic release in a substitute way.

Classification

Same-sex attraction and same-sex behavior in males and females cannot be attributed to a single cause which explains all cases. Each individual has a unique history and those discussing this issue should avoid simplistic generalizations.

Jon K. Meyer in a review of the literature on homosexuality in *Psychoanalysis: The Major Concepts* (1995) writes:

A large number of psychogenetic factors have been cited in homosexuality and no list can do them justice. Without any pretense at completeness, they have included seduction, distorted paternal and maternal relationships, narcissistic wounds, psychical injury, the viewing of actual or inferred injury, illness, untimely or ill-prepared hospitalization, surgical or other procedures, separations, losses, heightened separation and/or castration anxieties and schizophrenic, narcissistic, and borderline processes (358).

As early as 1905, Freud referred to homosexuality as "inhibited development, arrested development, developmental inhibition, sexual infantilism, and dissociation of development." He concluded that the presence of exclusiveness and fixation is a characteristic of psychopathology and proposed the following classification based on conscious and unconscious motivation: (1) absolute inverts, whose sexual objects are exclusively of their own sex and who are incapable of carrying out the sexual act with a person of the opposite sex or of deriving any enjoyment from it; (2) ambiguous inverts, whose sexual objects may be of their own sex or the opposite sex, because this type of inversion lacks inclusiveness; (3) contingent inverts, whose circumstances preclude accessibility to partners of the opposite sex and who may take as their sexual objects those of their own sex.

This classification is very strikingly similar to the classification used today, under which we divide homosexual behavior into reparative, variational, and situational types.

Treating these three in reverse order:

1) Situational homosexuality occurs where heterosexual contact is unavailable, and an individual whose fantasy life and previous behavior has been directed to nonheterosexual sex seeks homosexual orgasmic outlet. This can occur in prisons, single-sex schools, and isolated single-sex work environments. For example, in certain areas where men have emigrated to find work, women have fallen into homosexual relationships out of loneliness. It may also occur in societies where same-sex sexual activity is considered a normal part of the developmental process or when homosexual acts are incorporated into religious rituals. Such expedient acts are not compulsive and are normally dropped when heterosexual outlets are available.

2) Variational patterns occur in the individual who yields to the desire for an alteration of sexual excitation. In some cultures such surplus activity is part of the established social order. In other cultures, it is an entirely individual departure contrary to the social order. This kind of homosexual activity sometimes occurs among show business celebrities who combine extreme sexual practices with substance abuse.

3) Reparative homosexuality is characterized by an inhibition of heterosexual performance and the persistence of childhood fears. The individual experiences feelings of incompleteness or inadequacy particularly in his or her gender identity and seeks to "repair" the incompleteness or inadequacy through sexual intimacy with a person of the same sex. The process of repair works in the unconscious and is marked by a high degree of inflexibility. The individual depends on homosexuality to fulfill orgastic gratification in all circumstances. Though he may force himself to go through the motions of heterosexual genital activity, he cannot thereby obtain satisfaction.

A. Dean Byrd (1947) describes the pattern of environmental factors which can lead to a homosexual outcome:

> From a developmental perspective, the male child experiences his parents, particularly his father, as failing to assist him through the normal developmental phases. The result is a defensive detachment from the same-sex parent. This defensive detachment serves as a protection against hurt from males during childhood. In adulthood, it serves as a barrier to honest intimacy and mutuality between men. The resulting sense of incompleteness fuels a reparative drive or desire to complete oneself. This is manifested in the eroticization of other men, sexualizing that with which the male homosexual is

not identified. Homosexual attractions then represent distorted attempts to meet legitimate needs for affection, approval, attention, and masculine affirmation. Homosexual men seek out other men who have traits that are viewed by them as lacking in themselves, and attempt to vicariously participate in this perceived masculinity. Fathers of homosexual men are often viewed as underinvolved with their male child, emotionally withholding, failing to recognize and affirm the autonomy and masculine nature of the son. Because of their struggles, many of these fathers seem unaware of what is happening in these relationships or incapable of rectifying it. It should be noted that homosexual attractions do not emerge from difficulties in the father-son relationship. Rather homosexuality develops because of a deficit in the male child that makes him unable to relate to the father or masculine figure. Mothers of homosexual men failed to reinforce the developing masculine identity, fostered a false identity as a "good little boy," and developed a relationship with the child which is characterized by excessive intimacy. Other influential factors in childhood include peers. Many homosexual men report hurtful relationships with male peers. The pre-homosexual boy often experiences rejection and teasing from peers. Lack of peer bonding is characteristic of the preadolescent homosexual boy. Finally, a history of premature introduction to sexuality which may include homosexual experiences with peers or older men or victimization through sexual molestation is common in the histories of homosexual men.

There are three major forms of clinical, overt homosexual behavior: 1) Pre-oedipal; 2) Oedipal; 3) Co-existing schizophrenia and homosexuality.

1) Pre-oedipal homosexuality is characterized by anxiety and guilt associated with an inability to make the intrapsychic separation from the mother before the age of three. In the milder form, the client may present with surface clinical picture of oedipal conflict, but these may obscure the deeper and more important pre-oedipal conflict—the child had failed to detach or to separate from the mother and to identify with the father or male peers. A boy who does not successfully complete separation and identification may realize he is male, but internalize the concept "I am not like my father" or "I am different from other boys," or "I am more like my mother."

Numerous studies have shown that a large percentage of homosexually active adult males suffered from some form of gender defined sexual identity disorder or gender identification failure in childhood. Homosexual therapists such as Dr. Richard Isay may insist that homosexuality is a "normal variation," but at they same time admit that homosexual men suffer from a failure to identify with other males. In an article in the *Psychoanalytic Study of the Child* (1986) Isay wrote: "Each of the 40 gay men whom I have seen in psychoanalysis or analytically oriented therapy has reported that starting from about age 4 he experienced that he was 'different' from his peers."

The homosexual male experiences his own gender identity as a faulty or weak masculinity and/or as femininity. The female homosexual has a faulty, distorted and/or unacceptable feminine identity. The disturbance in gender identity is always present in pre-oedipal homosexuality, but may become apparent only when the patient's unconscious material is subjected to close analytic scrutiny.

The persistence of primary feminine identification in male pre-oedipal homosexuals is a consequence of the failure to traverse the separation/individuation phase (age eight months to three years) and develop a separate and independent identity from the mother. The failure to separate from the mother and to identify with the same-sex parent and peers affects the individuals' ability to relate to themselves and to others. Males suffering from pre-oedipal homosexuality are beset by chronic anxieties, which in most cases lead to a continual search for sexual partners.

Research on the transmission of the virus which causes AIDS uncovered the extent of the promiscuity in the gay male community. Researchers were forced to change their definition of promiscuity when they discovered that the majority of homosexually active men had over fifty sexual partners and many had hundreds or even thousands

Pre-oedipal anxieties include fears of engulfment, ego disassociation, a loss of self and ego boundaries, dissolution of self, self fragmentation, separation anxiety, and identity diffusion. A child feeling threatened or fearful can employ various defense mechanisms to deal with anxiety. A psychologically healthy adult overcomes these early fears. In the case of homosexuals these early fears and perceived threats continue to create anxiety. The homosexual act is used to alleviate that anxiety, to ensure ego survival, and to stabilize the sense of self, as well as to incorporate transiently the masculinity of the partner. Because the soothing effect of the homosexual act is short-lived, anxiety returns, and the act must be repeated. The pre-oedipal homosexual, thereby, experiences a compulsion to engage in homosexual acts.

It should be pointed out that some of the most severely disturbed homosexuals show no outward signs of anxiety because they continually engage in homosexual acts with others or masturbate with homosexual fantasy, and so neutralize anxiety. The enactment of any sexual deviation helps to keep the individual, who is beset with unconsciously motivated anxiety, in equilibrium. The sexual deviation has been unconsciously, but nevertheless specifically, constructed to neutralize anxiety.

The manner in which extremely promiscuous homosexual men reacted to the HIV/AIDS epidemic reveals the compulsive nature of pre-oedipal homosexuality. Even after homosexually active men were informed of the danger associated with certain behaviors and fully understood that infection with HIV would lead to a painful and probably deadly illness, they continued to engage in activities which spread the infection. While abstinence or testing and monogamy offered safety, a substantial portion of homosexually active men opted for continuing to engage in anal sex with multiple partners. Although condom use increased, failure to use condoms 100% of the time was the norm rather than the exception. In addition, homosexually active men frequently combined sexual activity and the use of alcohol and mind-altering drugs, virtually guaranteeing high-risk behavior and infection. The result has been that in spite of all the HIV education that has occured, for the foreseeable future one out of two men who have sex with men will eventually become HIV positive.

This problem has been amply documented by numerous studies. Gay activists Gabriel Rotello in his book *Sexual Ecology,* and Michael Signorille, author of *Life Outside*, present graphic evidence of homosexual men's high-risk behavior. Some homosexual advocates, such as Dr. Walt Odets, a homosexual therapist and author of *In the Shadow of the Epidemic*, have even argued that one should not stigmatize the way in which homosexual men engage in sexual activity because of the "psychological" costs of such criticism.

Those fighting the AIDS epidemic have frequently expressed their frustration in the face of almost suicidal behavior patterns of homosexual men. Dr. Ronald Stall, a leading AIDS, researcher and his co-authors in an article in the *American Psychologist* (1988) concluded: "The efficacy of health education interventions in reducing sexual risk for HIV infection has not been consistently demonstrated. More education, over long periods of time, cannot be assumed to be effective in inducing behavior changes among chronically high-risk men." The failure of anti-HIV education is in part a result of a failure to understand the compulsive nature of male homosexual behavior. A number of my patients have thanked me for saving their lives. They are convinced that if they had not received treatment for their homosexuality they would have contracted HIV and died.

How can a homosexual man continually and knowingly risk his life? Because he is driven by more primal fears. The aim of the homosexual act is ego survival. The pre-oedipal male homosexual achieves "masculinity" through identification with a male sexual partner; this lessens castration fear or fears of object loss. The female homosexual achieves "resonance identification" with a woman partner—this lessens castration fear. Female homosexuals may also use sexual acts to create a "good" mother-child relationship.

Once the underlying psychological mechanism which produces the homosexual adaptation is understood, the pathological character of that adaptation becomes clear, as Bieber et al. explain "Any adaptation which is basically an accommodation to unrealistic fear is necessarily pathologic; in the adult homosexual continued fear of heterosexuality is inappropriate to his current reality. We differ with other investigators who have taken the position that homosexuality is a kind of variant of 'normal' sexual behavior."

Levels of Functioning

At the highest level of functioning and fixation, the patient with specific narcissistic pathology may have no neurotic symptoms, a good surface adaptation, little awareness of any emotional illness except a chronic sense of emptiness and boredom, and be creative in his field with a superior intellect and achievement. However, there may be a severe degree of superficiality and flightiness in his relationships. He may come to treatment in middle or late age, secondary to the development of chronic depressive reactions and almost never for his homosexuality. Other symptoms are emptiness, boredom, immediate need for the approval of others. This type of man uses denial, devaluation, and hypomania episodes as a defense against depression.

At the middle range of pathology we find those who are fixated at somewhat lower levels who may exhibit symptoms of narcissistic personality. Their surface function shows very little disturbance. Diagnostic exploration, however, reveals an excessive degree of self reference in interaction with others and excessive need to be loved and admired.

Gay activists Kirk and Madsen in the book *After the Ball* (1989) noted that the DSM-III definition of narcissistic personality disorder described in a clinical manner their "straightforward list of honest gripes" about gay men.

Kaplan, writing *in Archives of General Psychology* (1967), offers an explanation of the relationship between homosexuality and narcissism

In a sense, the homosexual has much in common with the narcissist, who has a love affair with himself. The homosexual, however, is unable to love himself as he is, since he is too dissatisfied with himself; instead he loves his ego-ideal, as represented by the homosexual partner whom he chooses. Thus for this particular type of individual, homosexuality becomes an extension of narcissism.

The homosexual at this level evidences a curious contradiction between an inflated concept of self and a shallow emotional life. There is often a remarkable absence of the capacity for an integrated conception of others. A homosexual's relationship to others is often characterized by inordinate envy. They idealize those from whom they expect to fulfill their narcissistic needs and treat with contempt those from whom they don't expect anything (often former idols). Relationships to others may on the surface be charming, but are at the core exploitative and parasitic and in some cases, cold and ruthless. As regards their affective life, they are restless and bored when there are no sources to feed their self-regard. They may appear dependent because of their need for adoration and tribute, but in reality they are unable to depend on anyone, due to their own feelings of underlying distress and devaluation, unconsciously spoiling what they receive due to conflicts around unconscious envy. (In many instances such symptoms are not due to homosexuality directly but due to the associated narcissistic personality disorder.)

Homosexual individuals who have the severest degree of pathology may be considered on the lowest level of the narcissistic pathology. In these cases pathological grandiosity is prominent. Overt borderline features include generalized impulsively; lack of anxiety tolerance, disposition to explosive or disassociative rage reactions; and severely paranoid distortions of their interpersonal relations. These individuals may engage in joyful types of cruelty, self-mutilation, and express a combination of paranoid and explosive personality traits, rage attacks, and blaming others. If aggression has been integrated into some existing superego functions, they show a capacity for depression and/or self-directed aggression. Some individuals in this group direct their anger outward, deriving sexual pleasure from sadism and aggression. Sado-masochism appears to be more common among homosexuals than heterosexuals. A study done by Dr. Andreas Spengler published in *Archives of Sexual Behavior* (1977) found that of sadomasochistic men surveyed, 38% were homosexual, and 31% bisexual.

It is important to differentiate borderline personality disorder proper, and the most severe form of narcissistic pathology, from the narcissistic personality disorder structure proper. Borderline personality disorder, a mental disease in which the symptoms are not continually psychotic nor strictly neurotic, appears to occur more frequently among homosexuals than among the general public. A study comparing 61 patients with borderline personality disorder with 60 non-borderline patients by Dr. Joel Paris, et al., published in *The Journal of Personality Disorders* (1995) found that: The rate of homosexuality in the BPD sample was 16.7% as compared with 1.7% in the non-BPD comparison group. The study also found that The homosexual BPD group had a rate of overall [childhood sexual abuse] of 100%, as compared to 37.3% for the heterosexual BPD group. ... 3 out of the 10 homosexual borderline patients also reported father-son incest.

A study of consecutive admissions for borderline personality disorder by Dr. George Zubenko et al. published in the *American Journal of Psychiatry* (June 1987) also found a high occurrence of homosexuality among BPD patients. According to the abstract: The authors found that 12 (57%) of 21 consecutive male patients with borderline personality disorder who presented for psychiatric treatment at two distant geographic sites were homosexual. They then obtained the sexual histories of 80 patients who met the standardized criteria for borderline disorder and found that 17 (21%) of these patients were homosexual, four (5%) were bisexual, and nine (11%) had diagnosis of paraphilias (748). Charles Silverstein, an active proponent of extreme homosexual practices and a gay affirming therapist, also admits that gay people are currently more prone to be diagnosed with borderline personality disorder. Writing in the *Journal of Homosexuality* (1988) Silverstein blames this on the confusion in society [?]. According to Silverstein " ... the more the innovations in society favor the acceptance of variations in lifestyle, the greater the confusion in those groups that vary the most from the norm such as gay people.

Again, as discrimination is reduced, we should expect some gay people to experience more confusion" (209).

It should be noted that borderline personality disorder whether or not associated with homosexuality is extremely difficult to treat.

As for the non-pre-oedipal forms of homosexuality, the oedipal form of homosexuality does not carry with it the compulsivity and the severe anxieties associated with the pre-oedipal type. Space does not permit me to discuss oedipal homosexuality further.

As to schizophrenia and homosexuality, Bieber et al. in their study of 106 homosexual men in analysis found that "One-fourth of the homosexual cases were diagnosed as schizophrenic." They proposed that "schizophrenia and homosexuality represent two distinct types of personality maladaptation which may or may not coexist."

Gay-affirming therapists such as John Gonsiorek have also had to deal with the occurrence of schizophrenia and homosexuality: Gonsiorek (1982) writes:

> ... the emergence of homosexual behavior with genuine desire may precipitate a schizophrenic episode in a marginally functioning pre-schizophrenic individual. This may be especially true of homosexual individuals with late onset paranoid schizophrenia, who may experience a coming out crisis in late teens or early twenties (often with a paranoid flavor) with clear indications of homosexual desire and occasionally behavior (12).

Gonsiorek felt it important to warn gay-affirmative therapists about the danger of "minimizing or ignoring the client's schizophrenia":

> Perhaps most cruel of all is when such clinicians, out of ignorance, inexperience or anti-intellectualism, interpret aspects of schizophrenia (such as interpersonal awkwardness; chronic lack of desire; pleasure deficit; disordered thought process; pervasive ambivalence; etc.) as signs of "not really accepting one's gayness." ...Some years ago, this author had to hospitalize one such individual who became psychotic and suicidal as a result of such pressure in a coming out group, encouraged by a paraprofessional group leader who didn't believe in schizophrenia because it was 'medical-model garbage.'

Treatment

In 1968, this author introduced the pre-oedipal theory of causation—namely that obligatory homosexuals of the pre-oedipal type have not made the psychological progression from a mother-child unity of earliest infancy to individuation. Fixation in the pre-oedipal period leads to a tendency to regression to the earliest mother-child relationship. This is experienced by the homosexual as a threat of personal annihilation, a loss of ego boundaries, or a sense of fragmentation. My work with numerous patients in the subsequent years has confirmed this theory (1978, 1988, 1995). Others have reached similar if not identical conclusions.

If homosexuality is experientially derived, then once the anxiety and conflicts that originally caused the inhibition of development and led to homosexual attractions and behavior are removed through suitable psychological measures, the obtainment of heterosexuality and heterosexual object love is possible. This has been verified in approximately one-third to one-half of all such patients who undertake therapy with a sincere desire to change (Socarides 1978, 1988). These results have been confirmed by a number of other therapists.

According to D. West (1977), "Every study ever performed on conversion from homosexual to heterosexual orientation has produced some successes." In addition to the already mentioned study by Bieber et al. and a similar study by Kaye et al. on homosexuality in women, numerous therapists have reported on successful treatment of homosexuality. Among these are: Dr. Samuel Hadden, Dr. Lawrence Hatterer, Dr. Frank Caprio, Dr. Edmund Bergler, Dr. Daniel Cappron, Dr J.A. Hadfield, Fr. John Harvey, Dr. Richard Fitzgibbons, Dr. Gerard Van den Aardweg, Dr. Jeffrey Satinover, Dr. Joseph Nicolosi, Dr. Ben Kaufman, Dr. Elaine Siegle, and Dr. C.W. Socarides (1969).

Robert Goetze of New Direction for Life, a Toronto-based support group for persons seeking to change from homosexuality, published a monograph reviewing 17 published studies which document change from exclusively or predominantly homosexual. Dr. Warren Throckmorton, whose review of the literature on efforts to sexual orientation was published in the *Journal of Mental Health Counseling* (Oct. 1998), concluded: "... the available literature leaves no doubt that some degree of change is possible for some clients who wish to pursue it."

Ruth Barnhouse (1984) commenting on the evidence of change wrote: "the frequent claim by gay activists that it is impossible for homosexuals to change their orientation is categorically untrue. Such a claim accuses scores of conscientious, responsible psychiatrists and psychologists of falsifying their data." In another place, Barnhouse wrote: "The distortion of reality inherent in the denials by homosexual apologists that the condition is curable is so immense that one wonders what motivates it" (109).

We as clinical psychoanalytic researchers owe much and give special thanks to our patients' persistence and endurance in attempting an alleviation of their conditions, for their courage and their trust in the psychoanalytic process. The challenge and fulfillment of this clinical research has proven to be equal in measure for both analyst and patient. We trust that our experience will be of great help to the bishops here today as they work to fulfill their pastoral

234

responsibilities in every way, with kindness, compassion, understanding, tolerance, and knowledge.

Postscript

The conclusions of therapists who treat homosexuality have frequently been challenged, on the grounds that their clinical experience comes from working with a troubled population of persons seeking psychiatric help and is not applicable to non-client homosexually attracted persons. Two carefully designed studies published in 1999 in *Archives of General Psychiatry* [Herrel 1999, Ferguson 1999] have supported the association of homosexuality and psychological pathology. A birth cohort study done in New Zealand (Ferguson, 1999) found that 78.6% of homosexuals had multiple psychiatric disorders as opposed to 38.2% of the 979 heterosexual subjects. Dr. Richard Friedman, commenting on the studies, admitted some mental health professionals who opposed the successful 1973 referendum to remove homosexuality from the DSM-III will feel vindicated.

References

Barnhouse, Ruth. 1984. What is a Christian view of homosexuality? *Circuit Rider* (February): 12–15.

Barnhouse, R. 1977. *Homosexuality*: a symbolic confusion. NY: Seabury Press.

Bergler, Edmund. 1959. One thousand homosexuals. Patterson NJ: Pagent.

Bieber et al. 1962. *Homosexuality: a psychoanalytic study of male homosexuals*. NY: Basic Books.

Byrd, A. Dean. 1997. A developmental model of male homosexuality: the Greg Louganis story. *NARTH Papers*, 13–24.

Cappron, Daniel. 1965. *Toward an understanding of homosexuality*. Englewood Cliffs, NJ: Prentice-Hall.

Caprio, Frank. 1954. *Female homosexuality: a psychodynamic study of lesbians*. NY: Citadel.

Fergusson, David, John Harwood, and Annette Beautrais. 1999. Is sexual orientation related to mental health? Problems and suicidality in young people. *Archives of General Psychiatry* 56 (10): 876–880.

Fitzgibbons, Richard. 1996. The origins and healing of homosexual attractions and behavior. In *The truth about homosexuality*, ed. John Harvey, 307–343. San Francisco: Ignatius.

Freud, S. 1905. *Three essays on the theory of sexuality*, Standard Edition, 7: 125–145. London: Hogarth Press, 1953.

Friedman, Richard. 1999. Homosexuality, psychopathology, and suicidality. *Archives of General Psychiatry* 56 (10): 887–888.

Goetze, Robert. 1997. *Homosexuality and the possibility of change: a review of 17 published studies*. Toronto: New Direction for Life.

Gonsiorek, John. 1982. The use of diagnostic concepts in working with gay and lesbian populations. In *Homosexuality and psychotherapy*, 9–20. NY: Haworth.

Hadden, Samuel. 1967. Male homosexuality. *Pennsylvania Medicine*. (February): 78–80.

Hadfield, J.A. 1958. The cure of homosexuality. *British Medical Journal* 1:132.

Harvey, John. 1996. *The truth about homosexuality*. San Francisco: Ignatius.

Hatterer, Lawrence. 1970. *Changing homosexuality in the male*. NY: McGraw-Hill.

Herrell, Richard, et al. 1990. Sexual orientation and suicidality: a co-twin control study in adult men. *Archives of General Psychiatry* 56 (10): 867–874.

Isay, Richard. 1988. The development of sexual identity in homosexual men. *Psychoanalytic Study of the Child* 41:467–489.

Kaye, et al. 1967. Homosexuality in women. *Archives of General Psychia-*

try 17: 623–634.

Kaplan, E. 1967. Homosexuality: A search for the ego ideal. *Archives of General Psychology* 16: 355–358.

Kirk, M., Madsen, H. 1989. *After the ball.* NY: Doubleday.

Meyer, Jon. 1955. Homosexuality. In *Psychoanalysis: the major concepts,* ed. F. Moore and B. Fine. New Haven: Yale University Press.

Nicolosi, Joseph. 1991. *Reparative therapy of male homosexuality.* Northvale, NJ: Aronson.

Odets, Walt. 1995. In the shadow of the epidemic. Durham, NC: Duke University Press.

Paris, Joel, H. Zweig-Frank, J. Gryder. 1995. Psychological factors associated with homosexuality in males with borderline personality disorders. *The Journal of Personality Disorders* 9 (1): 56–61.

Rotello, Gabriel. 1997. *Sexual ecology.* NY: Dutton.

Satinover, Jeffrey. 1996. *Homosexuality and the politics of truth.* Grand Rapids, MI: Baker.

Siegel, Elaine. 1988. *Female homosexuality: choice without volition.* Hillsdale, NJ: Analytic Press.

Signorille, Michael. 1997. *Life outside.* NY: Harper Collins.

Silverstein, Charles. 1988. The borderline personality disorder and gay people. *Journal of Homosexuality* 15 (1 & 2) 185–212.

Socarides, C.W. 1968. *The overt homosexual.* New York: Grune and Stratton.

Socarides, C.W. 1969. The psychoanalytical therapy of a male homosexual. *Psychological Quarterly* 38: 173–190.

Socarides, C.W. 1978. *Homosexuality.* New York: Jason Aronson.

Socarides, C.W. 1988. *The preoedipal origin and psychoanalytic therapy of sexual perversions.* Madison, CT: International Universities Press.

Socarides, C.W. 1995. *Homosexuality: A freedom too far.* Phoenix, AZ: Adam Mangrave Books.

Spengler, Andreas, 1977. Manifest sadomasochism in males. *Archives of Sexual Behavior* 6:441–546.

Stall, Ronald, T. Coates, C. Hoff. 1988. Behavioral risk reduction for HIV infection among gay and bisexual men. *American Psychologist* 43(11): 878–885.

Throckmorton, Warren. 1998. *Journal of Mental Health Counseling.* (October): 20(4): 283–304.

Van der Aardweg, Gerard. 1985. *Homosexuality and hope: a psychologist talks about treatment and change.* Ann Arbor, MI: Servant.

West, D. 1977. *Homosexuality re-examined.* London: Duckworth.

Zubenko, George, et al. 1987. Sexual Practices among men with borderline personality disorders. *American Journal of Psychiatry* 144 (6): 747–752.

GAMBLING AS AN ADDICTIVE BEHAVIOR

RACHEL A. VOLBERG, PH.D.

Introduction

This paper presents information about gambling and problem gambling. As my remarks in person in Dallas made clear, this is an issue with which few people are familiar. My intent in the presentation, and in these written remarks, is to inform you about recent and rapid changes in the availability of legal, commercial gambling and about the risks that these changes present to some individuals in the general population. My hope is that you will discuss this information amongst yourselves and develop your own individual and organizational responses to the issues I have raised.

The Evolution of Legal Gambling

What Is Gambling?

Gambling is an ancient form of recreation in nearly all human societies. There is strong evidence of gambling in prehistoric cultures as well as among indigenous peoples (Gabriel 1996). In Western countries, gambling has played an integral role in society although, historically, attitudes about the acceptability of different types of gambling have fluctuated in different eras and cultures.

The author would like to acknowledge several collaborators—Max Abbott, Sue Cox, Henry Lesieur, and Richard Rosenthal—whose contributions to the present work have been invaluable.

At the end of the twentieth century, the term "gambling" refers to a collection of several distinct behaviors and activities. The common thread is that all of these activities involve risking the loss of something of value in exchange for an opportunity to gain something of far greater value (Thompson 1997). Gambling games can be classified in numerous ways and on the basis of many different characteristics: the availability and frequency of opportunities to participate, the ratio of prizes paid to amounts staked, the ratio of elements of luck to elements of skill, the degree of player participation, association with other attractions, cash or credit basis, the knowledge needed to enter the game, and so on (Abt, Smith, and Christiansen 1985; Volberg, Reitzes, and Boles 1997). Gambling games also differ in their intellectual and physical appeal, in the level of physical and social interaction, and in their speed.

The Worlds of Commercial Gambling

Several distinct types of legal gambling have become widely available in the last quarter of the Twentieth Century. These include lotteries, casino-style gambling, electronic gambling machines, pari-mutuel wagering on horse and dog races, and charitable gambling (i.e. bingo and pulltabs). Each of these types of gambling elicits different political and social responses; each has evolved in different ways to meet changing markets; each is associated with particular social worlds of customers, operators and regulators.

Lotteries. In the 1970s and 1980s, in response to declining tax revenues, governments around the world moved to legalize different types of gambling. In North America, only 13 lotteries were operational in 1975; a quarter-century later, in 1997, lotteries operated in 37 of the 50 states and the District of Columbia as well as in all of the Canadian provinces. The top ten countries in lottery sales in 1997 included the United States, Spain, Italy, Germany, United Kingdom, Japan, France, Canada, Malaysia, and Australia (McQueen 1997).

As lotteries have matured, they have introduced new, more exciting products to maintain and increase sales. Many lotteries now offer a multitude of games that blur the boundaries between their traditional products and other types of gambling, including instant or scratch tickets, daily numbers games, and electronic gambling machines offering keno, poker, blackjack and line games similar to slot machines at casinos. Except in the United States, where sports betting is largely illegal, sports lottery games blur the boundary between lotteries and legal bookmaking and pari-mutuel operations. Finally, there is the growing availability of lottery games on the Internet, including the Red Cross lottery based in Liechtenstein, the national lottery in Finland, and even a lottery offered by the Coeur d'Alene tribe in Idaho (McQueen 1997).

Casino-style gambling. Well-established casino industries in Australia, Europe, and North America dominate the gambling business worldwide and are considered mature markets. On all three continents, the modern casino era started as a tourist-based industry. Since 1990, casinos have grown increasingly dependent on local players for casino profits. City-centered casinos, serving a predominantly local clientele, were first established in the Canadian provinces. There are now city-centered casinos in five of the eleven Canadian provinces. In Australia and New Zealand, there are casinos in all of the major cities.

In France, casinos were once operated seasonally and only for tourists. In the 1990s, French casinos were established in permanent facilities and locals were allowed to play. It is likely that casinos will soon be permitted in several major French urban centers, including Lyon, Bordeaux and possibly Paris. Elsewhere in Europe, the Dutch have introduced casinos in Amsterdam and Rotterdam; there is a casino in Copenhagen; in Germany, there are casinos in Stuttgart, Hamburg and Berlin as well as in tourist resorts like Baden-Baden. In Spain, laws against casinos in city centers have recently been overturned, and Seville and Barcelona are expected to have urban casinos in the near future. In Great Britain, casinos have been located in city centers since they were first legalized in 1970; now, however, laws that prevent advertising and require membership registration are changing (Kent-Lemon 1998).

The Indian Gaming Regulatory Act of 1988 created a regulatory structure for gambling on Native American lands throughout the United States. By establishing a framework for negotiation between the sovereign tribes and state governments, Congress opened the door for American Indian tribes to establish casino-style gambling in any state where charitable or social gambling is permitted (Eadington 1991). There are now 24 states that have entered into compacts with 146 tribes to establish a variety of gambling operations throughout the United States (Bureau of Indian Affairs 1998).

Casino-style gambling spread rapidly through North America in the 1990s. Casino-style gambling outside Nevada and Atlantic City first came to several small mining towns in Colorado and South Dakota. These casinos offered limited-stakes table games such as poker and blackjack, as well as slot machines. Once the door was opened, other forms of casino-style gambling proliferated in the United States. The first riverboats, legalized in Iowa in 1991, placed strict limits on both wagers and losses. As riverboat casinos were legalized in other states, including Illinois, Indiana, Louisiana, Mississippi, and Missouri, these limits were lifted. While these casinos must be located on facilities that look like boats, few of the riverboats actually leave shore. In Mississippi, as well as in Iowa where the earlier restrictions have been eliminated, the term "dockside gambling" is a more accurate description than "riverboat gambling."

In contrast to the United States, where casinos tend to be privately owned and operated, the Canadian provinces have implemented casino gambling as a means to raise funds for charitable purposes. Provincial governments operate most of these casinos with the proceeds distributed to charitable organizations. In some cases, such as Ontario, charitable casinos are privately operated although some of the revenues paid to the provincial government are distributed to charitable organizations.

Electronic gambling machines. After the emergence of urban casinos, the trend with the greatest effect on gambling markets worldwide is the growing popularity of electronic gambling machines. Electronic gambling machines include traditional slot machines as well as government or privately owned machines that feature video poker, video blackjack, and/or video keno. In mature casino markets, table games are in decline vis-à-vis slot machines. In every country where statistics are available, slot machines have increased their market share and table game revenues are declining. In France, 87 percent of casino revenues are derived from slots; in the United States, slot machine revenues represent approximately 70 percent of gross gaming revenues (Kent-Lemon 1998; Heneghan 1995).

In addition to slot machines in casinos, electronic gambling machines are an established element in the mature gambling markets of Australia, Europe, and North America. In Australia and New Zealand, thousands of slot machines are permitted at social clubs as well as in casinos in major urban areas (Winton, McQueen, and Hepworth 1998). In Europe, there are thousands of AWP ("amusement with prizes") machines as well as true slot machines in bars, taverns, restaurants and arcades in Germany, Great Britain, the Netherlands and Spain (Becoña 1996; Brown, and Fisher 1996; Remmers 1997).

In North America, there are now twenty-four states and seven provinces where electronic gambling devices such as slot machines or video lottery terminals are widely available (McQueen 1998). In some states, these machines generate substantial revenues for private route operators, gambling establishments, and state and county governments. A recent study in Montana, for example, found that the state's 1,740 gambling establishments generated $219 million in gambling revenues and another $34 million in tax revenues in a state with a population of approximately 649,000 adults (Polzin, Baldridge, Sylvester, Doyle, Volberg, and Moore 1998).

Pari-mutuel industry. In contrast to lotteries and casinos, the pari-mutuel industry has struggled to compete in a vastly more competitive environment. In North America, racetracks have sought relief from taxation and have also sought to expand their activities. Initially, racetracks worked to increase access to their traditional product by establishing off-track betting systems and broadcasting races from other tracks at their facilities. More recently, racetracks have sought to compete by offering other types of gambling. In California, several racetracks now have card rooms where patrons may wager on poker and other games. In Delaware, Iowa and West Virginia, racetracks have been permitted to add electronic gambling machines to their traditional products with excellent results for their bottom line.

Charitable Gambling. Despite widespread prohibitions against gambling throughout the Twentieth Century, gambling for charitable purposes has a long history internationally. Indeed, bingo and casino nights run for or by charities and churches are often not even regarded as gambling. As with lotteries and casinos, however, charitable gambling in the 1980s and 1990s has evolved to include larger facilities, higher stakes, and faster games. Large-scale bingo halls, seating hundreds of players, are found in many provinces and states throughout North America. In the United States, American Indian tribes run many of these large-scale bingo operations. Electronic linking of bingo games in separate locales has meant that the prizes for some of these games can be extremely large. Finally, there is the development of electronic bingo that allows operators to sell far more cards per game to their players and, in some cases, to increase the speed of the game appreciably. Electronic bingo has proved especially popular in South American countries where casinos are still largely illegal (Handler and McQueen 1997).

Emerging Trends

There have been substantial increases in the availability and acceptability of commercial gambling in the last two decades of the twentieth century. There are many ways that legal gambling now reaches into modern society. The operation and oversight of gambling activities have become part of the routine processes of government. Gambling commissions have been established, gambling revenues distributed, constituencies of customers, workers and organizations have developed. Governments have become dependent on revenues from legal gambling to fund essential services. Many nongambling occupations and businesses have also become dependent on legal gambling. Lawyers, accountants, architects, public relations and advertising, security services, and financial services have expanded their activities to provide for the gambling industry. Convenience stores, retail operators, restaurants, hotels, social clubs, and charitable organizations have become dependent on revenues from legal gambling to continue to operate profitably.

On the horizon is the prospect of wagering on sports, casino games, and lottery games on the Internet. The potential market for Internet gambling is enormous. According to one analyst, the number of sites offering wagers on casino games has grown from 10 in 1996 to 40 in 1997. Online wagering internationally could reach $8 billion annually by the turn of the century if these operations were made legal (Sinclair 1997, 1998). Internet gambling is particularly appealing to a new group of gamblers – youth and young adults who are computer literate and can take advantage of the fact that age restrictions are difficult to enforce in cyberspace.

As the history of the United States with Prohibition shows, there are difficulties in making any widespread behavior illegal. Laws against gambling are difficult to enforce because so many individuals engage in these behaviors. Further, governments now permit many types of gambling and it is difficult for citizens to make distinctions between similar activities, only one of which is sanctioned by the state. For example, many governments sanction lotteries while laws against "numbers" or "policy" games (essentially, illegal lotteries) remain on the books. In legalizing gambling machines, many governments have made the argument that illegal, "grey" machines will be put out of business. However, citizens find it hard to distinguish between machines owned by the government and those owned by other, sometimes illegal, operators.

Problem and Pathological Gambling

Defining Our Terms

Most people who gamble are social gamblers. They gamble for entertainment and typically do not risk more than they can afford to lose. If they should "chase" their losses to get even, they do so briefly; there is none of the long-term chasing or progression of the pathological (or compulsive) gambler.

Pathological gambling lies at one end of a spectrum of problem gambling and was first recognized as a psychiatric disorder in 1980 (American Psychiatric Association 1980). Recent changes have been made to the psychiatric criteria for pathological gambling to incorporate empirical research that links pathological gambling to other addictive disorders like alcohol and drug dependence. According to the American Psychiatric Association (1994), the essential features of pathological gambling are:

- a continuous or periodic loss of control over gambling;

- a progression, in gambling frequency and amounts wagered, in the preoccupation with gambling and in obtaining monies with which to gamble; and

- a continuation of gambling involvement despite adverse consequences

Numerous similarities between pathological gambling and alcohol and substance dependence have been noted (Levinson, Gerstein, and Maloff 1983; Miller 1980; Moran 1970). While money is important, most male pathological gamblers say they are seeking "action," an aroused, euphoric state comparable to the "high" derived from cocaine or other drugs. Many will go for days without sleep and for extended periods without eating or relieving themselves. Clinicians have noted the presence of cravings, the development of tolerance (increasingly larger bets or the taking of greater risks to produce a desired level of excitement), and the experience of withdrawal symptoms (Meyer 1989; Rosenthal and Lesieur 1992; Wray and Dickerson 1981). In anticipation of gambling, some gamblers report a "rush," characterized by sweaty palms, rapid heart beat, nausea or queasiness. Other gamblers may exhibit different symptoms. For example, because many women gamble as an escape mechanism and are more passive in their gambling, their physical reactions may differ from those of the action-seeking male gambler.

To be diagnosed as a pathological gambler, an individual must meet at least five of ten diagnostic criteria established by the American Psychiatric

Association (1994). The ten criteria include: loss of control, tolerance, withdrawal, increasing preoccupation, gambling to escape problems and dysphoric feelings, chasing one's losses in an effort to get even, lying about one's gambling, jeopardizing family, education, job or career, serious financial difficulties requiring a bailout, and illegal activities to finance gambling or pay gambling debts.

It is not bad luck, greed, or poor money management that makes one a pathological gambler. Some individuals have sought help in the early stages of their gambling careers. They were astute enough to become concerned about their intense physical reactions or their preoccupation with gambling, which created problems at home or work. Others experience gambling problems without developing the progression or engaging in long-term chasing. The term "problem gamblers" (Lesieur & Rosenthal 1991; Rosenthal 1989) has been introduced to describe these individuals, who may be in an early stage of pathological gambling. The term is also used as a more inclusive category that encompasses pathological gambling at one end of a continuum of problematic gambling involvement. In this sense, ***problem gambling*** has been described as ***any pattern of gambling behavior which compromises, disrupts or damages family, personal, or vocational pursuits*** (Lesieur and Rosenthal 1991).

Epidemiological Research

The first question that people usually ask about problem gambling is: How many problem gamblers are there? There is a rapidly growing body of research on the prevalence of problem gambling and the characteristics of problem and pathological gamblers. However, due to the recent nature of much of this work as well as the small number of studies that have been published in scholarly journals, there have been few attempts to synthesize this literature and review the results from multiple studies.

North America. Since 1985, numerous prevalence studies have been conducted among adults in states and provinces in North America. There have also been studies of problem gambling prevalence among adolescents, college students and individuals in treatment or prison settings. A recent meta-analysis identified 120 studies of "disordered gambling" in North America carried out between 1975 and 1995 (Shaffer, Hall, and Vander Bilt 1997).

Some major conclusions of the meta-analysis were:

- "disordered gambling" is a robust phenomenon;
- the majority of North Americans gamble with few adverse consequences;
- between 1975 and 1995, gambling disorders increased significantly among adults in the general population but not among adolescents or among adults in treatment or in prison; and
- gambling disorders are more prevalent among youth, males, and those with concurrent psychiatric problems.

The majority of problem gambling prevalence studies have been conducted by telephone with randomly selected individuals in the general population. The number of interviews completed in each jurisdiction was generally
determined by balancing available resources, confidence intervals and the size
of the population. In these surveys, respondents are asked about their gambling involvement and their demographic characteristics. A standard screen,
based on the psychiatric criteria for pathological gambling, is used to identify
respondents as problem or pathological gamblers. Until 1995, the South Oaks
Gambling Screen (SOGS) was used to identify respondents as problem or pathological gamblers (Lesieur and Blume 1987). Since 1995, other screens based on
more recent psychiatric criteria have been developed, although none have
been as widely used.

Table 1 presents information about the prevalence of problem and probable pathological gambling from surveys utilizing the South Oaks Gambling
Screen (SOGS and SOGS-R) in the United States and Canada.

Risk Factors and Correlates of Problem Gambling

Clinical evidence has pointed to a variety of possible factors in the
development of gambling problems. However, the research evidence in support of these factors is often equivocal and varies from one jurisdiction or
study to another. These factors include the availability of gambling, modes of
gambling, a family history of gambling difficulties, and membership in disadvantaged groups.

Gambling availability and access. Researchers and clinicians have
long argued that increased availability of gambling leads to increases in the
prevalence of gambling problems. Clearly, the availability of all kinds of gambling has increased in the past twenty years. The North American meta-
analysis established that both past year and lifetime prevalence of gambling-
related difficulties have increased significantly in this period. However, the
links between gambling availability and increases in the prevalence of gambling-related difficulties are not necessarily straightforward. In some jurisdictions, replication studies have shown significant increases in the prevalence
of problem gambling following the introduction of casinos or electronic gambling machines. In other jurisdictions, replication studies have not shown
significant increases. In still other studies, significant increases in problem
gambling prevalence have been identified in spite of the fact that there were no
changes in the availability of gambling.

Gambling mode. Since the early 1990s, increasing clinical evidence has
pointed to the different "careers" experienced by individuals with gambling
problems. Early research suggested that individuals with gambling difficulties
preferred wagering on horse races and that their difficulties took many years to
develop (Volberg and Steadman 1988). More recent evidence suggests that a
growing number of individuals with gambling difficulties prefer to wager on
electronic gambling machines and that their difficulties develop within two to

three years. The media and some clinicians have even labeled electronic gambling machines the "crack cocaine" of gambling (Bulkeley 1992).

The question of the impact of gambling machines is especially salient because of the growing reliance of the gambling industries on these devices. In mature casino markets, 70 percent to 80 percent of industry revenues come from slot machines. Electronic gambling machines represent the fastest growing segment of gambling markets internationally. Depending on the jurisdic-

Table 1

Prevalence Rates in North America (percentages)				
Year	Jurisdiction	Current Problem	Current Prob./Path.	Current Total
United Sates				
1993	South Dakota	0.7	0.5	1.2
1992	North Dakota	1.3	0.7	2.0
1994	Georgia	1.5	0.8	2.3
1997	Colorado	1.8	0.7	2.5
1992	Washington State	1.9	0.9	2.8
1996	Connecticut	2.2	0.6	2.8
1995	Texas	2.2	0.8	3.0
1995	Iowa	2.3	1.0	3.3
1997	Oregon	1.9	1.4	3.3
1997	Michigan	2.1	1.3	3.4
1996	New York	2.2	1.4	3.6
1998	Montana	2.0	1.0	3.6
1994	Minnesota	3.2	1.2	4.4
1995	Louisiana	3.4	1.4	4.8
1996	Mississippi	2.8	2.1	4.9
Canada				
1994	Saskatchewan	1.9	0.8	2.7
1996	British Columbia	2.8	1.1	3.9
1996	Nova Scotia	2.8	1.1	3.9
1995	New Brunswick	1.9	2.2	4.1
1995	Manitoba	2.4	1.9	4.3
1998	Alberta	2.8	4.8	2.0

247

tion, these machines can be located in casinos, social clubs, bars, restaurants, taverns, amusement arcades, and convenience stores. The machines are appealing to young people familiar with video games played on computers at home and school and to women who may be uncomfortable with more traditional casino table games.

In jurisdictions where electronic gambling machines are widespread, such as Montana, Oregon, and South Dakota, prevalence studies show that problem gamblers are just as likely to be women as men (Polzin et al 1998; Volberg 1997; Volberg and Stuefen 1994). Again, however, longitudinal research needed to identify more precisely the development of gambling difficulties associated with gaming machines and the risk factors that accompany this evolution, such as linking the availability of gaming machines to alcohol service.

Gambling involvement. Two findings are consistent across every survey of gambling and problem gambling in the general population. Problem gamblers in every jurisdiction and from every population group (adult, adolescent, college, etc.) are significantly more likely than nonproblem gamblers to gamble weekly or more often and on more than one type of gambling (Volberg 1996). In every jurisdiction and in every group in the population, problem gamblers report spending significantly more on gambling activities than nonproblem gamblers.

Demographics. The recent meta-analysis of prevalence studies in North America identified several demographic risk factors associated with the development of gambling problems. "Being young, male, in college, having psychiatric co-morbidity, or a history of antisocial behavior are factors that represent meaningful risks for developing gambling-related problems" (Shaffer, Hall, and Vander Bilt 1997: 56).

Although gambling availability and problem gambling prevalence rates vary across jurisdictions, problem gamblers are strikingly similar across different jurisdictions. Problem gamblers are significantly more likely than nonproblem gamblers to be male, under the age of 30, non-Caucasian, and unmarried. Problem gamblers in the general population are significantly less likely than nonproblem gamblers to have completed secondary education (high school in North America). Problem gamblers in the general population recall starting to gamble at a significantly younger age than nonproblem gamblers (Volberg 1996).

One interesting change that has occurred in recent years is an apparent increase in the proportion of problem gamblers who are relatively well to do. In the earliest surveys of problem gambling, the annual household income of problem gamblers was significantly lower than the annual household income of nonproblem gamblers (Volberg 1994). In more recent surveys of problem gambling, the annual household income of problem gamblers is not significantly different from the annual household income of nonproblem gamblers (Volberg 1996). One explanation is that these more recent surveys have been carried out in jurisdictions with generally lower income levels. Another possibility is that more middle-class individuals are gambling and getting into difficulties with these activities, as predicted by Rosecrance (1988).

Disadvantaged groups. Substantially higher rates of problem gambling have been identified among certain socioeconomically disadvantaged groups. Disadvantaged groups with high rates of problem gambling include New Zealand Maori and American Indians in Montana and North Dakota (Abbott and Volberg 1996; Polzin et al. 1998). High rates of problem gambling have also been identified in the general population in Puerto Rico (Volberg and Vales 1998).

Despite great differences among indigenous peoples throughout the world, there are similarities in the conditions under which many of these groups live. Poverty, unemployment, and dependence on welfare are widespread. Many such groups have been subject to a history of colonization and accompanying policies of economic exploitation and many remain relatively disadvantaged in socioeconomic terms. Like other indigenous groups, Maori, American Indians, and Puerto Ricans have relatively low levels of formal education and household income. These groups also have high unemployment rates and high levels of morbidity and mortality on a wide range of indices, including particularly high rates of alcohol and substance misuse.

Table 2 (see following page) shows that problem gambling prevalence rates are far higher among disadvantaged groups than in the general population. In another context, it has been suggested that, in contrast to the upper and middle classes, the working and lower classes represent subcultures where gambling is a socially sanctioned activity that gives status to the participants (Volberg, Reitzes, and Boles 1997). Combined with the stresses that are part of working class and lower class life, gambling represents a challenging opportunity to beat the system, get some action, demonstrate one's skills, and gain prestige among one's friends. We can hypothesize that the extremely high prevalence rates among American Indians in Montana and North Dakota, the Maori in New Zealand, and in Puerto Rico all emerge from the role played by gambling in these highly impoverished cultures.

The Impacts of Problem Gambling

There are few systematic studies of the financial or social impacts of problem and pathological gambling on individuals, families, or communities. However, based on what is known about pathological gamblers in treatment and/or attending Gamblers Anonymous, the following statements can be made:

Individual impacts. By the time he or she seeks treatment, a pathological gambler has generated substantial financial debts and, as a result, has withdrawn from work activities as well as from family and social life. As these relationships and activities deteriorate, there is depression secondary to the guilt, shame, and helplessness over mounting problems. Several studies have shown that one out of five pathological gamblers attempts suicide (Custer &

Table 2

Prevalence Rates Among Disadvantaged Groups				
Year	Jurisdiction	Current Problem	Current Prob./Path.	Current Total
1992	NZ Maori	4.6	2.2	6.8
1998	Montana Indians (hh)	3.5	5.0	8.5
1998	Montana Indians (res)	6.5	2.8	9.3
1997	Puerto Rico	4.4	6.8	11.2
1992	North Dakota Indians	5.8	6.6	12.3

Custer 1978; Lesieur & Blume 1990; Livingston 1974; McCormick, Russo, Ramirez, and Taber 1984; Moran 1969; Thompson, Gazel, and Rickman 1996). This rate is higher than that for other addictive disorders and second only to suicide attempt rates for depressive disorders, schizophrenia, and a few hereditary neurological disorders.

There may be an exacerbation of other mental disorders, such as manic depressive illness, alcoholism and substance dependence, anxiety states, and various personality disorders. Pathological gamblers typically are at risk for a number of stress-related physical illnesses. Hypertension and heart disease are common (Lorenz and Yaffee 1986).

Family impacts. There are multiple effects on the family; the most obvious of these are lack of financial support, neglect, and divorce. The spouse of the male pathological gambler is three times more likely than her counterpart in the general population to attempt suicide (Lorenz & Shuttlesworth 1983). There is also a high rate of stress-related physical illnesses in the spouse, notably hypertension, headaches, gastrointestinal disturbances, and backaches, which are eight times more common than in the general population (Lorenz and Yaffee 1988). A recent survey of members of Gamblers Anonymous in Montana found that 33% of the respondents had been involved in incidents of gambling-related domestic violence (Polzin et al. 1998).

The children of pathological gamblers do worse in school than their peers, are more apt to have alcohol, drug and gambling problems, or eating disorders and are more likely to be depressed. They attempt suicide twice as often as their classmates (Jacobs 1989; Lesieur and Rothschild 1989).

Social impacts. Addictive disorders such as alcoholism, substance dependence and pathological gambling are major causes of illness, disability and premature death. The monetary burden on society of the most serious consequences of these disorders can be estimated although some of the conse-

250

quences, such as pain, suffering, and family disruption, are not quantifiable.

While there is little information on the costs of pathological gambling to society, there are well-established parallels between pathological gambling and addictive disorders such as alcoholism. These include similar psychiatric criteria as well as similar demographic characteristics. One estimate of the cost of alcoholism to society is $11,532 per alcohol abuser per year (Rice, Kelman and Miller 1991). If the cost of pathological gambling to society is similar, the economic benefits of legal gambling may be quickly outweighed by its social costs.

In the workplace, gambling problems eventually lower productivity and cause inefficiency, absenteeism, and theft. Research on members of Gamblers Anonymous and on individuals entering treatment supports these findings. For example, a recent survey of Gamblers Anonymous members in Wisconsin found that 65% of the respondents had missed work due to gambling while 21% of the respondents had lost or quit their jobs due to gambling (Thompson, Gazel and Rickman 1996).

The already-overburdened criminal justice system can be affected by pathological gambling. Studies have shown that two out of three pathological gamblers commit illegal acts in order to pay gambling-related debts and/or to continue gambling. Such acts typically are turned to out of desperation and occur late in the disorder (Brown 1987; Lesieur 1984; Rosenthal and Lorenz 1992). The majority of crimes committed by pathological gamblers are nonviolent, and many involve embezzlement or fraud. One survey of Gamblers Anonymous members found that 47% had engaged in insurance fraud or thefts where insurance companies had to pay the victims (Lesieur and Puig 1987). A more recent survey of Gamblers Anonymous members found that 22% had declared bankruptcy, 20% had been involved in civil court cases and 14% had been arrested and prosecuted for gambling-related crimes (Thompson, Gazel and Rickman 1996).

Issues for the Church

In concluding, I would like to draw attention to some issues related to the links between legal gambling and the Church. These include the international nature of the expansion of legal gambling, the impacts that legal gambling is already having on your parishes, the support received by the Catholic Church from charitable gambling, and the need for a more informed clergy when it comes to the issue of problem gambling.

International Aspects

The evolution of legal, commercial gambling internationally has followed similar trends in many developed countries. Recent events in South America and South Africa suggest that the evolution of commercial gambling will follow a similar pattern in less developed countries as well.

The Catholic Church is an international institution, with the power to affect policies and programs in many countries. The rapid expansion of legal gambling presents a challenge to the Catholic Church because it has occurred in so many countries and because it has occurred in such a relatively short period of time. Individual clergy, and their congregations, may find themselves working with a surprising array of partners to address issues of gambling and problem gambling. There are three clear choices to the clergy in addressing gambling issues. These are to ignore the issues outlined here; to oppose the expansion of legal gambling; or to respond by learning more about gambling-related problems, educating yourselves and others about problem gambling, and working to ensure that adequate services are available for individuals and families harmed by legal gambling.

Impacts on Parishioners

Gambling involvement can have severe impacts on individuals and families. Members of the Catholic Church reside in these communities and, in ministering to their congregations, see many of the individual and family impacts on a regular basis.

Until the 1980s, problem gambling was viewed as a "sin" or a "vice" rather than as a treatable disorder. Problem gambling is still not widely recognized, even by mental health and addiction treatment professionals. When parishioners seek help with personal or family difficulties, it would be helpful if their pastors were familiar with the issue of problem gambling and knew enough to elicit information about whether gambling was a contributing factor. Early intervention of this kind could save many individuals and families from the despair and desolation of pathological gambling.

Conflicting Roles of the Church

Given the moral authority of the Catholic Church, it seems ironic that the Church has relied on bingo and "casino nights" for fund-raising purposes for many years. While there is evidence that bingo can provide important social rewards (Dixey 1987; Martin and Nayowith 1988; Parker and Wagner 1988), a recent study identified extremely high prevalence rates of problem and pathological gambling among regular bingo players (Volberg and Glackman 1995). Among regular bingo players in Vancouver, 12.5% scored as problem gamblers while 13.0% scored as probable pathological gamblers.

The bingo players surveyed in Vancouver were predominantly older women of European ancestry with relatively low levels of education and income. The majority of these bingo players planned their bingo outings and played bingo with a group of friends. These women acknowledged numerous negative impacts of their bingo play on family relationships and family finances.

How reliant is the Catholic Church on bingo for fund-raising purposes? How dependent is the Church, therefore, on a small but highly troubled group of players for these much-needed revenues? These are questions that I believe must be addressed as the Catholic Church moves forward into the Twenty-first Century.

The Pastoral Role – Linking with Available Services

Finally, given the likelihood that more of you will be seeing the impacts of legal gambling on your parishioners (and perhaps even your colleagues) in the coming years, I believe that every one of you should learn more about gambling-related difficulties. Certainly, this workshop is a first and important step in educating yourselves and your colleagues about a heretofore unrecognized issue. Future steps could include training in how to recognize individuals with gambling-related difficulties, development of a referral network so that parishioners who do experience gambling-related difficulties can not only be recognized but referred to appropriate treatment. Finally, I believe that the Catholic Church must examine its own dependence on gambling and ask whether there are better ways to raise revenues for much-needed programs.

References

Abbott, M. W., and R. A. Volberg. 1996. "The New Zealand National Survey of Problem and Pathological Gambling." *Journal of Gambling Studies*, 12 (2): 143–160. Special Issue on International Prevalence Studies and Related Treatment Developments.

Abt, V., J. F. Smith and E. M. Christiansen. 1985. *The Business of Risk: Commercial Gambling in Mainstream America.* Lawrence: University Press of Kansas.

American Psychiatric Association. 1980. *Diagnostic and Statistical Manual of Mental Disorders*, Third Edition. Washington, D.C.: American Psychiatric Association.

_____. 1994. *Diagnostic and Statistical Manual of Mental Disorders*, Fourth Edition. Wash., D.C.: American Psychiatric Association.

Becoña, E. 1996. "Prevalence Surveys of Problem and Pathological Gambling in Europe: The Cases of Germany, Holland and Spain." *Journal of Gambling Studies* 12 (2): 179–192.

Brown, R. I. F. 1987. "Pathological Gambling and Associated Patterns of Crime: Comparisons with Alcohol and Other Drug Addictions." *Journal of Gambling Behavior* 3: 98–114.

Brown, R. I. F., and S. E. Fisher. 1996. *The Social Implications of Casino Gambling.* London: The Home Office.

Bulkeley, W. M. 1992. "Video Betting, Called 'Crack of Gambling,' Is Spreading." *Wall Street Journal* (July 14, 1992): B1.

Bureau of Indian Affairs. 1998. "The Tribal State Compact List." Website accessed July 21, 1998. *www.doi.gov/bia/foia/compact.htm.*

Custer, R. L., and L. F. Custer. 1978. *Characteristics of the Recovering Compulsive Gambler: A Survey of 150 Members of Gamblers Anonymous.* Paper presented at the Fourth National Conference on Gambling, Reno, NV.

Dixey, R. 1987. "It's A Great Feeling When You Win: Women and Bingo." *Leisure Studies* 6: 199–214.

Eadington, W. R. 1991. "Public Policy Considerations and Challenges and the Spread of Commercial Gambling." In *Gambling and Public Policy: International Perspectives*, W. R. Eadington & J. A. Cornelius, eds. Reno: University of Nevada Press.

Gabriel, K. 1996. *Gambler Way: Indian Gaming in Mythology, History and Archaeology in North America.* Boulder, CO: Johnson Books.

Handler, B., and P. A. McQueen. 1997. "Lands of Opportunity: Gaming in Latin, Central and South America." Supplement to *International Gaming & Wagering Business* 18 (11).

Heneghan, D. 1995. "Wealth Machines," *International Gaming & Wagering Business* 16 (10): 108–111.

Jacobs, D. F. 1989. "Illegal and Undocumented: A Review of Teenage Gambling and the Plight of Children of Problem Gamblers in America." In *Compulsive Gambling: Theory, Research, and Practice,* H.J. Shaffer, S.A. Stein, B. Gambino, and T.N. Cummings eds. Boston: Lexington Books.

Kent-Lemon, N. 1998. "Global View: Cities and Slots are the Future." *International Gaming and Wagering Business* 19 (4): 34–35.

Lesieur, H. R. 1984. *The Chase: Career of the Compulsive Gambler.* Cambridge: Schenkman.

Lesieur, H. R., and S. B. Blume. 1987. "The South Oaks Gambling Screen (SOGS): A New Instrument for the Identification of Pathological Gamblers." *American Journal of Psychiatry* 144: 1184–1188.

_____. 1990. "Characteristics of Pathological Gamblers Identified Among Patients on a Psychiatric Admissions Service." *Hospital and Community Psychiatry* 41 (9): 1009–1012.

Lesieur, H. R., and K. Puig. 1987. "Insurance Problems and Pathological Gambling." *Journal of Gambling Behavior* 3: 123–136.

Lesieur, H. R., and R. J. Rosenthal. 1991. "Pathological Gambling: A Review of the Literature (prepared for the American Psychiatric Association Task Force on DSM-IV Committee on Disorders of Impulse Control Not Elsewhere Classified)," *Journal of Gambling Studies* 7: 5–40.

Lesieur, H.R. and J. Rothschild. 1989. "Children of Gamblers Anonymous Members." *Journal of Gambling Behavior* 5: 269–282.

Levinson, P. K., D. R. Gerstein, and D. R. Maloff (eds). 1983. *Commonalities in Substance Abuse and Habitual Behaviors*. Lexington, MA: Lexington Books.

Livingston, J. 1974. *Compulsive Gamblers: Observations on Action and Abstinence*. New York: Harper & Row.

Lorenz, V. C., and D. E. Shuttlesworth. 1983. "The Impact of Pathological Gambling on the Spouse of the Gambler." *Journal of Community Psychology* 11: 67–76.

Lorenz, V. C., and R. A. Yaffee. 1986. "Pathological Gambling: Psychosomatic, Emotional and Marital Difficulties as Reported by the Gambler." *Journal of Gambling Behavior* 2: 40–49.

_____. 1988. "Pathological Gambling: Psychosomatic, Emotional and Marital Difficulties as Reported by the Spouse." *Journal of Gambling Behavior* 4: 13–26.

McCormick, R. A., A. M. Russo, L. R. Ramirez, and J. I. Taber. 1984. "Affective Disorders Among Pathological Gamblers Seeking Treatment." *American Journal of Psychiatry* 141: 215–218.

McQueen, P. A. 1997. "Special Report: Gaming on the Internet: Lottery. Bordering on Growth." *International Gaming & Wagering Business* 18 (4): 55.

_____. 1998. "North American Gaming at a Glance." *International Gaming & Wagering Business* 19 (9): 20–22, 109.

Martin, M. A., and S. A. Nayowith. 1988. "Creating Community: Groupwork to Develop Social Support Networks with Homeless Mentally Ill." *Social Work with Groups* 11: 79–93.

Meyer, G. 1989. *Glucksspieler in Selfsthilfegruppen: Erste Ergebnisse einer empirischem Untersuchung.* Hamburg: Neuland.

Miller, W. R. (ed). 1980. *The Addictive Behaviors.* Oxford: Pergamon Press.

Moran, E. 1969. "Taking the Final Risk." *Mental Health* (London): 21–22.

_____. 1970. "Gambling as a Form of Dependency." *British Journal of Addiction* 64: 419.

Parker, S. D., and C. E. Wagner. 1988. "The Most Underrated Activity in Nursing Homes." *Activities, Adaptation and Aging* 12: 87–90.

Polzin, P. E., J. Baldridge, D. Doyle, J. T. Sylvester, R. A. Volberg, and W. L. Moore. 1998. "From Convenience Stores to Casinos: Gambling— Montana Style." *Montana Business Quarterly* 36 (4): 2–14.

Remmers, P. 1997. *A Dutch Treat: The Gaming Industry's Response to Problem Gambling in the Netherlands.* Paper presented at the 10th International Conference on Gambling and Risk Taking. Montreal, Canada. (May–June 1997).

Rice, D. P., S. Kelman, and L. S. Miller. 1991. "The Economic Cost of Alcohol Abuse." *Alcohol Health & Research World* 15 (4): 307–316.

Rosecrance, J. 1988. *Gambling Without Guilt: The Legitimation of an American Pastime.* Belmont, CA: Wadsworth.

Rosenthal, R. J. 1989. "Pathological Gambling and Problem Gambling: Problems of Definition and Diagnosis." In *Compulsive Gambling:*

Theory, Research, and Practice, H.J. Shaffer, S.A. Stein, B. Gambino, and T.N. Cummings, eds. Boston: Lexington Books.

Rosenthal, R. J., and H. R. Lesieur. 1992. "Self-reported Withdrawal Symptoms and Pathological Gambling," *American Journal on Addiction* 1: 150–154.

Rosenthal, R. J., and V. C. Lorenz. 1992. "The Pathological Gambler as Criminal Offender: Comments on Evaluation and Treatment." In *Psychiatric Clinics of North America* 15 (3) (Special Issue on Forensic Issues): 647–660.

Shaffer, H. J., M. N. Hall, and J. Vander Bilt. 1997. *Estimating the Prevalence of Disordered Gambling Behavior in the United States and Canada: A Meta-analysis.* Boston, MA: Harvard Medical School Division on Addictions.

Sinclair, S. 1997. "By the Numbers: Internet Casino Growth Predicted." *International Gaming & Wagering Business* 18 (3): 17.

_____. 1998. "By the Numbers: Cybergaming's Limited Market." *International Gaming & Wagering Business* 19 (3): 12.

Thompson, W. N. 1997. *Legalized Gambling: A Reference Handbook.* Santa Barbara, CA: ABC-CLIO. Series in Contemporary World Issues.

Thompson, W. N., Gazel, R., and Rickman, D. 1996. The Social Costs of Gambling in Wisconsin. *Wisconsin Policy Research Institute Report 9(6):* 1–44.

Volberg, R. A. 1994. "The Prevalence and Demographics of Pathological Gamblers: Implications for Public Health." *American Journal of Public Health* 84 (2): 237–241.

_____. 1996. "Prevalence Studies of Problem Gambling in the United States." *Journal of Gambling Studies* 12 (2): 111–128.

_____. 1997. *Gambling and Problem Gambling in Oregon.* Report to the Oregon Gambling Addiction Treatment Foundation.

Volberg, R. A, and W. Glackman. 1995. *Bingo Play in Vancouver: Report on a Telephone Survey of Active Bingo Players in Vancouver.*

Report to the Mount Pleasant Starship Community Charitable Association.

Volberg, R. A., and H. J. Steadman. 1988. "Refining Prevalence Estimates of Pathological Gambling." *American Journal of Psychiatry* 145: 502–505.

Volberg, R. A., and R. M. Stuefen. 1994. *Gambling and Problem Gambling in South Dakota: A Follow Up Survey.* Report to Citizens Uniting for Gambling Reform.

Volberg, R. A., and P. A. Vales. 1998. *Juegos de Azar y el Problema de Juego en Puerto Rico [Gambling and Problem Gambling in Puerto Rico].* Report to the Puerto Rico Department of the Treasury.

Volberg, R. A., D. C. Reitzes, and J. Boles. 1997. "Exploring the Links Between Gambling, Problem Gambling and Self-Esteem." *Deviant Behavior* 18: 321–342.

Winton, K., P. A. McQueen, and K. Hepworth. 1998. *Australia and New Zealand Gambling Report 1998.* (August 1998). Supplement to *International Gaming & Wagering Business* 19 (8).

Wray, I., and M. G. Dickerson. 1981. "Cessation of High Frequency Gambling and 'Withdrawal' Symptoms." *British Journal of Addiction* 76: 401–405.